Tom
HAPPY 65th
BIRTHDAY

Paul Patty

Ryan

THE
SHADOW OF
KILIMANJARO

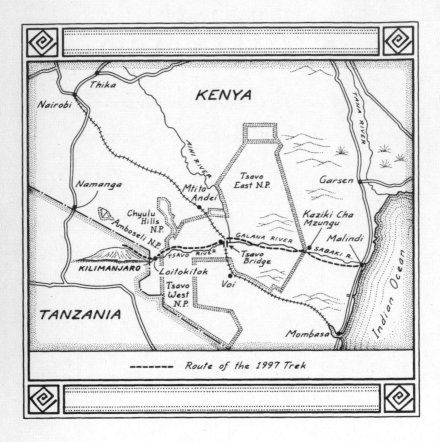

-------- Route of the 1997 Trek

THE
SHADOW OF
KILIMANJARO

On Foot Across East Africa

RICK RIDGEWAY

An Owl Book

Henry Holt and Company • New York

Henry Holt and Company, LLC
Publishers since 1866
115 West 18th Street
New York, New York 10011

Henry Holt® is a registered trademark
of Henry Holt and Company, LLC.

Published in Canada by Fitzhenry & Whiteside Ltd.,
195 Allstate Parkway, Markham, Ontario L3R 4T8.

Library of Congress Cataloging-in-Publication Data
Ridgeway, Rick.
The shadow of Kilimanjaro : on foot across East Africa /
Rick Ridgeway.
p.   cm.
Includes index.
ISBN 0-8050-5390-5
1. Tsavo National Park (Kenya)—Description and travel.   2. Ridgeway,
Rick—Journeys—Kenya—Tsavo National Park.   3. Hiking—Kenya—
Tsavo National Park.   4. Natural history—Kenya—Tsavo National Park.
5. Kilimanjaro, Mount (Tanzania)—Description and travel.   6. Ridgeway,
Rick—Journeys—Tanzania—Kilimanjaro (Mount).   7. Hiking—Tanzania—
Kilimanjaro (Mount).   8. Natural history—Tanzania—Kilimanjaro (Mount).
I. Title.
DT434.T73R54   1998   98-15970
916.762'3—dc21   CIP

Henry Holt books are available for special promotions and
premiums. For details contact: Director, Special Markets.

First published in hardcover in 1998 by
Henry Holt and Company, Inc.

First Owl Books Edition 1999

Designed by Jessica Shatan and Paula Szafranski

Printed in the United States of America
1   3   5   7   9   10   8   6   4   2

To
Connor, Cameron, and Carissa

Learn as though you're going to live forever,
but live as though you're going to die tomorrow.

Introduction

I love long walks, and I would trade them for the life I have spent as a mountaineer, if forced to choose. Once in Punta Arenas, the southern tip of South America, I was waiting for the weather to clear to fly to Antarctica with a group that was dog sledding across the continent. I was in a bar with Reinhold Messner—considered the most accomplished high altitude mountaineer of our day—who was also going down to make a traverse, but on foot, wearing skis. "It is the long walks that attract me now," he said "The long walks across open places."

In the last fifteen years, the journeys that have left me with an urge to return have been the trips to the open plains, the deserts, the savannas. I would love someday to walk across the high and uninhabited plateau between the snow peaks of the Chang Tang region in Western Tibet, and in a curious way the ice plains of Antarctica invoke the same yearning. Looking across the ice cap from high in the Ellsworth Mountains is the only place I've ever been on the planet where you can see the horizon bend down on the edges and know by looking that the Earth is round. On another more recent trip to Antarctica I was in Queen Maud Land, a very remote region of mythical rock spires that rise two thousand vertical feet out of flat ice, like towers from some book of fables. One day at our base camp I wandered off alone, skiing in a long and distant line away from our tent. I stopped to gaze from my highland vantage down and across the ice where I could see the tops of the rock spires peering above the sharp horizon line at a distance I knew was well over one hundred miles, and I had an urge to keep skiing. To keep going, one sliding foot in front of the next. This was not a death wish because once I thought it through and imagined my walk slowing, then stiffening, then freezing, the urge vanished; but the point is that the allure was there, and it was real: the urge to keep walking.

As much as Antarctica, the acacia bushlands of East Africa have left me with indelible images that seem to tap some deep yearning. When I close my eyes and imagine East Africa, what I see is grass savannas framed by umbrella thorn trees, the elephant, the giraffe, the companies of grazing zebra, the stalking predators, and in the blue distance the white mantled dome of Kilimanjaro. It is a scene, emblematic and timeless, lodged in my consciousness with a gravitational weight that pulls me back time and again to this part of the world.

The last time I was in East Africa, several years ago, I had a chance to make a short walk through the thornbush country with my friend Iain Allan and a park ranger who accompanied us to provide armed protection from dangerous animals. We were following a *lugga* (a Swahili word used in East Africa to describe a sand river that is dry in all but flash floods) when we chased out of the bush a large lioness. She ran along the edge of the riverine thickets, then turned and disappeared, and we followed to try to get a closer look. The ranger, a six-foot-seven-inch Samburu named Mohamed, raised his semiautomatic rifle to his shoulder and clicked off the safety. We entered the bush. I knew from my reading, and from stories Iain had told, that the lions of Tsavo more than those of anyplace else in Africa are famed man-eaters, but my mind didn't need an academic analysis to tell my body to have every synapse ready to close and open at the speed of light. My hand folded around my camera and I was wishing it was instead folding around a spear tipped with a sharp steel point; or even better, around the grip of a rifle like Mohamed's.

"There!"

Mohamed spun in response to Iain's cry, and my eyes whipped sideways just in time to see the tawny back of the lion disappear thirty yards away into the saltbush. "We had a glimpse, didn't we," Iain said.

At that moment I had a glimpse of more than the back of that lion. I had tasted what it was like to walk in a true wildness. Henry David Thoreau did not write that in *wilderness* is the preservation of the world, as he is oft misquoted, but wrote that "in *wildness* is the preservation of the world." (Italics mine.) There is a difference, and it is significant. A wildness is intact. In wildness, all the original pieces are there. My own backyard mountains in California, from the Coastal Range through the Sierras, are in many places wilderness, but none of it is wildness because the grizzly is gone. We may have the grizzly on the state flag; having it there, however, is not a celebration of our heritage but a burlesque of what we have done to the most noble patriarch ever to walk the land. The last grizzly in California was gunned down in 1922, and as it died so did an essential element of our relationship with our land and the animals we are designed to share it with.

◈

So I was eager to visit on foot a wildness that still had all the predators in place. What would it be like to walk for one month in the close company of animals that put me several links down on the food chain? The chance came when Iain proposed an idea: to walk from the summit of Mt. Kilimanjaro all the way to the Indian Ocean, crossing the vast Tsavo, the largest national park in East Africa. Despite the poaching that Tsavo suffered in the 1980s, the elephant have made a comeback, and other than rhinoceros, which have been poached to near extinction, the ecosystem is complete. It is eight thousand square miles of wildness; and traversing it on foot would be like walking across an entire country.

The trip therefore held promise to be distinct. As I think back to some of my other adventures, the ones that are most memorable are also ones that held surprises, that brought experiences that were not anticipated, or revealed lessons that in advance were not considered. This walk was going to be such a journey. After spending a month on foot and at eye level with the large mammals of Africa, I was going to reflect considerably on my relationship with them. Then, six months after the trek, I was going to return to Africa, this time to look more closely at the nature of our species's relationship to these animals over time: as hunters, and as conservationists.

It would be a trip such as the Italian anthropologist and adventurer Fosco Maraini referred to when he spoke of the only true kinds of travel, the journeys where the signposts are unfamiliar, and where the new worlds you see reveal elements in yourself that you never even knew existed.

RICK RIDGEWAY
Ojai, California, 1998

PART ONE

Kilimanjaro

The Ascent

I open my eyes and check my small travel alarm next to my head and know that I must have slept but it doesn't feel like it. I lie in my sleeping bag and in my mind go through the checklist: first the headlamp next to the alarm, then long underwear on and baggie shorts over that, socks and boots in the corner, camera bag is ready, ice ax and crampons go in Iain's pack. Put everything else in the duffel, ready for the porters to carry around to the other side of the mountain where we'll meet them at day's end.

I reach for the headlamp, pull on the underwear and then the baggies over that.

"It's that time already?" Iain asks.

"Five to twelve."

"Oh dear," he says in a self-mocking tone with his British Kenyan accent.

Outside I look up and see the clouds over the summit have gone and stars alone light the lava rocks like a dim photograph. I look the other way and the Southern Cross and the Magellanic clouds bring a memory of when I was eighteen and won passage as a novice crew on a small sloop with four other kids and the guy who owned the boat. We sailed to Tahiti and each night on watch this southern sky was revealed inch by inch.

I call to the others that it's time and I'll meet them in the mess tent. Up the hill to where the porters pitched our tent next to the metal hut where they have slept and cooked, and beyond in the black where dozens of other climbers have pitched their tents I hear their murmurs and complaints. In the tent everything is laid out so I pour tea and force down some biscuits

*and then pour more tea and the others arrive. Danny looks haggard. He lies
in the doorway and I hand him a tin mug of tea and tell him he has to drink.
He hasn't finished dressing so with no words between them Bongo laces his
boots for him and then snaps on his gaiters. No thanks is given but none is
needed because they're brothers.*

"It's almost one," Iain says.

*I offer to take Danny's day pack because I have only my shoulder bag of
camera gear and though it's heavy I feel strong. Rustus, our head porter,
who will go with us, asks if we're ready, and when we say "let's go" he leads
the way. Above there is a great black hole the shape of the mountain cut out
of the studded nightsky and in the center a vertical line of twinkling lights
of those trekkers even more foolish than ourselves who have beat us out of
camp. Our own world is reduced to the cones of light from each man's headlamp except Danny, who has never climbed before and didn't have all the
equipment or a headlamp, but whoever is behind him takes care to aim his
light at Danny's feet.*

*I find a rhythm and try to lose my thoughts to it but feel the first pain of
a stomach cramp and then another, and I feel the nausea starting and the
headache that I recognize all too well. People assume I must be good at altitude because I've done it a lot, but the truth is I acclimatize slowly and
when I first go up to 18,000 and higher I get sick even more than others,
and if I have an advantage it's only that I know what's coming. I catch up.
The only sound is our boots crunching the lava gravel and the metal clank
of someone using an ice ax as a walking stick. The pain is sharp in my head
and my cramping is still with me; if I feel this way how is Danny doing with
no sleep and nothing in his stomach from the vomiting after dinner? I can
see him ahead passing in and out of the light beam as he steps stiff with his
arms straight at his sides and his wool mittens looking oversized like he's a
kid who has borrowed them from his dad. What if he doesn't make it? Will
he want to continue the trip knowing that he didn't even reach the starting
point?*

*For that matter will I make it? This is worse than I usually feel at this al-
titude for the first time going up—maybe there's something else wrong with
me? We stop to rest and Iain says we are making good time and asks how
we feel. I confess my nausea and Iain offers to take my camera bag and I
discover that was the problem, the shoulder strap has been restricting blood
around my neck and the nausea leaves but the headache is still there, but so
what. I don't wear a watch and I don't know the time other than what I can
gather from the stars and a vague graying of the black sky to the east behind*

what I can just make out as the sharp-tipped summit of Mawenzi. Lift one foot and then the other, just enough to place it higher; don't use any more energy than you need to and breathe deeply between each move. Rhythm is everything, rhythm and pacing, and when you are in it your thoughts go and it is dreamlike, but you are still here in the moment, the cone beam of light coming from your forehead tying you through the blackness to the lava slope of this mountain that in your mind you see rising to a rare glacial height above the acacia-studded plain of Africa.

Look up and the vague light of the coming sunrise is just enough to see the glacier coming down from the rim like a white tongue. Remember the story of that German missionary one hundred and fifty years ago seeing this ice from far away below and thinking first it was a cloud but then realizing it was snow and back home in Europe no one believed him. Not snow on the equator. And twenty years later another missionary even more intrepid climbs up here to the snow line, but on the way back his porters desert and he dies from lack of supplies and never gets word home of what he has found. Then remember the story of the leopard? The climbers after the First War finding the remains of a leopard on a rocky point just above where we are now with glaciers on both sides, the mummified body stiff and hard as old leather and the fur bleached in the ultraviolet sun but the spots are still there, and as Hemingway said in the opening of his famous book no one knew what the leopard was looking for.

I am wearing only my long underwear with my baggies pulled over and I have been warm enough as long as I kept moving, but the sun brings a wind so we stop and pull anoraks from our packs, then keep going. As though to herald our arrival we reach the crater rim just as the first rays from the sun break over the horizon, but it's like I am on the moon because the light warms one side of my face only. We cross the rim and look into the caldera and the mineral colors look like ground spices, like they should each own a distinct taste, and on the far side a long wall of ice sits on top of the sulfurous rock like an ancient temple. To our left the trail follows the inside edge of the crater, and now I give Danny his day pack and take my camera bag from Iain, thanking him twice, and walk up the trail weaving between towers of twisted lava until we get to a wall of ice striated with zebra varves and a frozen pond at the base big enough to skate on. Iain is saying this is where we leave the trail and walk the glaciers to the top.

I sit and strap on my crampons, and Bongo helps Danny who has only twice ever seen snow and now at 19,000 feet he is apprenticing in the art of walking on ice. But Danny is not complaining and I know he feels as lousy

*as I do but both of us are smiling and with our spikes on our boots we walk
up the glacier to the crest, and the squeak of the steel biting into the ice is
nostalgic and reassuring. The slope steepens and we have a short hill to
climb that rounds off below us and disappears into space, and on this
smooth ice if you slip you would gain speed faster and faster as you flew
over that edge. I pause to turn and watch Danny but he moves carefully and
I have been in this position before with beginners that you know are okay
because they realize they cannot afford to fall and so they don't. The sun is
above the horizon and the light specular off the ice and I watch Danny and
Iain and Bongo and beyond them all of Africa awakening to a new dawn.*

*I turn and continue and to my right see the main trail, and Rustus and
our other porter and Pete with his handicam who is helping me make a film
of this trip, and around them above and below on the trail maybe ten other
trekkers heading for the top only a hundred meters farther. We keep walking on the ice and our glacier route turns and joins this main track, and in a
few minutes we make the final steps to the highest point. It is eight in the
morning. There are maybe twenty other trekkers here and I sort the conti-
nental Europeans dressed in nylon jackets with neon colors and contrasting
shoulder panels from the Americans in drab enviro greens, blues, and
browns. Everyone takes turns holding the summit signboard, long detached
from its post, that says:* YOU ARE NOW AT UHURU PEAK. THE HIGHEST POINT IN
AFRICA. ALTITUDE 5895 METERS A.S.L. *An Italian in chartreuse pants and silver windbreaker offers to take my camera while we hold the sign; we get our
summit photograph and thank him. Then a young American woman comes
over and even though we are strangers we are sharing this summit so she
smiles and says, "Guess what?" I say, "What?" and she points to a young
man and says, "My boyfriend just proposed to me." So I smile back and ask,
"Did you accept?" and she looks at him and says with mocking uncertainty,
"I don't know . . ." then laughs and says, "I guess I do!" and they kiss. Another woman who appears to be in her early fifties makes slow and painful
steps past me and she has only ten more feet to go so I say, "You made it,"
and she answers, "Thank God." Sensing my thoughts Iain puts his hand on
my shoulder and says in his trickster voice, "And we've only two hundred
and fifty more miles to walk, and we'll be there, too."*

1

Natural Selection has designed us—from the structure of our brain-cells to the structure of our big toe—for a career of seasonal journeys on foot through a blistering land of thorn-scrub or desert.

—*Bruce Chatwin*, The Songlines, *1987*

Iain Allan is widely regarded as the most experienced mountaineer in East Africa. As a teenager, while his classmates played cricket, he was away on weekends ascending Mt. Kenya where today (with his lifelong climbing partner, a British ex-pat named Ian Howell) he has made more first ascents of new routes than anyone. He was born in Scotland, and his parents immigrated to Kenya when he was eight. Today he lives in Karen, a suburb of Nairobi where houses have manicured gardens and wide lawns. His wife is a doctor who is partner in a neighborhood clinic, and they have two young boys, and a teenage daughter by Iain's previous marriage. Their house is old and colonial, and the living room is filled with books on the history of East Africa. Iain's other passion is films, and there are stacks of videos in the corner shelves and elsewhere in the house. To make his living, Iain owns and operates a guide service that takes climbers and trekkers up Mt. Kenya and Kilimanjaro (it was on one of these treks where he met his wife, who is Australian), and he is the only outfitter in East Africa to offer walking safaris in the two great Tsavo National Parks that together form a game land preserve roughly the size of Israel.

For Iain mixing his avocation for climbing with his vocation as a guide has not diminished his zest for mountains and rock crags. When we go climbing I tease him about his budding mid-age girth, but the truth is he can still make moves that are beyond me. He loves good wine and food as much as he loves good books and films, and in the bush he insists on being comfortable whenever there is a choice (and there almost always is). In this regard I compare him to the Duke of Abruzzi, the Italian aristocrat turned mountaineer and explorer. From the 1870s until just before the Great War, Abruzzi made, among many expeditions, the first ascent of Saint Elias, in Alaska, the first climbing exploration of the Mountains of the Moon, and the highest elevation reached by climbers on any mountain during an expedition to K2, in 1909. On that last one, he had porters carry his brass bed 150 miles to base camp, but he was the only one left going when they turned back at over 21,000 feet.

I first met Iain ten years before when I received an assignment to write a screenplay based on the book *No Picnic on Mt. Kenya,* a true story about three Italians imprisoned in a World War II camp at the base of Mt. Kenya who, as a very original antidote to the boredom of prison life, plot to break out, climb the mountain, then turn themselves back in. So I could write more accurately about the climbing part of the story, the producer sent me to Africa to ascend Mt. Kenya, and I hired Iain as my guide. That's when I was first exposed to how safaris and even climbing outings in Africa are organized, at least by Iain. We carried only day packs to the base of the mountain, where Iain has his own hut (actually owned by the Kenya Mountain Club, but used most frequently by Iain), and where his cook, Kahin, got up at one A.M. on summit morning to prepare our substantial breakfast of eggs, sausage, and excellent toast from bread that he had baked fresh for our climb. We were ascending an alpine route called the Ice Window, and when we arrived at the hardest part—a bulge of near-vertical ice—Iain said with a crafty grin, "I forgot to tell you. We have a long tradition in this country that the crux pitch always goes to the visitor." I led the section, and on the 17,000-foot summit I was feeling the combined effect of altitude and jet lag, and by the time we returned to Iain's hut, in the last light of the day, I was thoroughly exhausted.

"How many times have you climbed this peak?" I asked.

"This was my twentieth ascent," he said, "but I've never climbed it this fast before."

"How is that?"

"We always have an extra day to acclimatize. But you being a big Himalayan climber, as well as one of those Hollywood types, always in a hurry, I thought we should speed it up."

Since my first climb up Mt. Kenya I have returned several times to Africa to climb and to trek with Iain. I've enjoyed his mischievous humor his encyclopedic knowledge of East African history, his campside conversation about books and films, his commitment to comfort while climbing or trekking. A few years ago, when we were following a hippo trail along the Galana River in the vast parkland of Tsavo East, Iain mentioned an idea he had to make a foot safari from the summit of Kilimanjaro to the sea. He wanted to follow the watercourse east, first along small rivulets that course down the monumental dome. Then, as the streams gather and grow and feed into the Tsavo River, he would follow hippo trails that border the water as it flows fast and straight through the wild country of Tsavo West. After the river joins the Athi, and the combined waters, now wide and open, become known as the Galana, he would cross the bushlands of Tsavo East, then, when the river leaves the park and its name changes again to the Sabaki, he would continue down trails edged by coconut palms that cut between the slow, bending oxbows, until finally the waters of Kilimanjaro are delivered into the Indian Ocean.

"If that sounds like something you would like to do, let me know."

It was very much something I wanted to do. I realized after that first visit to Tsavo that foot safaris are the only way to gain a tactile knowledge of Africa's wildlands and wild animals. I had stood in the roof hatch of a Land Rover watching a herd of elephant in the Masai Mara, and I had stood on foot watching a herd of elephant in Tsavo East. In the vehicle, while it was still fascinating to watch the animals browse in the open fever tree savanna, I was a detached observer. It was like going to a large zoo where I was the one in a cage. Watching elephant on foot was altogether different. On foot, I studied the direction of the wind, I watched every animal's movement to make certain they hadn't detected us. I heard their breathing and the sound of their ears flapping and their stomachs rumbling. I smelled their dung. I felt the sandy soil under my feet and the acacia scrub scratch my legs as we approached the herd. And I moved stealthily, taking great care not to step on any branches.

So I had no doubt about wanting to extend that experience into a one-month foot safari. The only thing preventing my making the trip was figuring out how to pay for it. Extended safaris in East Africa are expensive. Fortunately, I make my living following various pursuits connected to the world of outdoor adventure, and I have experience figuring out how—by book or film or photographs or lectures or endorsements—to finance such endeavors. This professional interest started one day in 1976 at about 24,000 feet on the side of Everest's Lhotse Face. I was asked by a CBS crew that was filming our expedition to climb with them up the face, an expanse of ice about the size of a vertical Central Park. As the cameraman climbed into position, then signaled me to start, it dawned on me that we were both doing the same thing: climbing. Only there was one difference: He was getting paid.

When I returned from the Everest climb I called the film's director, Mike Hoover, who was then at the forefront of adventure filmmaking. "The most important things you need," he told me, "are good ideas." I had those. In fact, I had a folder in my file cabinet labeled "good ideas," and in it were notes from reading Baron von Humboldt's *Travels to the Americas,* written in 1802, that included references to mysterious rock towers rising out of the Venezuelan jungle. One in particular had a cave piercing the summit side to side, like the eye of a needle, and was said by locals to be the lair of a dinosaur-like creature that at night descended the mountain and raided villages. I wrote up a proposal, Hoover sent it to ABC television, and we were on our way.

The climb was exciting, and while there was no dinosaur in the cave, ABC liked the film. That started me on a series of adventure films, and Hoover was my mentor. We made a film documenting a skiing and climbing adventure to Antarctica, in 1979, before it was a popular destination for mountaineers. The only way to get there was to book passage on a tour boat, and once there we had the captain let us off in a glacier-lined bay with gear, enough food for two months, and two rubber Zodiacs with outboards. The only thing we didn't have was a ride home. We skied, climbed, and explored in our small boats, and at the end of our two months we spotted the British icebreaker that services their bases leaving the coast and heading out to sea. We panicked and gave our outboards full throttle and didn't catch the ship until we were five miles offshore. We paced alongside yelling and waving, but it was still some minutes before a deckhand happened to see us. The captain ordered the icebreaker head-to-wind, and the full crew gathered on the rail and stared down at two thirteen-foot rubber boats with the four of us wind-burnt and wet in the twenty-nine-degree water. They didn't say anything and neither did we until my boatmate yelled up, "We were just wondering if you had any beer you could spare?" They nodded and one of them left and came back in a moment and lowered a case of McEwans Scotch Ale over the side. All of us except Beverly, who chose not to participate in these male antics, forced ourselves against the cold to open a can each and take big drafts, and then look up and say, "We were also wondering if we could hitch a ride north, maybe to Argentina?"

By 1980 I had produced my first adventure documentary for television, and since then I have made one or two a year, on the average. When a film producer called and said he needed a one-hour program for a new adventure series, I remembered Iain's idea. The producer liked the sound of a Kilimanjaro Summit-to-Sea trek, so I called Iain and he was immediately enthusiastic and said he would think about who else to invite. The first person who came to mind was Bill Woodley. Bill had been assistant warden of Tsavo East for ten years. He had climbed Kilimanjaro twice. He had been senior warden of Mountain Parks (now divided into Aberdare and Mt. Kenya National Parks), then senior warden of Tsavo West. He had probably walked more miles in those places than any nonnative in history. There was only one problem. Bill Woodley had died in 1995.

Two of Bill's sons, however, were following his footsteps, and Iain proposed to invite them to join our trek. At the time, Bongo Woodley was thirty-two years old and senior warden of Mt. Kenya National Park, where he had climbed the peak several times and gained basic mountaineering knowledge as well as mountain rescue skills. He had sandy hair and tanned skin from his life outdoors, and, like his father, he had experience bush walking and knew how to handle himself in the presence of wild animals. While he had poor eyesight, corrected by substantial glasses, he was nevertheless an expert shot. Bongo grew up in the Mt. Kenya area when his father was warden there, and later, during breaks from boarding school, he walked the bush on patrol with his father after Bill was transferred to Tsavo West. Iain knew that if Bill were alive, he would jump at the chance to make this trek, so he assumed that Bongo would also be up for the adventure. He was right. Bongo didn't hesitate to accept. "I haven't had a chance to walk that bush country in Tsavo since Dad died," he told Iain.

Bongo's younger brother Danny also worked for the national park system (called the Kenya Wildlife Service), leading a team that controls problem animals in the inhabited areas adjacent to the parks, mostly rogue elephant that invade farmers' fields. His father had been transferred from Mountain Parks to Tsavo West when Danny was a small boy, and Danny grew up sitting in the backseat of his father's small plane helping him spot poachers. Danny had clear, tanned skin, short-cropped hair the same sand color as Bongo's, and a quick smile that exposed even, white teeth. He wore the same style of thick-lensed glasses that Bongo favored, and while it is easy to tell they are brothers, Danny seemed to be the one to have inherited his father's mischievous habits, and certainly his father's appeal to women. When he was a teenager, Danny was widely known as a prankster and was

regarded by everyone as rebellious. While now he was very committed to
helping preserve Kenya's wildlands and wildlife, he still enjoyed a good
party, always had time for a good story, and loved telling jokes, all traits that
were characteristic of his father.

Like Bongo, Danny also signed up immediately when he was invited to
join the trek, although he was in equal measures enthusiastic about walking
across Tsavo and apprehensive about climbing Kilimanjaro. Not only did
Danny have no mountaineering experience, he had seen snow only twice in
his life; what he remembered most from those experiences was how much
he hated being cold. If that was the price, however, for the chance to walk in
one continuous line across Tsavo, and then continue from the boundary of
the park all the way to the ocean, he was willing to pay it.

2

Think of your life in nature—daily to be shown matter, to come in contact with it,—rocks, trees, wind in our cheeks! the solid earth! the actual world! the common sense! Contact! Contact!

—Henry David Thoreau,
from "Ktaadn" in The Maine Woods, *1864*

Most of my adventuring has focused on climbing mountains, and one aspect of long expeditions to remote ranges that I have enjoyed has been the approach marches, the sometimes very long walks through roadless regions. The Kilimanjaro trek was going to be an approach march in reverse: We were going to climb the mountain first, and then make our long walk *away* from it. Iain estimated that including the climb up one side of Kilimanjaro and down the other, we would walk about five hundred kilometers, and that to do it would require a little over three weeks' time. Iain also told me, after studying maps of the area, he had determined that for most of our route once off the mountain, he could position our campsites in places accessible to his four-wheel-drive vehicles. That meant that for the most part we would not have to take porters.

"There are dirt roads that reach the river here and there, so Kahin and the men can drive the vehicles from one campsite to the next while we walk on the game tracks alongside the river. There may be one or two places the vehicles cannot access, and there we may have to carry our gear in larger packs, but otherwise we can get by with day packs. Don't worry, it will be well organized."

I wasn't worried. I had been with Iain enough to know that "well organized" meant it would be a Duke of Abruzzi trip. It meant "Iain's men" (the very competent and very affable Kenyan crew who work for his adventure travel company) would each day have our tents set up for us by the time we walked into camp; that we would have one community mess tent with a folding table and chairs where we could gather for dinner and breakfast; we would have a portable shower with warm water heated over the campfire and poured into a collapsible bucket suspended over our heads; there would be a cold box with dry ice and chilled beer; and, most important, we would have Kahin, the expert campfire cook, preparing our meals. We would have to average twenty-five kilometers a day, and we would have to walk in sometimes oven-hot temperatures, but still it would be, compared at least to the expeditions I most commonly went on, a luxury trip.

◈

Luxury or not, the trip held promise to be much more than just another climb up a mountain or trek across a wilderness. One element that had captured my fancy was a particular interest that Danny had in the final section of our walk. Once we left Tsavo East and followed the Sabaki River into the ranchland regions outside the park boundary, we would be in country that once was the stronghold of a hunting tribe known as the Waliangulu. Danny had never met a Waliangulu, but as far back as he could remember his father had told him stories about these People of the Long Bow who were the greatest native elephant hunters on the continent of Africa. He remembered his father telling him about the size of their bows, and more, about their legendary draw weights. They were said to be the most powerful bows ever made by any native peoples in the world. He also knew that his father had learned the nuances of hunting elephant from these Waliangulu, and it was his skills as a hunter that Danny most admired about his father. Danny considered those skills the most valuable thing his father had passed to him.

When Bill Woodley was nineteen years old he had been posted to Tsavo as a junior assistant warden and charged with the task of ascertaining the extent of poaching in the new park by native bow hunters. Bill crossed part of Tsavo East on foot, walking many of the game trails we would follow on our trek, and there he discovered vultures darkening the sky over the carcasses of clephant with their tusks hacked out. He soon learned most of this poaching was the work of these mysterious Waliangulu: a small adaptable group that made their living hunting elephant. He also soon realized that when the new park was created, no one had told the Waliangulu that their hunting lands no longer belonged to them but to the government. No one had explained that what they had been doing for centuries was now against the law. No one thought to consult them because none of the park's founders really understood that the Waliangulu were as fundamental to the ecosystem as the elephant themselves.

So it fell to Bill to tell the Waliangulu they could be jailed for something they had been doing for centuries. Bill then pursued the Waliangulu for ten years and made several hundred arrests. At the same time he developed a deep respect both for their hunting skills and for their guileless honesty. Whenever they were released from prison, he worked hard to win them jobs as park rangers, game scouts for safari outfitters, trackers, and gun bearers. The Waliangulu, however, weren't successful in making the conversion from hunters to workers-for-hire; when they were let go by their new employers they walked back to their villages, and the outside world forgot about them.

At that time, in 1996, it was not known if any of the bow hunters were still alive, or, if they were, what had become of them. Danny wanted to find out.

◈

I had my own particular interests regarding the trek, and foremost was to see what it would be like to walk for an extended period in the close company of potentially dangerous mammals. I had experienced encounters with dangerous animals a few times before in my wilderness travels, but all of these had been brief. Once navigating in native dugouts along the Casiquiare canal, a natural waterway that connects the Amazon to the Orinoco, with a mix of Yekuana and Yanomami Indians, we stopped for the evening to pitch camp. As we stepped out of the canoe, one Indian pointed excitedly to a paw print at river's edge. It was a jaguar, and it was so recent the water was still filling into the mud cast. We cut saplings and lashed them with vines to construct a pole frame to hang our hammocks, and we slept cheek by jowl and through the night I could feel the big cat watching us. Like a fish finding comfort swimming in the middle of the school, I was glad I was not on either of the two end positions.

I have only felt this hyperalertness, this caution like a warning buzz in my ear, twice when hiking in the United States. Once in Montana's Bob Marshall, the largest contiguous wilderness in the lower forty-eight states, I found my eyes scanning the hillsides like radar seeking brown-humped blips that would indicate grizzly. Another time in the Sespe Wilderness of my own backyard mountains in California, I was walking with my five-year-old boy at a time when a hiker in the area had been recently mauled by a mountain lion. Without thinking, I placed my boy directly in front of me and kept him within a ten-pace distance as our trail entered a rocky defile.

The image of the stalking lion stayed with me through our hike, but there was another image that was missing. Had I been a Chumash Indian two hundred years earlier I would have held in my vision the image of both the mountain lion and the grizzly bear. The Chumash had a significant village in the valley of Ojai where I now live in the coastal range twelve miles inland, and early missionaries and visitors reported that in all these villages in Southern California it was common to hear stories of Indians killed by bear, and even more common to see inhabitants that bore the scars of direct encounters. In his logbook of his voyage up the California coast in 1602, the Spanish navigator Sebastian Vizcaino reported seeing the carcass of a whale on the beach with grizzlies crawling over it thick as flies. In my own backyard, the Ventura River was once a corridor for bear coming down from the mountains to the beach; one Spaniard, on his way up the river from the Buenaventura Mission, near the beach, to his ranch in Matilija Canyon in the hills just behind Ojai, reported counting over one hundred grizzlies in a single day. Although the river is now tamed by a dam and an attendant diversion canal, it is still undeveloped in places and many times, driving the road that parallels it, I have imagined how it was when wholly wild.

The flood bed is a field of river rock covered with dried gray algae and within the wild buckwheat I see a large brown alpha bear on his way from the pine mountain backcountry to the beach to fish and dig clams and maybe even find a stranded whale, the bear himself moving like a land whale, and there downriver from my vantage is a Chumash stalking through the gravelbed chaparral hunting for small game. The Indian follows a single quail that lags the covey, and he moves like a stalking lion so focused on the bird he misses the bear coming down the same game trail until he hears the deep exhale and then it is too late. The brown bear rears on his hind legs and the hunter can smell the animal's warm, stale breath and his own smell of fear and death and he knows his arrows are nothing but he knows too what to do because he has thought this through many times in his life and he has been taught by the elders whatever you do don't

run but force yourself still and talk to the bear and tell him in soothing voice
that you are only looking for your food as he is looking for his and then
slowly turn your head and present your neck because the bear knows this is
submission. The great bear holds ground, then lowers and exhales and
breathes again and lets the Indian live.

As a species we evolved to survive encounters such as this, and to my
mind there can be no doubt that vestiges of these skills remain with us today
even as we have driven the beasts out of our lives and into the caves of obliv-
ion. Today we no longer worry about living among stalking predators until
on rare occasion a mountain lion takes a boy while he is out hiking with his
family, and then we are outraged and our hired agents hunt down and destroy the beast that has trespassed from our primitive past to make such a
shocking affront to our modern present. We are safe. But at what cost?

It was my hope on our walk to see if I could find out.

3

The creation of order, of which man is an example, is realized also in the number of species and habitats, an abundance of landscapes lush and poor. Even deserts and tundras increase the planetary opulence. Curiously, only man and possibly a few birds can appreciate this opulence, being the world's travelers.

—Paul Shepard,
"Ecology and Man—A Viewpoint,"
published in The Subversive Science, 1969

We descend from the summit rim of Kilimanjaro down a wide swath of scree that's like a miniature glacier of pea-sized pumice that advances ever so slightly downhill with each of our footsteps. We make wide strides, breaking on occasion into a series of hops, like skiers with no skis. We lose elevation quickly and my headache disappears. Iain is ahead and waits when he reaches a small trail that breaks off east toward the Kenya border. When I arrive I take a rest and enjoy the view. To our right the summit of Mawenzi is now above us; to our left the trail we are about to follow continues for miles down the sloping volcanic dome until both trail and dome roll over the edge into a soft floor of cloud that spreads east to the horizon.

Assisted by gravity, leavened by the memory of morning light glistening on equatorial ice, we descend the single-track trail in full jaunty strides, and within an hour the first scrub bushes reappear between the basalt rocks, and Bongo stops to examine a set of tracks crossing our trail. "Eland," he says. "Some days old." He stands and gazes across the open chaparral toward Mawenzi. Earlier Iain had told us that in this alpine desert region on Kilimanjaro we might see duiker, one of the smallest of the antelope—about the size of a large jackrabbit—or, if we were truly fortunate, eland, the largest of the antelope—about the size of an ox and weighing up to a ton. Eland are found abundantly in certain mid-elevation grasslands in East Africa, but there is also a secluded population on the higher plateaus buttressing the flanks of Kilimanjaro that has adapted to the cold by growing long, shaggy hair. They are, however, rare and elusive, and Iain said in his twenty-two previous trips up this mountain he has never seen them. They used to be common in the high tussock between Mawenzi and Kili. In his book, *Snow on the Equator,* the redoubtable British mountaineer H. W. Tilman, on a solo climb in 1933, described seeing a herd of twenty-seven eland only a short distance from where we stand over these prints. "They seemed to be subsisting very happily on a diet of shale, and were very shy."

They are now even more shy for they have been poached to near extinction by the Chagga tribesmen who live around the base of the mountain. And not just the eland. When we climbed up the Umbwe route on the Tanzanian side, the *Podocarpus* forest was dead of any game even though our trail was remote and sees comparatively little traffic from trekkers or mountaineers. Higher on the mountain the only mammals that seem to have survived intact against the years of hunting and poaching are the hyrax, a rabbit-sized animal that looks something like a marmot, and the leopard that travel to higher elevations to hunt the hyrax.

◈

At our first camp on the way up the mountain, Iain told us a disquieting story about an encounter with a leopard when he had last ascended the Umbwe track, twenty years earlier. "I was with two friends, a husband and wife, coming up to do the Heim Glacier route. They had been in Africa only a few weeks, so they were still new to the place. Shortly after going to bed we heard a leopard in the forest but I told them it was nothing to worry about. Then in the middle of the night Barbara sat up and said, 'There's something outside.' About ten feet from the tent we heard this horrible growl. It was the leopard. I yelled and it ran off, so I said, 'It's gone now, there's nothing more to worry about.' Then about ten minutes later it was back, but this time from the opposite side. I told everyone to shout because I didn't want the leopard to get used to only my voice. We succeeded again in scaring him off, but he was back once more in ten minutes, and we yelled again, at a different pitch. This went on until dawn, and each time we had to figure out a new way to scare him, and each time he came back he seemed to return that much more emboldened. By dawn we were all exhausted.

"We packed the tent and started up the trail, and traveled only a short distance when ahead I heard this heart-stopping growl, and just in front of us I caught a glimpse of the leopard as it jumped off a rock. By this point I was more than just frightened: I was worried for our lives. A week earlier a solo Japanese climber attempting this same route had disappeared, and although it was assumed he had wandered off route in the forest and fallen or died in some other way, I now suspected this leopard had taken him. I decided then and there to abandon the climb and get out, but even walking down the trail was frightening: We kept looking over our shoulders."

That night there were no leopard around our camp, and the next day, once we climbed above the forest and entered the zone of the giant groundsel (a Jurassic-looking plant that grows to thirty feet and has cabbage-shaped rosettes of green leaves on the ends of naked, palmlike trunks), we saw several specimens of leopard scat deposited in the middle of the trail. "There are leopard everywhere," Iain had said.

"It's probably only one animal," Bongo replied as he bent over the droppings. "And likely a male, laying scat in one area." Bongo poked the dropping with a stick. "This fur's a bit thin for a hyrax or duiker, so it could be a small rodent, perhaps the groove-toothed rat or the stripy field mouse." He broke the scat and looked closer. "Leopards eat mice all day long, like they were Mars bars."

"How high do they normally range?" I asked.

"There's the case of the famous one up on the main dome of Kibo itself."

Bongo referred to the carcass of a leopard that was discovered in the early 1920s at about 18,500 feet on the main route just below the crater rim, and it inspired the famous preface in Hemingway's short story "The Snows of Kilimanjaro" where he wrote that "close to the western summit there is the dried and frozen carcass of a leopard. No one has explained what the leopard was seeking at that altitude." The rocky promontory where the carcass lay became known as Leopard's Point, and in 1926 a local pastor climbing the mountain boasted that he cut off one of the animal's ears as a souvenir. On his 1933 climb Tilman reported the desiccated remains were still there.

"I have never heard any explanation of how it came to be there," Tilman wrote, "but presumably it went up on its own volition."

Other than the hyrax, the leopard scat was the last sign of any mammal we've seen until these eland tracks. I glass the slopes with my small binoculars, then hand them to Iain, but neither of us spot anything. We continue down the trail. This track we are descending, known as the Loitokitok-Rongai route—after the town nearest the trailhead—crosses the border out of Tanzania and into Kenya while still on the mountain's flank, and it has only been in the last two years that an earlier political estrangement between the two countries has thawed sufficiently that trekkers are again allowed to climb up and down this side of Kilimanjaro. Iain has gone one step farther, however, and succeeded in arranging for us special permission to traverse the mountain up the Tanzanian side and now down this way, and we are the first party allowed to do so in many years.

Our goal is Third Cave, one of the traditional campsites on the route, and soon we arrive at this clamshell-shaped opening in the side of the lava flow that appears to have been formed as a natural bubble in the cooling magma. There is smoke coming out the entrance, where our porters are gathered around a fire.

"What time is it?" I ask.

"Eleven thirty," Iain says.

"No way. It feels like four thirty."

We have already put in nearly a twelve-hour day, but we all feel like we can keep going. "What do you say we carry on to Second Cave," Iain suggests. "That will lessen the distance tomorrow, which otherwise could be quite a full day."

Iain is concerned that we pace ourselves or otherwise we might not hold up the entire distance. I'm more optimistic even though I recognize there is always the chance one or more of us could get knocked out by illness, or more remotely, injured by a charging animal, or a crocodile. It is even possible we could encounter poachers or bandits and get mixed up in a shoot-out. But as far as having the mental stamina to keep stepping one foot in front of the other, I suspect from these first few days together, we are all capable.

The only foreboding I have is the heat I know we will encounter in Tsavo. When I was there two years ago, my family was with me, and it was hot. My

wife had asked whether it was a good idea to have our three young children
out walking two and three hours at a stretch. "It's not that hot," I had assured her, but then the glue holding the rubber soles on my Nikes melted
and I had to secure the bottoms with duct tape. "That's nice, Rick," my wife
said after she had asked what the tape was about. "I wonder what the heat is
doing to the kids' brains?" That evening I quietly asked Iain if they kept a
thermometer in camp. "It was up to 125 today," he said. "In the shade. In
the sun I think it was closer to 150."

All in all, Iain's point about pacing is valid, and by the time we reach Second Cave we are all fatigued. The cave is large and has a sandy floor and the
ceiling, about fifteen feet high at the entrance, is blackened by the resinous
accretion of hundreds of campfires. It will be a good bivouac for the porters.
We pitch our tents on a nearby flat covered with clumps of tussock and have
our meal. The mountain is shrouded in gray cloud, and now that the sun is
down the chaparral around our camp has also turned gray. By the time we
crawl in our tents we have been awake for twenty hours. Lying in my bag, I
feel a sudden depression that is a strange counterpoint to the euphoria of
the summit morning, and the pleasure of the afternoon walk. It's as though
I have somehow acquired Iain's uncertainty, and now I'm not as self-
confident as I was even an hour ago. It's not that I doubt we can make it, but
it's more that I don't have my usual enthusiasm.

Lying in my bag, reflecting on the last four days, the trip, to this point,
feels in overview a disappointment. Not that it hasn't been beautiful, especially the first two days on the Umbwe route. Even in the rain I enjoyed hiking through the cloud forest, the *Podocarpus* almost a hundred feet high, the
Spanish moss in the branches giving the forest a kind of fairy-book enchant-
ment. The undergrowth was thick with tree ferns that overhung the trail,
and water dripped off the ends of their feathered fronds. Then on the second day the *Podocarpus* dwindled to a few scraggly dwarfs, and we ascended in a forest of giant heather, and through occasional openings we
could see the southern glaciers of Kilimanjaro.

I had enjoyed it, but then at high camp the Umbwe merged with one of
the two main routes up Kili, and the site was crowded with over fifteen tents
from other groups, and was littered with garbage and smelled like someone
had locked me in a well-used outhouse. There are over twenty thousand
people a year who now climb Kilimanjaro, and the mountain is suffering
under such traffic.

More disappointing, however, was to discover the mountain bereft of wild
animals. I wanted to see the long-haired eland running across alpine tundra

framed between backdrop glaciers. Where were the mountain elephant with their short ears and squat bodies more adapted to cold? The colobus monkeys with their black and white tuxedo coats?

I know there will be wild animals when we reach Tsavo. I know my funk is related to the fact it has been twenty-one hours since I last slept. I turn to Iain to say good night, but he is already breathing steadily and deeply as people do who fall asleep from a pervading exhaustion, and in a few minutes I also drift out of the sentient world.

4

Just because I am an officer doesn't mean I have to sit in an office.

—*Bill Woodley,*
in a frequent comment to his friends

The sun strikes my side of the tent, and I am awake. The sky is clear, the mountain bright, and on the summit of Kilimanjaro the line where the ice meets the sky is sharp, white against blue. I feel not only cheerful but vibrant. My uncertain thoughts last night about the negative aspects of the climb were just that, negative thoughts. I make note to be vigilant of mixing gray landscapes under gray skies with no sleep.

We have a leisurely morning washing up and shaving, then we begin the day's walk. The trail continues in a straight line, dropping off the edge of the dome toward a quilt of clouds that blankets the lowlands. We walk through a maze of ten-foot-high bushes with bright orchid-shaped yellow flowers and tiny leaves the shape and color of oregano. Nearby I recognize the song of the hunter's cisticola, and in a turn of the trail I spot them at the top of a bush, two nondescript brown birds, their throats pulsing first one and then the other, sharing the distinct parts of their song in such perfect and continuous harmony that if Iain hadn't told me earlier how they sing in duet, I would have assumed it was a single bird.

Yesterday Bongo and Danny spotted prints of buffalo near Second Cave, but otherwise there is still no sign of wildlife. We cross the nascent gully

of a seasonal stream, and in the bottom is a small olive tree, stunted from
its vanguard position at the very edge of the tree line. We step over another streambed, with small pools of clear water lined with emerald moss.
The olive trees now become more frequent, and many have branches
blackened from a recent fire. "Honey hunters," Bongo says, "trying to
smoke out bees."

We pass First Cave, the traditional bivouac of the beginning stage of the
Rongai section of the Loitokitok ascent. The trail merges with the road head
of a four-wheel track that is covered with a fine, shoe-deep dust that pow-
ders our leg hairs. There are flowering protea along the trailside, and Bongo
points out the first East African pencil cedar. These tall, hearty evergreens
grow to over a hundred feet and are common in the mid-elevation zones on
the equatorial mountains of Africa. Like the American red cedars, their
wood is used to manufacture pencils, and also like the American trees, these
are not true cedars, but rather junipers. (It's interesting that most of the
trees that are commonly called cedars are often something else, and that
there are only four true cedars in the world: the historical cedars of
Lebanon, the atlas cedar of North Africa, the deodar of the Himalayas, and
the Cyprian cedar of its namesake island.)

In only fifteen minutes we complete the transition from open bush to
gallery forest. One of the aspects I enjoy most hiking the glacial mountains
of equatorial Africa is the speed with which you pass through almost every
climatic zone on Earth; it's like taking a supersonic transport from the high
Arctic to the low equator. The canopy closes over the road, and Bongo identifies East African olive as well as a very large fig, the biggest tree in the forest, with its great trunk made of a dozen or more columns, some freestanding
and then joined higher up.

"You know these trees quite well," I say to Bongo. He answers that most
of them occur in the forests that ring Mt. Kenya, and there he has made a
personal effort to learn their natural history. Bongo has been warden of Mt.
Kenya for six years, and his jurisdiction includes not only the mountain, but
also the surrounding moorlands and forests. I ask him what a typical day is
like on his job.

"I usually start with a morning flight in my small plane over the mountain.
With good weather I take a look at the three main climbing routes, to make
sure any parties on the mountain are safe. I look for fires, animals on the
moorlands, parties of tourists that may be having trouble. Then I go into the
office for the rest of the day, attending to paperwork. I have seventy people
under me. In the evenings I try to get out again, for either another flight or
a drive up one of the tracks.

"With my father a warden," he continues, "I grew up in the national parks, on Mt. Kenya, and across the way, in the Aberdares. Now being a warden myself, I'm still there, in the parks. So you see, it's the only life I've known."

It was the only life his father knew as well. I knew a little of Bill's history from previous conversations with Iain, and one evening during our climb up Kilimanjaro he told me more. We were camped at the top of the Umbwe track and all of us had stayed out to enjoy the alpenglow on the summit glaciers, until we finished the single bottle of whiskey we had brought on the climb. I shared a tent with Iain, and once we were snug in our bags we got on the subject of Bill Woodley.

"He was a big influence on my life," Iain said. "I met him when I first started climbing on Mt. Kenya, when I was fifteen or sixteen. He was at that time warden of the park, and he very quickly had me on his rescue team, and was very supportive when I started my climbing guide service. Then in 1979 there was a total eclipse of the sun and the epicenter was to be in Tsavo, and I had a group of American scientists who wanted me to take them there. By then Bill had been transferred to Tsavo West, so I went down to see him, to work out the details. It was only a few months after he had returned from surgery, to treat his stomach cancer. He took me up in his plane, to fly around and have a look. We were over the Tsavo River, and I remember looking down at the hippos lining the banks, the doum palms, the rock face of Kichwa Tembo framing everything, and Bill turning to me and saying, 'Great country down there. You should think about doing walking safaris.'

"And now those safaris are the mainstay of my business. So you see, I owe him a lot, and not just from a business point of view, but because he was such an honorable man; I think he influenced me even more in that regard. It's a shame we never stopped that time to visit him."

Iain referred to a time a few years before when I was in Africa scouting locations for that film project based on the story *No Picnic on Mt. Kenya.* Iain and I had again climbed the peak, and on the way back to Nairobi he proposed we stop and chat with Bill and Ruth Woodley. Bill had by then left Tsavo and retired to a small house on the slopes of Mt. Kenya, where Ruth enjoyed the cool air, but we were late getting off the mountain, I had a return flight to catch, and we postponed the visit. Ruth died the next year, and Bill followed soon after.

"If I had that one to do over I would postpone the flight, not the visit."

The next day, as we hiked a contour trail that connected the Umbwe to the main track, all of us stopped for a rest and I asked Bongo to tell me about the first time he had climbed Kilimanjaro.

"I was fourteen, and it was just Dad, my brother Benjamin, two rangers, and myself. My most enduring memory is arriving at Marangu Hut and finding a German who had died of a heart attack. There was another casualty still alive, but they had the dead German on the only stretcher, and I remember Dad taking charge and removing the body to free up the stretcher for the sick person, who had priority. Mountain rescues were the talk of our household, so the incident didn't bother me that much."

"How would your dad have felt about a trip like the one we're doing?"

"He would have been right in it," Danny said. "He was a walker."

"One day shortly before he died," Iain said, "he told me that when he first started in Tsavo he had to walk, because there were no roads, and he wondered then what it would be like to drive. Then one day he was driving and he wondered what it would be like to fly, and now that he was retired from flying he said it was time to go back on foot, to do more walking. But of course by then his health was gone."

"So maybe he's walking with us in spirit," I said.

Danny smiled and said, "Except he's got the bottle of whiskey, and we don't."

❧

Later I would ask Bongo and Danny what they thought the most important thing was they had learned from their father. "The love of the bush," Bongo said. "Love of the outdoors, of life in the national parks. He paused, then added, "and integrity. That was the main thing. To his dying day he was the most honest man I've known, and I like to think I've got a bit of that in me, too."

I turned to Danny. "The most important thing for me," he said, "was to be taught to think like a hunter."

"How is that?"

"We were brought up with the belief that to be a good warden you have to be a good hunter. Dad believed that nobody knows an animal better than the man who has had to hunt it. I think of myself as a hunter because I enjoy the way of living that revolves around hunting. Being in a dangerous moment, relying on every sense you have: tracking skills, hearing, seeing, smelling, your reaction time in a split second to a very dangerous situation."

"Your father was a hunter even while he was a park warden?"

"There was always control work to be done, buffalo harassing people, elephants raiding *shambas*. Apart from that, Dad would take out a license for an elephant each year, especially when he was younger because an assistant warden's salary didn't come to much, and a good pair of tusks made a nice supplement. He hunted outside the parks, the Tana River and such, so it was all legal, of course."

"It wasn't seen as a conflict?"

"No, not then."

"Later?"

"Later all hunting became illegal. It was banned."

It seemed to me like a contradiction: to be a warden dedicated to the conservation of wild animals, and at the same time to hunt those animals for sport and for their ivory. It also seemed like a contradiction to arrest and jail the Waliangulu, the tribe whose entire culture revolved around hunting elephant but then, given the choice, head out to do just the same.

As our trek continued, and I came to know and understand Bill better, and after our trek, when I would talk to many of his friends, I would discover that most of his contemporaries who were park and game wardens were also active hunters. Most of them, like Bill, had come to conservation from a background of professional hunting, usually as safari guides, but sometimes, like Bill, as professional ivory hunters. All of them had grown up in an era when, if you loved life in the wild bush, you nearly always pursued that love through hunting.

It would take some thinking and some research before I came to understand this, but when I did, I would also understand how they justified their arrests and punishments of the Waliangulu. Understanding this would help me to understand better the differences that exist today between Africa's conservationists over not only the preservation of wildlife, but also the conflict between that wildlife and Africa's rural populations; this, in turn, would allow me to see better the possible futures that lay ahead for this vast bushland and its wild animals.

5

Above all do not lose your desire to walk.

—*Kierkegaard,*
as quoted in Bruce Chatwin, The Songlines, *1987*

We realize the *bandas* that Iain has arranged for our lodging this evening are some miles to the east and south, so we begin to contour first across fields, then through a grove of nursery pine that has been planted in perfect rows so the trunks blink stroboscopically as we walk through. Somewhere at the edge of the grove a chainsaw makes its keening wail. We gain another road and soon we can see the cabins.

"I recognize where we are now," Bongo says. "We could have descended the Naro Moru route and ended up right here."

"I've never come down that way," Iain replies. "So I didn't realize that."

"Bloody would have saved two hours walking."

Iain doesn't respond, and after a pause Danny says, "The porters may not have been able to come down that way, though, if it isn't in their concession."

"Nevertheless, it's still piss poor planning," Bongo says.

Iain still doesn't reply, and there is a residual tension that lasts until we arrive at the cabins. They are attractive bungalows arranged around a large, open lawn at the edge of the forest, and constructed recently in the hope that the newly opened Loitokitok route would attract quantities of trekkers. The fresh pine walls smell resinous, and the beds have laundered sheets.

Within a half hour, two vehicles arrive from Nairobi with Kahin the cook, the other camp assistants, and the provisions we will need for the next week or so. We pay off our Kilimanjaro porters, and their manager, who by previous arrangement has driven around the mountain from the Tanzanian side to take them back. All is according to the plan that Iain designed weeks before, and it unfolds without delay.

❖

I wake at first dawn and listen to the birds in the forest as they begin their songs. Sleeping in a bed has been an unexpected luxury. The temperature is about sixty degrees, and I indulge myself lying between the sheets for a few extra minutes, thinking that today is the autumn equinox, which means, from our latitudinal position not quite three degrees south of the equator, the day will be very much the same length as the night.

We all gather for a hearty breakfast prepared by Kahin, who I remember fondly from my previous safaris with Iain. Kahin is a Kikuyu who lives on a small family *shamba* outside of Nairobi where he farms in the off-season. He is five foot six, and like all of Iain's staff, he has a ready smile, but with Kahin you have the impression that behind the smile his thoughts are distracted, and you soon learn that indeed he spends nearly all his time concentrating on his cooking. He is the most accomplished open-fire chef I have ever encountered. He has coerced Iain into paying for subscriptions to most of Europe's food magazines. He may be the only African featured in an article in the English edition of *Gourmet*. He has an instinctive palate, and he is completely self-taught. He will take a recipe from a magazine and know how to adapt it to the local ingredients available to him; or he will read a recipe and use it only as a base of inspiration for his own creation. All of this on a bed of coals using Dutch pots and a coal-fed oven.

After breakfast we hire a local to guide us down trails that shortcut the dirt roads into town. With the camp supplies that arrived yesterday all of us also received our personal kit for the lowland part of our walk, and this morning Danny and Bongo are dressed in khaki shorts and shirts, and in addition Danny has knee-length mowgli-green socks. They both look like wardens.

We begin the day's walk, passing a sign that reads NARO MORU TRAIL, and Iain says, "If we would have come down this trail yesterday we could have saved two hours. Think of that, two whole hours!"

Everyone laughs, including Bongo, and whatever rancor existed the day before is gone. The sky is blue, the air is cool, and I'm in a good mood even knowing that today will probably be the least pleasant of our trek. We have to walk fifteen kilometers along the road that rings Kilimanjaro, until we reach a small drainage called the Mogoini that we then follow as it flows eastward into Masai land.

It's market day in Loitokitok, and in the town commons hundreds of farmers display their produce on squares of colorful cotton *kikois* spread on the ground. We pass a carpentry shop that makes furniture, and Iain pauses to study the small wooden building, then says, "This used to be a bar, owned by an old half-caste Singh, where I stopped whenever I was through here on safari to have a beer. The old man used to tell me his bar had been a favorite of the great American hunter Hemingway. I took the story with a grain of salt, until one time he pulled out a box from under the counter, and showed me a letter addressed to him, and at the bottom it was signed 'Your Friend, Ernest Hemingway.'"

There aren't many visitors now to Loitokitok, especially ones entering on foot through the back door of town, and passersby slow and gawk. Down the street we see the vehicle that has brought the three Kenya Wildlife Service rangers who will accompany us from here all the way to the ocean. They are all three dressed in camouflage field uniforms, and each has a semiautomatic assault rifle resting upright on his thigh. They are here to protect us as we walk through Tsavo from potentially dangerous animals (especially buffalo, crocodile, and hippo) and, as we walk through the remote ranchland country below Tsavo, from Somali bandits and poachers who are known to frequent the area and would think nothing of robbing and murdering a group of *mzungus* traveling on foot.

Two of the rangers are from the proud and warlike Nilotic tribes of Northern Kenya. Mohamed—a sergeant and the most senior of the three—is the six-foot-seven Samburu; Lokiyor is a six-foot-four Turkana. Galogalo, at five-foot-eleven, is Rendille, a tribe also from Northern Kenya, but descending from peoples of Hamitic origins. The three crawl out of the open-backed Land Rover and stand on an elevated curb, guns at their sides, as Danny introduces them to Pete, our cameraman, and to me. I already know Mohamed from the foot safari I had made with Iain two years before. He made such a vivid impression on me at that time that in the interim I have wondered if my memory has built him into something larger than life. But his face is just as I remembered: the pierced ears, the lower lobes distended, as is the Samburu custom; the knife scar across one half of his face; the impossibly red eyes, like the eyes of a night-stalking animal. Those two years before, Iain had arranged to have Mohamed first meet us at a tourist hotel near the entrance gate to Tsavo. We were at poolside, with dozens of other tourists, when Mohamed approached. Then, as now, he was dressed in camouflage fatigues and black field boots. Narrow-eyed and set-faced, he had crossed the lobby in wide strides, *and* he was carrying his assault rifle. The tourists instinctively edged toward their children, and Iain lowered his beer and said, "Look, here's Mohamed," and I said, "No, here's Rambo." Now I shake his hand, which is at my eye level, and smile, but Mohamed peers down at me without any recognition in his hard-set expression.

"I don't think he remembers me."

Iain speaks to him in Swahili, and Mohamed answers without changing expression. "Of course he remembers you," Iain says. I look back at Mohamed, and this time he nods, and I nod back.

"Shall we begin our walk?" Bongo says.

❖

We follow a dirt path alongside the paved road. Buses and trucks slow and farmers stop plowing as we pass. When the sun reaches its zenith I mention to everyone it is the equinox, and Iain, the inveterate movie buff, sings the theme from *High Noon* ("Oh don't forsake me, oh my darlin' . . ."). It does in fact feel like we're in a Western, the guns, the dust, and in the distance the heat shimmers that turn the asphalt into tantalizing pools of desert water rippled with wavelets. For one of the few times in my life traveling the back roads and trails of remote countries, I realize I no longer have that little caution buzzer in the back of my head reminding me always to be alert for robbers and hustlers. I realize I have no fear of militia or armed police or bandits dressed up like armed police. Now, for the first time in my career as an adventure traveler, I *am* the armed police.

The pavement gives way to dirt, or more accurately, to dust, and each truck and bus leaves a roiling contrail that encloses us in an apocalyptic brown cloud. We cut squares from a cotton *kanga* and fold them on the triangle to make bandannas that we tie bandit-style over our mouths and noses. The dust still clogs our throats. It's hot, and over our shoulders the perceptual summit ice of Kilimanjaro glimmers in a narrow band across the top of the dome that already seems a surprising distance away. Farms revert to stretches of thornbush, then back to farms. We pass a colony of candelabra *Euphorbia*, a forty-foot-high tree with spreading succulent-like branches that make the plant look like a giant cactus; if broken the branches produce a sticky latex so toxic that a drop of it in the eye can cause blindness.

By mid-afternoon we reach the Mogoini drainage that, at this elevation and season, is only a dry bed of gray rock. We rest under the spreading crown of a large tamarind tree. "It might be best if we stop this time each day," Bongo says, "and wait for it to cool before we finish the day's walk."

"I'd just as soon put up with the heat and get to camp," Danny replies.

No one answers and we rest for ten minutes, then by an unspoken consensus lift our day packs and continue, following a footpath that connects the huts of the farmers who cultivate small plots adjacent to the streambed. We walk another hour until the footpath crosses a narrow four-wheel-drive road with fresh tracks that lead toward a group of tall tamarinds that mark the bank of the Mogoini. There are Iain's vehicles, and there we set up camp.

❖

Our eyes look like they have been glued onto our dirt faces. Our feet are sore from the pavement, and Iain and Bongo both have hot spots they fear are developing into blisters. But we are all in a good mood, and after we rest and clean up Danny says, "There's an area not far from here where elephants have been raiding the *shambas* nearly every night. I suspect I'll be sent there soon to sort it out. Why don't we drive out so you can see the situation for yourself?"

Like Danny, Lokiyor—the Turkana ranger—is also part of the Kenya Wildlife Service's Problem Animal Control, and Danny instructs him to put his shoes on, get his rifle, and come with us. When the rangers arrived in Loitokitok they had brought with them Danny's Belgian FN, a semiautomatic assault weapon, as well as Bongo's elephant gun, a rare and vintage Rigby .416 that had belonged to their father. Danny now picks up his FN and we load in Iain's Land Rover and leave. I don't ask, but I assume we are armed not because we expect to encounter a rogue elephant, but rather to confirm our status with the villagers as officials of the Kenya Wildlife Service (or KWS, as it is commonly known). This military appearance—camouflage fatigues, black field boots, webbing vests, semiautomatic rifles—also surprises tourists visiting Kenya's national parks, who sometimes assume that it has something to do with a dictatorial government. The real reason is that KWS is a paramilitary organization that has fought a real war against poachers who shoot real bullets, and not just at animals.

In the vehicle Danny tells us more about the conflict between elephant and farmers. "This area is Masai land and historically they only herded their goats and cattle here, but recently—all within the last few years—they have leased some of the land to farmers from other tribes such as the Wakamba, Kikuyu, and Chagga." (There is also an undercurrent of resentment between the Masai and these other tribes, as there almost always is the world over between pastoralists and arablists.) "When it was just Masai they were able to live in reasonable harmony with the wildlife, but now all that's changed."

We leave the main dirt road and follow a small track to a series of cultivated fields. The silhouette outline of Mawenzi frames the background as the sun sets behind the peak, casting heraldic rays that create a crown over the summit. We stop a farmer walking back from his fields and Danny asks him about the elephants. "He says they're marauding nightly. He'll show us the damage." We get out of the vehicle and follow the farmer, walking on berms between cultivated plots that now hold only the bent brown stalks of maize already harvested, although there is some kale, ground tomatoes, and small red chilies. All these fields have been claimed out of the wild bush within the last ten years. Irrigation water is channeled from the nearby Rombo River that flows off Kilimanjaro. We pass the remains of a campfire and a scrap of corrugated metal siding, and Danny explains that young boys rotate sentry duty building fires and beating sticks on the tin to scare the elephants. "It's a problem because they're up all night, then they're expected to go to school all day."

The farmer leads us to a field still soft from a recent irrigation and planted with a local type of bean. Pocking the field, like small craters from a mortar attack, are the deep foot holes left by browsing elephant. "He says the elephants were in here last night, and they couldn't scare them away." Danny inspects the tracks and concludes it is a matriarchal herd of perhaps five or six animals. "My unit will probably be sent here soon, to scare them off."

The Problem Animal Control, in its current charter, was formed in the early 1990s because of an increasing conflict between farmers and elephants. Ironically this problem developed only after the poachers were finally contained (and the elephant population had reduced from an estimated one hundred twenty thousand at the beginning of the 1970s to a little more than twenty thousand at end of the 1980s, when the rate of poaching was finally reversed, although some of this reduction was the result of a drought in 1971 and 1972). The Nairobi newspapers, which had only a few years earlier published frequent stories of the rampant poaching, were now running lurid headlines of elephants menacing farmers, terrorizing schoolchildren, trampling villagers to death. With poaching controlled, the papers claimed, the elephant population was out of control. But in fact the problem was not so much a sudden increase in the elephant population (because of their long gestation and weaning period, elephant can increase their herd size by only about four to five percent a year), but rather that the human population continued to encroach on elephant habitat. Joyce Poole, a young field researcher who had spent most of her professional life studying elephant in Amboseli National Park, to the north of Kilimanjaro, explained the problem in her memoir *Coming of Age with Elephants*. "With the poaching pressure off . . . the elephants had come out of the forests and national park refuges and back along their traditional migration routes, only to find human settlements crowding their old habitats."

Regardless of who was to blame, however, KWS knew it had to do something, or face increasing political pressure that could weaken their other programs, especially efforts to keep the lid on poaching. The organization tried community-based projects and even fencing, but in the end the only policy that seemed feasible was to dispatch to a problem area a small military unit to teach the marauding elephant a lesson. The strategy was to single out from a herd an individual elephant, usually a juvenile, and shoot it. Theoretically this would so traumatize the rest of the animals that they would then stay away from the farmers and their fields, often for years. Ironically it was Joyce Poole, in her new role at KWS, who was in charge of administering the program, and Danny who was given the duty of carrying it out.

"This is not an ideal solution," Danny says as we stand examining the elephantine footprints in the farmer's field. "Killing elephants to save them."

Before leaving on this trek I had read Joyce Poole's book, and what struck me most poignantly in her story was that she had lived for so long in such close company with individual elephant that they had become her family. She knew, regardless of whether she could prove it scientifically, the joy her study elephant felt when they greeted long-absent relatives, as well as the fantasy world that young elephant entered when they played. She knew that elephant own a sense of self that in the animal world is shared perhaps only with the great apes and *Homo sapiens*. She witnessed the mourning of an elephant family over the death of a loved one and wrote: "There is something so grand about the life of an elephant, its great size, strength, and age, that in death its loss is equally monumental."

"It must have been hard on Joyce when she was in charge of this program," I say to Danny. "To spend your life studying an animal and trying to save it, only to have to order its death."

"She didn't talk about that," Danny answers. "But I suspect you're right."

I suspect so, too, and I make a note to ask Joyce when we see her, for we have arranged to have her join us for two days when we cross the lowland expanse of Tsavo East where, at this time of year, the elephant congregate in large numbers along the Galana River.

※

Dozens of villagers have now joined us and we all stand in a circle around the elephant prints and the damaged crops. Each of the women in the group has at a minimum three young children either in her arms or hiding behind her dress; peering from behind one cotton skirt, I count seven little faces. The farmer who has been escorting us seems to grow more angry with each example of crop destruction. "You must come back here tonight," he demands, indicating Danny's gun. "Come back and shoot the elephants. Shoot all of them."

6

I am not an empire builder, I am not a missionary, I am not truly a scientist. I merely want to return to Africa and continue my wanderings.

—*Joseph Thomson,*
in a letter to his brother, 1896

At first light I hear the woodnote call of the tropical boubou, a black-and-white shrike whose monochromatic looks are made up by its remarkably clear obolike call, a *hoooo-l-hoo, hoooo-l-hoo.* This call, like that of the hunter's cisticola, is a duet made by a male and a female, one *hooo*-ing and the other *l-hoo*-ing. Since the weather is so stable, we have slept without rainflies over our tents, and now, through the mosquito netting that forms the roof of my shelter, I watch the sky lightening.

"Good morning, Mr. Rick."

It is Chui, the perennially happy Kikuyu camp assistant. (Chui is tall and lean for a Kikuyu, a Bantu-speaking group originally from the central highlands; most of the others on Iain's staff suspect there is some Masai in his bloodline.) He is now bringing me a plastic tub of hot wash water. This is a courtesy that Iain had first encountered trekking in the Himalayas, where the Sherpa porters bring hot water each morning to your tent, and he thought his clients on his walking safaris in Africa would enjoy the same hospitality. He is right.

After breakfast we're joined by a local Masai who will be our guide for the next two days. Between here and the park boundary we will be walking through Masai land, and it will be invaluable to have someone lead us through the maze of cattle trails that follow, in general direction, the course of the Mogoini, but cut occasionally cross-country between bends in the river. We leave camp at seven thirty, not as early as I had expected, but it took time for Danny and Bongo to prepare their rifles. Even in this area of human habitation I am told it is possible to encounter elephant, or more likely buffalo, and as we leave Bongo has his heavy rifle balanced on his shoulder.

Our Masai guide is in the lead. He is short for a Masai, perhaps five foot six. He is dressed smartly in a matching cinnamon-brown jacket and pants, and a full brim hat of the same color. He carries a hardwood spear tipped on one end with a two-foot flat blade, and on the other with a tapered steel point. When they walk in the bush, male Masai are never without their spears, and taking a lion with only a spear is the favored way that a Masai boy becomes a Masai man, a *morani* or warrior.

My favorite Masai spear story isn't about gaining manhood, however, but rather takes place at a cattle auction attended by hundreds of Masai men. A local government official has arranged to show a film, and it is the first time any of the Masai have seen a movie. They sit transfixed, staring at the moving pictures. But then a close-up shot of a lion appears, and suddenly several of the warriors leap up and launch their spears at the screen, slicing it to shreds.

Masai boys grow up herding cattle and goats, and they know how to walk. Our guide is no exception. He walks sprightly, making each step off his toes so that his body rises in small jumps. We're all breathing hard to keep up, except Lokiyor and Mohamed, the Turkana and the Samburu, both whose Nilotic tribes are related to the Masai, and whose long legs move at half the speed of mine. After an hour we call for a rest, and as we catch our breath I reach in a bag of goodies I have brought on our trek and hand each man a chocolate-covered espresso bean. Our guide swallows his, sits still for a few seconds, then jumps up and takes off. "Now you've done it," Danny says.

We pass the first manyatta, a circular wall of woven thorns enclosing the wattle and daub Masai huts. This one looks in ill repair, and the only occupants visible are a few small children peeking suspiciously through the opening in the thorn wall. I was surprised when I first learned we would be walking through Masai country: I didn't know their homeland extended this far east. We are, in fact, on the very edge of their nation. From here their territory extends roughly northwest along the Great Rift Valley past Nairobi, west across the Masai Mara grasslands and south to the Serengeti, then east again, crossing the Ngorongoro crater and continuing back to Kilimanjaro; it's a region split roughly in two between Kenya and Tanzania.

We follow our Masai guide through thick *Acacia mellifera,* one of the smallest of the acacia, growing in a shrub five to ten feet high, with short but very effective hooked thorns. Here at the end of the dry season the dun thornbush is leafless and looks dead, and we walk in zigs and zags to find our way through. We chase up a flock of superb starlings, with plump chestnut breasts and iridescent blue backs, that squawk like parrots as they scramble into the bush. The Masai stops at an even smaller bush and says to Bongo in Swahili, "This is for venereal disease."

"You better eat some of that," Pete, our cameraman, jokes.

"Not to worry," Bongo answers, no doubt referring to his bachelor life at the base of Mt. Kenya. Earlier in the morning Bongo had also referred to his bachelorhood, in a more tangential way, when he told me the story about how he was given his name. I had always assumed Bill and Ruth had named their firstborn after the bongo, one of the rarest of the antelopes, but I never knew why. "When I was a small baby at home with Mum," Bongo explained, "Dad would often be out on lengthy safaris in distant areas of Kenya, and the only means of communication was over the national park radio network. But personal matters weren't allowed to be discussed, so it occurred to my father, as a way to get around this, to ask my mum, 'Well, how's the baby bongo?' Once my father's guest on safari was the governor of Kenya, Sir Patrick Renison, and one day when Sir Patrick heard this he said, 'Oh, I didn't realize you had a baby bongo. I should like to see it, so please bring it to Government House next time you are in Nairobi.' So Mum and Dad took me along and introduced me to Sir Patrick, who was very amused, and then and there, with whiskey and ginger, he anointed me and said, 'I hereby christen thee "Baby Bongo."' So the name stuck, only now there are only some people who can call me baby."

"Who's that?" I asked.

"I'm still looking," Bongo replied.

The *mellifera* scrub, with its very proficient hooked thorns, is the Masai's favored bush for constructing walls around their manyattas, and now we pass clearings where this bush has been stacked in long rows to protect farm plots from marauding animals. This experiment in agriculture is new for the

Masai, and it is something they are being forced to pursue as their pasture-
land is more and more controlled by national parks and ranches, or is leased
by them to agriculturists from adjacent tribes. Converting from a pastoral to
an agricultural subsistence places them in immediate conflict with wild animals, who maraud their fields, and Danny tells me it is also something for
which they often as not have neither skill nor passion. "They're likely to
fail," he adds. "This land is just too arid. But they'll try, and then the government will have to give them assistance, and then they'll come to depend
on that."

A white-bellied go-away bird, large and long-tailed, flies from bush to
bush in protest of our approach, squawking loudly "g'way, g'way." Other
than a few birds, there are hardly any wild animals, just the sere bush, occasional cattle, and occasional manyattas. The Mogoini has now cut a gorge
into the underlying rock, and for most of the morning we navigate through
the flats above the river, but as it nears mid-day, the trail we follow descends
into the gorge where we can see it climbing steeply up the opposite bank.
We pass a dobra tree, green and out of place against the dry scrub, a desert
topiary with a perfect round trunk supporting a perfect ball of foliage colored a perfect green. It's a Martha Stewart tree.

At creekside we take off our hiking shoes and wade through clear, cool
water. Upstream I spy the wagging tail of the African pied wagtail, and on
the opposite bank we sit to dry our feet and attend to blisters. Both Bongo
and Iain have suppurating bare wounds, and we still have about two hundred miles to walk. "This could slow or even stop us," Iain says.

"We have to be aggressive with them," Bongo adds as he cuts patches of
moleskin plasters.

With new bandages on our blisters, we follow our Masai guide, climbing
steeply out of the gorge. The pace is fast, but it feels good to exercise muscles that we haven't been using walking the flats. At the top we pause and
look back, and there in the far distance is the dome of Kilimanjaro, and we can
just make out the summit glaciers. In this heat I can understand how those
first reports in 1848 of snow on the equator by the two German missionaries
were met in Europe with such skepticism. (Local Africans were also oblivi-
ous of the true nature of snow. In his personal journal published as *Kenya
Diary 1902–1906*, a British subaltern named Richard Meinertzhagen described Kikuyu tribesmen around Mt. Kenya as believing "that snow came
out of the ground and must be very hot—in fact, 'white hot.' ")

Looking in the opposite direction to our right we can see the Taita Hills,
and to our left the rocky crags of the Ngulia Hills and a distinctive formation

with a right-angle prow known as Kichwa Tembo, the Elephant's Head. Somewhere out there the Mogoini joins the Tsavo River, and the Tsavo then flows under Kichwa Tembo, and even though this formation looks far in the distance, I take heart knowing it is no farther away than Kilimanjaro is in the opposite direction. All that is required is a steadfast one foot in front of the other, and I recall something that Iain had said at the beginning of the trip: "Slowly, slowly catches the monkey."

We are in the heat of the day, and I finish my water bottle. The ground is hot and dry. We enter a length of *Commifora africana*, another thornbush that is so dominant in some of the desert regions inland from the East African coast that the habitat is sometimes referred to as *Commifora* woodland. It's a small, deciduous tree, most of the year drab and leafless, about twenty feet high, with gray-green bark that peels away from the trunks like scrolls of dry parchment. (Close relatives of this bush found in Ethiopia and Arabia are the source for frankincense and myrrh.) The *Commifora* is soon displaced by the accurately named wait-a-bit thorn, a low scrub acacia that grows under the taller thornbush and has wiry branches lined with small hook-ended thorns that grab your clothing, or skin, and once you're hooked, you are hooked: You have no choice but to "wait a bit" as you carefully remove the thorns at precisely the reverse angle in which they penetrated. This bush was the bane of all early explorers in East Africa, and it was referred to as "wait-a-bit" even in Lugard's journals over one hundred years ago.

"The army has another name for it," Bongo says. "It's referred to as the 'where-the-fuck-do-you-think-you're-going' thorn."

We climb, descend, climb, descend, and from the top of another hill we are awarded a wide prospect across the savanna. "See those palms in the far distance?" Iain says. "They mark the Tsavo."

The doum palms suggest an oasis, and more, the promise of wild country that still holds wild animals. So far we haven't seen anything. The gray ground is peppered with small lava rocks, and in a dry wash deposits of metallic sand reflect flashes of the equinoctial sun. Up another hill we encounter a new acacia with dark, rough bark and branches ornamented with black galls. "Whistling thorn," Iain says. It soon thins and allows open ground between the bush.

"Fresh signs of ele here," Danny says, "so keep a sharp eye."

"Will do," Bongo replies as we pass the megafaunal prints of elephant crossing our path. I keep a sharp eye myself, but if there is game here, it is shy and elusive. I wonder, is this paucity of wild animals because of the Masai? Do their cattle compete with the game for grass and browse? Or perhaps the Masai *morani*, hunting for meat as well as for social accolade, have driven them into the park? Whatever the reason, they are not here, at least in any abundance, but there is no doubt they used to be. Iain and Bongo have both told me that Joseph Thomson, one of the first Europeans through this same country we now walk, reported in the late nineteenth century that there were huge quantities of game animals in the bushlands and savannas east of Kilimanjaro.

❖

Joseph Thomson was six feet tall, lean and strong. His older brother described him as "gentle, lovable, lively, energetic, fearless, studious, industrious and full of fun." He was born in Scotland in 1858, and as a young boy he was fascinated by accounts of African explorers such as Livingstone and Stanley. Thomson was working in the family construction business when he answered a newspaper ad for a position on an expedition to Lake Nyasa in East Central Africa. He had trained in the university as a geologist, so he had the idea to offer the expedition his services as a field naturalist for no charge. The tactic worked, and he was soon outward bound to what Livingstone had already characterized as the Dark Continent. It was 1878, and he was twenty years old.

Within weeks of arriving in Africa the expedition leader fell ill and died, and Thomson, who was the only other European on the trip, took over leadership. The expedition was a success, Thomson was invited to speak at the Royal Geographical Society, and he published an account of the expedition that saw several reprints. At home in Scotland he found himself returned a hero.

At that time the greatest prize in African exploration had already been won: the discovery of the source of the Nile in the great lakes of Central Africa. What remained, however, was somehow to march successfully from the coast directly to those central lakes. The problem was that the direct route necessarily traversed the heart of Masai land, and the Masai were the most fearsome warriors in Africa, as dreaded and as warlike as the Apaches were in the American West. Indeed, all the other tribes of East Africa feared above all the raids of the Masai *Il-Moran*, the warrior-age set of men in their teens to mid-twenties whose cultural mandate was to prove their manhood through hunting lion and raiding other tribes, leaving in their wake a scorched earth policy of death and destruction.

By 1882, the Royal Geographical Society was ready to mount an expedition that would depart the coast, cross under Kilimanjaro, then somehow traverse Masai land without being slaughtered. The Society would have preferred a more experienced Africa hand for the job, but anyone with experience would have insisted on an army of porters and soldiers, and there was no budget for that. The young Thomson, however, was willing to give it a try with only a little over one hundred porters (most expeditions had at least three hundred), convinced that by wile and guile he could figure out how to deal with the Masai. "I had great faith in the Italian proverb, 'He who goes safely goes gently, he who goes gently, goes far.' "

He left Dar es Salaam early in 1883 and proceeded inland toward Kilimanjaro, following the route of earlier explorers that traversed the southern and western slopes of the mountain. There he made his first contact with the Masai. "A war-chant was heard in the distance, and soon a party of *Il-Moran*, in all the glory of a new plastering of red clay and grease, appeared, marching in single file, and keeping step to their song, their murderous spears gleaming in the sun as they gave them now and then a rotary movement." To placate the warriors Thomson laid out loops of iron wire, strings of beads, and bolts of cloth. The Masai went after the booty in a free-for-all that Thomson said was liking watching "a pack of half-starved wolves let loose on small animals . . . they rave and tear . . . drawing swords and wielding knobkerries. Two men thus received some ugly flesh wounds, which did not however draw forth any comment from the on-lookers."

Things seemed to go okay for the next two days, but then Thomson received word the Masai were plotting an attack and that night, as silently as possible, he stole out of camp and retreated toward the coast. He left his caravan in an outpost town on the south side of Kilimanjaro, made a forced march back to the coast to resupply, then returned to try again. This time his fortune improved when he learned a large trading caravan led by coastal Swahilis was about to depart for Masai land. Even though he knew they were slavers, he made a deal to join them. This time, the caravan chose a route that contoured around the east side of Kilimanjaro, and Thomson therefore had to have crossed the Mogoini River somewhere very close to where we now walk. At that time, only a handful of Europeans had ventured that way before. The first were the two German missionaries who, beginning in 1848, made several journeys inland from Mombasa in the hope of establishing missions. Their journals were little more than factual reports of their trips. The next missionary in the general area, Charles New, in 1871, supplied a few more adjectives to his descriptions, but still left no sense of passion or awe in seeing lands and animals so few Europeans had ever witnessed.

Then there was Joseph Thomson. He saw Africa with the wide eyes of a child, and his enthusiasms transferred through his pen into his extraordinary journals:

Such is the country; but see its inhabitants! There, towards the base of Kilimanjaro, are three great herds of buffalo slowly moving up from the lower grazing grounds to the shelter of the forest for their daily snooze and rumination in its gloomy depths. Further out on the plains enormous numbers of the harmless but fierce-looking wildebeest continue their grazing, some erratic members of the herd gamboling and galloping about with waving tail and strange, uncouth movements. Mixed with these are to be seen companies of the loveliest of all large game, the zebra, conspicuous in their beautiful striped skin, here marching with stately step, with heads down-bent, there enjoying themselves. . . . Look! Down in that grassy bottom there are several specimens of the great unwieldy rhinoceros, with horns stuck on their noses in a most offensive and pugnacious manner; over the ridge a troop of ostriches are scudding out of reach of danger. . . . See how numerous are the herds of hartebeest, and notice the graceful pallah [impala] springing into mid-air with great bounds, as if in pure enjoyment of existence . . . among the tall reeds . . . the dignified waterbuck . . . the wart hog . . . clears off in a bee-line with tail erect and with a steady military trot truly comical. . . . Turn whatever direction you please, they are to be seen in astonishing numbers, and so rarely hunted that, unconcernedly, they stand and stare at us. . . .

I turn in every direction and see nothing but dry dun bush. We walk another hour and finally scare up a lone impala, and I just glimpse its cinnamon fur as it crashes through the whistling thorn. We stop while Bongo fixes our position, consults a map, and indicates our course. We reach a narrow sand river that we follow to our right, and around the corner we see a grove of *Acacia xanthlophloea*, the tall green-barked fever tree, said to be named by early explorers who sat under its protective shade to sweat out their malaria. Next to the river we spy the gray and blue nylon walls of our tents.

We spend the late afternoon soaking our feet in the cool stream water, and the next morning a troop of vervet monkeys scolds us from the fever trees as we leave camp. We follow a primitive four-wheel road, and in the dirt there is a confusion of cattle tracks mixed with a loping line of hoofprints from a solitary giraffe. A young Masai boy dressed in a blue-checkered *shuka* wrap waves from the roadside where he stands, staff in hand, next to his charge of goats. We walk the open margin of a large lugga that heads north toward the Chyulu Hills. Even though the rhumb line toward our destination is east, a range of low thornbush hills in that direction suggests it's easier to follow this sand river until we can turn to our right. As soon as the hills begin to diminish, we leave the open floodbottom and cut overland, through scrub bush and lava rock. For the first time in several days we find grass growing in stalky clumps.

"Look, there," Iain says, pointing. At a distance of some five hundred yards I can see the tawny shape of an animal that is too far away to identify with the naked eye. I'm lifting my binoculars when Iain says, "fringed-eared oryx." (I am often amazed at Iain's ability to identify game at extreme distances with his naked eye. He once told me that it has less to do with sharp eyesight than with recognizing telltale signs of shape, color, movement, and location.) To our right we see two male ostrich looking like land ships crossing the savanna. To our left there is a herd of grazing impala, maybe twenty animals. There are no signs of cattle. The grass in places is now knee-high, and even at the end of the dry season the country feels fresh and wild.

Without discussing the matter, Mohamed takes the lead. Bongo follows, then Iain, myself, the others, and Lokiyor, bringing up the rear. We follow an elephant path through the grass. We make only a few yards when Mohamed stops and points to a print in the dirt and says, "Simba." Bongo kneels and studies the pugmark. "Lion. Very recent."

Mohamed scans the grass and the tall bush. He looks at us and nods very slightly, then continues in the lead, carrying his assault rifle at waist level, his index finger poised on the trigger guard, his thumb positioned on the safety. He raises his hand and motions us to stop. He stands straight-backed, rifle at his side, and with his narrowed red eyes he studies the Chyulu Hills to our left, the low hills to our right. He then slices the air in a line with his large, flat hand, and says, "Hapa Ni Mpaka."

We are now in Tsavo.

PART TWO

Tsavo

7

You woke up in the morning and thought: Here I am, where I ought to be.

—Isak Dinesen (Karen Blixen),
Out of Africa, *1937*

It has been two hours since we walked across the unmarked border into Tsavo and already we have seen several species of antelope: impala, Grant's gazelle, waterbuck, and fringe-eared oryx, the latter with lancelike horns three feet and more in length, said to have inspired the myth of the unicorn. We follow a knoll fifty yards from the river where we see above the riparian bush the periscope necks of two giraffe, and hear the tuba snorts of several hippo. We also spot the gray humps of three elephant; they look like the backs of whales surfacing from the high bush, and when they smell us they move away with a slow and monumental grace.

We walk in single file behind Mohamed who stops abruptly and in the same instant lifts his hand motioning us to stop *and* be quiet. He raises his gun across his chest, and Bongo, Danny, and Lokiyor do the same. Through the thornbush we see a vague dark shape that takes me a only heartbeat to recognize as a large Cape buffalo, the most aggressively temperamental of Africa's megafauna. The animal stands motionless, eyes locked on us. We also remain frozen, waiting for the buffalo to make the next move. We wait, ten, twenty, thirty heartbeats. Suddenly the beast snorts, turns away, and gallops in a crash through the bush. This triggers more crashing, and we realize there is not one buffalo but a full herd. Our only movement is a slight turn of our bodies as we track the sound of crashing brush and beating hooves. Then ahead, through an opening cut by our trail, we get a quick glimpse of each one as it runs past—ten, twenty, maybe thirty animals—a thunder of hooves and rising dust. We wait for them to pass, and when we see them crest a small rise about a hundred yards away, Mohamed lowers his rifle, as do the others, and we continue.

Suddenly Mohamed jerks to a halt and instantly shoulders his rifle. We follow his eyes to a large bull who has remained behind. We are directly between him and the rest of his herd. The beast snorts and shakes his head, and Mohamed motions us to move away. We follow Mohamed, who walks quickly but stealthily, keeping his head sideways to maintain his fix on the buffalo. Thirty paces farther he lowers his rifle, as do the others, and we keep walking.

"Welcome to the hot zone," Iain says in a voice toned not with apprehension, but with enthusiasm that we have at last entered wild Africa.

❖

It literally is the hot zone, too. By early afternoon the temperature is 105 degrees. We stop to rest and Bongo fixes our position with his GPS. While he fiddles with the instrument I ask if I can look at his rifle.

"The safety's on," he says.

"This is a lot of weight to carry two hundred and fifty miles."

"My father carried it a lot farther than that."

"He didn't use a gun bearer?"

"Only if he had more than one gun. On a paid hunting safari the role of the gun bearer was to carry the client's gun, not the guide's. There would also be a tracker, and the gun bearer and the tracker were the most bush savvy. If an animal was wounded, the client wouldn't be allowed to enter the bush after it, but the guide, gun bearer, and tracker would go in."

"The only guide I've known whose skill in the bush matched the Africans' was Dad," Danny said. "Sometimes it was just he and Elui, and Elui was unarmed."

I had already heard Bongo and Danny mention Elui, but I didn't know much about him.

"Elui was a Wakamba hunter and an expert tracker who taught Dad much of what he knew about the bush," Danny said. "Dad was nineteen

when he met Elui, and he was close to him the rest of his life. When I was
just a kid Elui would come to Kamboyo [park headquarters for Tsavo West]
to visit Dad, and they would sit under a tree and tell stories into the
night."

When Bongo has our position fixed I hand the rifle back and we continue.
Soon the trail turns into a dusty four-wheel track, and to our right a mile or
two away the green tops of doum palms create a converging line that Iain
says marks the flow of the Tsavo River.

"And camp?" Bongo asks.

"There, at the base of Rhodesian Hill. Maybe six more kilometers."

"None too soon," Bongo replies.

"It's a very easy day from there to the next camp, so we can catch up on
our reserves."

"If we continue with these sorts of days it will wear us down, and we
mightn't finish the job."

There's a tone of criticism in Bongo's remark that once again Iain chooses
to ignore. I watch Iain's expression to see if I can detect any frustration with
what is now becoming a pattern of critical comments from Bongo, but Iain
seems to shrug it off, and we continue. Iain is not meek, however, nor is he
the kind of person who avoids conflict, and I consider the possibility that if
he develops a frustration that then builds and lets go, we could have one hell
of a row on our hands.

Iain's staff has located camp along the river in a grove of high fever trees.
Another of Iain's vehicles has arrived from Nairobi with fresh supplies. We
sit in the shade and tempers cool and moods brighten. Bongo is cleaning the
dust out of the old Rigby, and I ask more about the rifle's history.

"It was ordered by an Italian count, in 1927, for a hunt in Abyssinia, then
picked up by Tiger Marriott, who gave it to Dad."

"Tiger Marriott?"

"Colonel Tiger Marriott. He was an officer in the Fourteenth Bengal
Lancers, and fought the warlords in China, the Pathans in Afghanistan,
pretty much all over the world."

"How did he end up in East Africa?"

Bongo hesitates and with a smile looks at Danny, who shrugs. "Well, I'll
tell you the story, but if you write a book I'm not sure you should print it."

"Only with your permission."

"Tiger was on leave from the Western Front in the First War when he visited a lady friend who was having some sort of problem with a blackmailer. Tiger said he would take care of her problem, and he met the blackmailer, and they didn't see eye to eye, and in the melee Tiger grabbed a poker from the fireplace and cracked the fellow's skull and killed him. He left immediately for the trenches and never really went back to Britain but ended up in Africa. Dad was only seventeen or so when he met Tiger, who invited him on an ivory hunting expedition to Portuguese East Africa, now Mozambique."

"Why the name Tiger?"

"He had a tiger tattooed on his arm. We have his swords at home, two ceremonial and one fighting sword, a fine work of art that has killed seven Turks."

"And nine Germans," Danny adds.

"Well, one at least," Bongo corrects. "A German officer, in a cavalry charge in Mesopotamia. So he did his bit."

"Was he your father's mentor, then?"

"Dad's father died when he was nine," Bongo replies. "He grew up on the Athi plains, just outside of Nairobi, and spent his childhood wandering around with a couple of African boys, shooting game for the pot."

"Did you know Tiger?"

"He died before I was born. If you want to know more about him, we should go along after our walk and see Dad's sister, Judy."

Six months after we had finished our trek, I returned to East Africa and we visited Aunt Judy. She lived in Malindi, a block off the beach, in a smartly kept bungalow with a wide lawn framed by coconut and redolent of frangipani. She was tall and lean with short-cropped hair that still held a mix of natural brown. She was sixty-five years old and had lived by herself since her husband, Donald Destro, died. We sat on her screened porch, and her eyes went quickly from Bongo to Danny. She was sharp and alert, and I didn't detect a sentimental bone in her body.

"Did you hear about Vera? I tried to get up and see her, but the roads were dreadful. Next thing I know she goes and pegs out."

She sat straight-backed and no-nonsense, like a schoolteacher who takes her job seriously. She wore a cotton print dress with an apron tied around, blue flip-flops, and a wristwatch with a functionally oversized dial: I had the impression she was a person who liked to know the time.

Bongo had by then decided it was okay to print Tiger's story—he couldn't imagine anyone wanting to resurrect a case that happened so long ago under such vague circumstances—so I asked Judy if she could recall Tiger.

"He was a striking chap," she said. "Big and tall, hefty but not fat. He always wore jackets and sleeved shirts because of his fair skin. He was wonderful to Bill, and Bill needed that because he'd grown up without a father."

Bongo and Danny listened attentively, as though they might learn something they hadn't heard before.

"Mother was always too soft on Bill, and that's why he was so wild. He was beaten severely in school, always coming home with plasters on his backside, but it didn't seem to affect him. I remember when he was eleven or twelve he wanted to join the army. He simply wasn't interested in school, or in sport. Only the outdoors, that's what drew him, and Tiger recognized that. It was Tiger who really set the direction of Bill's life, taking him down to Portuguese East where Bill shot his first elephant. I still have two small tusks from that trip."

Bongo looked at Danny and raised his eyebrows. "You do?"

"Inside, in that old trunk. A rhino horn, too. I should give them to Moi, I suppose," she said, referring to Kenya's president.

"No, you should give them to us," Bongo replied. "We're authorized to hold ivory."

Judy walked to her living room and opened an ornately carved trunk and returned with two short tusks and the rhino horn. "What a relief, to finally get rid of these things. Too dangerous, what with all the Arabs around."

We stood to leave, and I asked her if she knew anything about the alleged murder, and why Tiger came out to the colonies. She looked at me sharply and said, "That was an unsolved murder," and I knew from her tone the case was closed.

After we left, I sat in the car and ran my thumb over the sharp point of the rhino horn.

"How much do you think this is worth?" I asked Bongo.

"About three thousand dollars," he replied.

"Do you think Aunt Judy realizes that?"

"I'm sure she does."

When Bill was growing up on the Athi plains, Kenya was then part of British East Africa, and the colony was famous as a playground for titled

British gentry, remittance men, and big-game hunters. Nairobi was founded in 1897 as the highland center for the railroad then under construction that was to link Mombasa to Lake Victoria in Uganda. By 1902 the town was a collection of bungalows and tents arranged in perfect rows so that it looked more like a military encampment than the site of a future capital. Richard Meinertzhagen, the young English subaltern who had been seconded to the fledgling King's African Rifles, described the settlement's only hotel as a "wood and tin shanty," and the only shop as a "small hut which sells everything from cartridges at eight pence and beer at five shillings a bottle to sardines, jams, tinned food . . ." The new commissioner of the protectorate, Sir Charles Eliot, was intent, however, on making the new colony not only grow but also pay its own way, including a return on the five-million-pound cost of the railroad; he oversaw a land dispersal that gave away a million acres with 999-year leases to any settlers willing to forge farms out of the highland bush. Sir Charles told Meinertzhagen that he foresaw thousands of Europeans with their families arriving, "the whole of the country from the Aberdares and Mount Kenya to the German border divided into farms."

By 1909 the Norfolk Hotel was well established (it remains today the hotel of preference for visitors coming to Africa "on safari"), and Nairobi's main street was lined with stores and shops, some two stories high. Settlers arrived by the hundreds. The First War was a distraction that slowed development, but in the years between the two wars the settlers new and old created a haven for white gentry intent on transferring English gentility to the new colony. "They had polo grounds, their racecourses, their country clubs, their gymkhanas and lunch parties," James Fox wrote in *White Mischief.* "And always a limitless supply of champagne."

There also appeared to be a limitless supply of wild animals to those attracted to the new colony for its big-game hunting. A month after he had arrived in Nairobi, Meinertzhagen wrote in his journal:

"I counted the game on the Athi plain south of Nairobi this afternoon in an area of about 10 square miles. It amounted to 2430 zebra, 967 wildebeeste, 846 Coke's hartebeeste, 932 Grant's gazelle, 546 Thomson's gazelle, 146 impala, 8 steinbock, 2 duiker, 46 eland, 19 giraffe, 1 rhinoceros, 86 ostrich, 1 cheetah, 5 hyaena and pack of 7 hunting dogs."

Meinertzhagen was himself an avid sports hunter—as were most British army officers in Kenya—but his shooting outings paled alongside the safaris organized by wealthy big-game hunters from Europe and America. The most prestigious safari in the years before the First War was Theodore Roosevelt's visit in 1909; it was also the most extravagant. Sponsored by Andrew Carnegie, Roosevelt and his entourage employed 265 natives to porter their tents, tables, crockery, field kitchen, camp chairs, cots, liquor supply, and library of leather-bound books. The expedition drew worldwide press coverage, firmly established Kenya as the mecca of big-game hunting, and made *safari* a household word (with Arabic origins, *safari* is Swahili for "traveling on foot," and was originally conscripted into English by the redoubtable explorer and linguist Sir Richard Burton).

The golden era of hunting safaris, however, was during the years between the wars. To stage a proper safari it was essential to retain a reputable hunting guide, and if you were well moneyed, or of royal lineage, you retained a guide only from a select roster of the most elite hunters. This group included Bror Blixen and Denys Finch Hatton; both gained prominence in later years because the first was Karen Blixen's husband, and the second her close confidant and probable lover; together they were immortalized in Blixen's memoir *Out of Africa*. (This book is regarded by most as the best invocation of the ineffable magic of Old Africa. When Ernest Hemingway won the Nobel Prize for Literature, in 1954, he said in his acceptance speech that the award should have gone to Karen Blixen, and that her book had been a major influence on his own writing.)

Finch Hatton was the eminent dean of the hunting guides, leading wealthy Americans, British aristocracy and even the Prince of Wales on safaris. "No detail during Denys' preparation for safari was too small," Errol Trzebinski wrote in *Silence Will Speak*, her biography of Finch Hatton. "Tents were inspected for rents, missing ropes or poles, and had to be at least eight feet high so that (quoting Finch Hatton) 'a man of some inches may stand straight in it and be at ease.' " One American client, in a memoir about his safari with Finch Hatton, wrote that the guide could "hunt up some corner of the world and make it more English than the home island itself."

Karen Blixen found in Finch Hatton an irresistible counterpoint to her boorish husband (whom she later divorced). In *Out of Africa* she wrote that what impressed people most about Finch Hatton was "his absolute lack of self-consciousness or self-interest, and unconditional truthfulness which outside him I have only met in idiots." He was comfortable by himself, or with only the company of African companions on safari, and this ease with solitude was something that made him to other people mysteriously inaccessible and at the same time enchantingly attractive.

Karen Blixen may also have been his only friend who recognized the depth of Finch Hatton's love for the African bush. He was especially fond of the region along the Galana River and the *nyika* bushlands to the north; this was the wildest and least-known country in the colony, and much of it would later be encircled by the boundaries of Tsavo East. He cleared from the thick *Commifora* along the Galana a landing strip for his Gypsy Moth biplane, and established a riverside camp, framed by doum palms and native poplars, where he would sometimes take his wealthy clients.

"It was in the month of May," Karen wrote in *Out of Africa*, describing one of Finch Hatton's frequent trips. "Denys went down to Takaunga for a week. . . . He went away in his aeroplane and was intending to make his way home round by Voi, to see if there were any elephants there for his safaris. The natives had been talking much of a herd of elephants which had come on to the land round Voi from the West, in particular one big bull, twice the size of any other elephant that was wandering in the bush there, all by himself.

"I asked him to let me come with him. First he said yes, and then he changed his mind and said no. He could not take me; the journey round Voi, he told me, was going to be very rough, he might have to land, and to sleep in the bush, so that it would be necessary for him to take a Native boy with him. . . .

"He went off on Friday the eighth. 'Look out for me on Thursday,' he said when he went, 'I shall be back in time to have luncheon with you . . .' "

But he did not come back in time. After taking off from Voi he circled "low at 200 feet and . . . suddenly the aeroplane swayed, got into a spin, and came down like a bird swooping. As it hit the ground it caught fire."

Denys Finch Hatton was buried in the Ngong Hills, behind Karen's farm, and his grave was marked by a brass plaque inscribed with words from "The Rime of the Ancient Mariner":

> *He prayeth well, who loveth well*
> *both man and bird and beast.*

That same year Karen sold her farm to land developers and returned to her native Denmark. (The subdivision became known as Karen, and it is where Iain Allan and his family live today in their colonial-period home a short distance from Karen's farm, which now is a museum open to the public and a popular tourist attraction, especially since the release of the movie *Out of Africa* that starred Meryl Streep and Robert Redford.) In her later years Karen Blixen became reclusive, refusing most visitors, except one. She did respond to a letter from a young and very handsome American photographer who had adopted Kenya as his second home when he became infatuated with the country after reading *Out of Africa*. In 1962 Peter Beard was a houseguest of Karen's, and he made the last photographs of her, shortly before she died.

In her late life Karen had a daily habit that was noted by one of her staff. Each evening she would go to a particular window and gaze out. After watching her do this for fourteen years, the employee finally asked the reticent baroness if this habit held any significance. Karen indicated the window and said that it faced the direction of Africa. What she didn't say, however, was that also in a frame positioned near to the window was a portrait of Denys Finch Hatton.

◈

For several years preceding his death in 1931, Denys Finch Hatton embraced, with his usual passion and enthusiasm, the art of wildlife photography. (It would seem likely that this parallel interest is why Karen Blixen late in her life broke her seclusion to see one Peter Beard.) Finch Hatton found satisfaction in this work, and several of his photographs were published in leading magazines of the day. In addition to pursuing photography for his own pleasure, he also began to advocate that hunters consider shooting pictures instead of bullets.

He began to guide clients interested primarily in photography safaris. These were not always tame and safe outings, to be sure; to capture a close-up image of a dangerous and agitated animal would require Finch Hatton to stand by with his rifle loaded and ready in case things got out of hand. On one occasion he did have to shoot and kill a charging rhinoceros just as it was about to impale his American client who stood in harm's way staring transfixed into his viewfinder as the rhino pounded straight at him.

At the root of Finch Hatton's fascination with wildlife photography was his desire to find a way to enjoy the satisfactions and excitements of hunting safaris without having to kill animals. He was a hunter, but he also was a conservationist. He was quick to criticize anyone he thought was gratuitously or unnecessarily shooting game, or breaking the game laws, and in a letter to *The London Times*, in 1928, he castigated "shooting visitors to East Africa who are anxious to fill their bag as quickly as possible. . . . I have heard of one party which came away from a fortnight's trip with nearly thirty assorted lions, lionesses and cubs—an orgy of slaughter." He then went on to advocate closing sections of East Africa from all lion hunting, countering the in-

evitable reaction that revenue from hunting licenses would be lost by arguing that more revenue would be gained from "people willing to pay for the
privilege of seeing game (from motor cars) and for photographing rather
than shooting them." (This was an amazingly prescient vision if you consider
that today you can daily witness in the Masai Mara—the segment of the
Serengeti Plain within Kenya—a dozen or more four-wheel-drive vehicles
gathered around a single leopard sleeping in a tree with tourists pointing
and whispering above the background noise of their whirring motor-driven
cameras.)

Finch Hatton wasn't the only big-game hunter to advocate game conservation. Even as early as 1902, Meinertzhagen, who was otherwise a passionate hunter, was loathe to shoot elephant. "Soon after leaving camp we
saw a party of 7 elephant," Meinertzhagen wrote in his journal. "One of
them was a fine old tusker. Now, much as I might desire to shoot an elephant
in self-defense, I have never had any desire to kill them for sport. . . . it is
a pity that an intelligent creature like the elephant should be shot in order
that creatures not much more intelligent may play billiards with balls made
from its teeth." In another passage he chastises a fellow soldier for shooting
three rhinoceros that were undersize. "He had a long tale about being
charged, but some of my men who were out with him at the time tell me that
these 3 rhino were deliberately stalked and shot, without any provocation. It
was pure slaughter, as none of the 3 had a decent horn among them. Apart
from the lie, it was an unsportsmanlike action and a breach of the game
regulations."

Meinertzhagen accepted and advocated big-game hunting, but not if it
was in breach of the game laws. Like many of his hunting brethren, he
viewed these game laws as designed to ensure the preservation of game
(even if the underlying motivation was to ensure that the animals would be
there to hunt. These same laws also ensured that the animals available to
hunt would be there only for those who could afford the licenses, which excluded all native peoples). Meinertzhagen also advocated game reserves
that would be off limits to farming. "I suggested to Blaney [Percival, who
was the new colony's first "game ranger"] that he put up a scheme for a very
large area in the country unsuitable for white settlement where game can
remain for ever. . . . Blaney promised to formulate a scheme."

In 1909 Kenya set aside the Northern and Southern Game Reserves. No
hunting for game animals was allowed within the reserves, but at the same
time it was very difficult for only a handful of wardens to patrol such a vast
area and enforce the laws; further, these wardens had to spend more time

protecting inhabitants within the reserves from marauding animals than they did controlling hunting. Further, the boundaries of the reserves themselves were in no way sacrosanct, and land on the edges was frequently deeded to ranchers under exclusions with the obfuscating titles of "Temporary Occupation Licenses" that were, in fact, permanent occupation rights. In other parts of Africa there was growing pressure to create parks that not only had firm borders, but also excluded all native peoples and their livestock.

In 1925 Prince Albert National Park was established in the Congo, and the following year Kruger National Park in South Africa. These two parks became both models and inspiration to wildlife conservationists in other parts of Africa, and led to a nascent movement to create a national park system in Kenya. The concept of wildlife preservation, however, fell on many deaf ears both within the colonial government and the home government in London. A dispatch in 1937 from the British secretary of state not only to Kenya but to the other colonies in Africa stated that any of the national parks then being considered should allow hunting and disallow any developments that might attract tourists who would get in the way of the hunters.

To understand how the foreign office of the British government, in the 1930s, could have held such a position, it is useful to take a brief look at the history of game laws and game reserves. "The preservation of game for sport hunting is an old practice," Alistair Graham writes in *Gardeners of Eden.* "It was well developed in Egypt as early as the time of King Sahure. . . . The Persians in 525 B.C. had numerous walled game parks containing a variety of wildlife, including tigers. The conquering Alexander records organizing a hunt for his troops in these parks, during which 4,000 animals were bagged."

In a similar pattern the first game laws in England were declared by William the Conqueror to protect animals so he could pursue his passion for hunting. "He took away much land from God and man, converting its use to wild beasts and the sport of dogs, demolishing thirty-six mother churches and driving away the inhabitants of many villages and towns," noted a chronicler of the times. A hundred years later (in the twelfth century) Henry II codified the game laws and the punishments for poaching. "He who does wrong in the King's forest touching his venison shall be blinded and castrated." This was not well received by a populace who, until the Norman invasion, had been free to hunt in the native forests, nor were the gamekeepers, who were empowered to enforce the royal laws, very popular.

As the forests in England were increasingly cut first to provide timber for the growing shipping industry, then to fuel the industrial revolution, game animals, in particular deer, were increasingly confined to the remnant woods set aside for their preservation, and hunting for stag became the exclusive domain of the king and select nobles. This led to the development of the hunting of other game animals, and also to the sport of angling. At the same time, game laws became increasingly restrictive, and in 1671 it became illegal to kill, without permission of the royal government, any game animal anywhere, even on private lands.

Things loosened somewhat in 1784 when the prime minister, William Pitt, introduced laws that allowed the public to purchase hunting licenses. Since the only game animals that remained were on private lands, however, would-be hunters had also to obtain permissions from landowners, and consequently hunting remained the domain of only the most privileged. That's not to say the urge to hunt among commoners was in any way alleviated. After the French peasantry stormed the Bastille, the next thing they invaded was the king's hunting grounds. In England, despite punishment that included exile to the Australian penal colonies, one out of every six convictions in the 1830s was for poaching.

When the English expanded their empire overseas, then, it is not surprising they arrived in the colonies with this desire to hunt. "When European sportsmen began coming to East Africa in the late nineteenth century," Alistair Graham writes, "they could hardly believe their hart-starved eyes. With the sight of a good stag already just a memory for most of them, here suddenly was an unbelievable multitude—'Stag' of all shapes and sizes leaping about by the hundreds of thousands; a vast forest devoid of royal prerogatives."

❖

In addition to their passion for hunting, the English brought to Kenya their traditions of game laws and game reserves. Implied in these laws is the concern and the desire to preserve wild animals, and while it is easiest to assume the motivation behind these laws was to ensure the preservation of trophy animals for hunters, I believe the reality is more complex. The English carried with them the knowledge of what they had done to their own wild forests and wild animals, and this history was not lost on men like Denys Finch Hatton.

Nor was it lost on another man of Finch Hatton's subsequent generation named Mervyn Cowie who, in the 1930s, became the leading advocate of the national park movement in Kenya. Born in Nairobi in 1909, Cowie was for a number of years himself a hunter, but eventually he came to realize that what had seemed like inexhaustible herds of wild animals were in reality imminently threatened unless something were done to protect them beyond the half measures of the existing game reserves and game laws.

Cowie sensed there might be sufficient support in the white community for a national parks initiative—many were aghast at the growing slaughter, especially by settlers expanding their grazing lands—but he needed some way to galvanize people into voicing their opinions. Cowie then landed on what turned out to be a brilliant idea.

He wrote a letter to the *East African Standard*, Nairobi's newspaper of the day, signing it anonymously "Old Settler." "How can any progress be made in a new farming country unless the danger and damage by game is removed?" the letter read. "What is the object of keeping thousands of useless creatures merely to eat all the grass which cattle should have, or to spoil crops and kill livestock? Better to rid the land of all this nonsense. Put the army on to destroying them with machine guns; it would be good training practice. Destroy the females so that they could breed no more. Put down poison for all the predators. Nothing could be easier."

The subterfuge worked. There was a call to have the "Old Settler" himself shot. A public meeting to discuss creating a national park system was packed with hundreds of supporters. The government relented, appointing a committee that advocated as a first step creating a national park out of the game-rich plains on the outskirts of Nairobi. The proposal was delayed by the war, but in 1946 Nairobi National Park was established and Cowie was head of its board of trustees. Cowie then set his sights on creating a second park out of the game-rich *nyiki*.

The National Park Board's first choice was the area that until then had been encompassed within the vast Northern Game Reserve. In addition to thornbush woodlands, this region had several mountain ranges with montane forests and spectacular scenery. It was, however, also home of the Samburu—as well as other tribes—and the government was reluctant to displace these people. Cowie then turned to the huge tract of *Comnifora* dryland known as the Tsavo. He had heard stories from Finch Hatton, Blixen, and Percival about the region's abundance of animals. The tract was enormous, over eight thousand square miles. Cowie and his colleagues thought that other than a few Wakamba hunters and migrant Orma herders, there were no inhabitants. (It would turn out, however, that native hunters and animal herders were using Tsavo much more extensively than Cowie or anyone else imagined.) Indeed, the powers in the colonial government considered the place next to worthless for anything other than wild animals, and in 1948 Tsavo National Park became the second park in the new system.

❁

The first warden appointed to oversee the new park was a Nairobi pharmacist who didn't even know how to camp, and if he were to have any hope of succeeding, he would need two assistants who had as much bush experience and wildlife knowledge as possible. Word went out in Nairobi that applications were being accepted for two positions as junior assistant wardens of the new Tsavo park. The pay was only six hundred shillings a month (about sixty dollars), and as anyone with extensive wildlife and camping experience could get a much more lucrative position working for a safari outfitter, the job was expected to attract only young men who were just starting out. Even then there were 120 initial applicants. The list was winnowed to twelve, then to six. The first one accepted was Peter Jenkins, a seventeen-year-old white Kenyan recently out of high school who was then working in Nairobi National Park driving tractors and doing menial tasks. Pete's family had spent most holidays on safari in the Masai Mara, so he had the camping and wildlife experience the hiring committee was looking for. The committee next turned to the other applicants to fill the additional vacancy.

It was then that Bill Woodley arrived back in Nairobi from Portuguese East Africa where, with Tiger Marriott, he had successfully shot over ninety elephant. He was nineteen years old, making his living as an ivory hunter, and was considering applying to one of the safari companies for a position as a hunting guide when he ran into Pete Jenkins, a school acquaintance, who told him about his new job at the national park in Tsavo. Bill had been in the bush so long he didn't even know Tsavo had become a national park. He also was having second thoughts about the safari business: It was difficult to imagine himself spending the rest of his active adulthood playing handmaiden to wealthy American and European hunters. Further, the idea of actually trying to conserve wildlife had an appeal; even at the young age of nineteen, he had seen enough dead elephant that he was uncertain he wanted to dedicate his life exclusively to killing more of them.

The window for submitting applications for the remaining job position, however, had closed the day before. Bill went to the national park office anyway, and there he was surprised to find that the woman in charge of accepting applications was a distant aunt. She told Bill to go ahead and fill out the form, and she would do her best to get it in. It was a propitious coincidence that a relative happened to be working in the office that day, because she did manage to have the application accepted past deadline, and that small effort on her part set the course of Bill Woodley's life.

8

The game is both the hunt and the hunted, the sport and the trophy. The game is killing the game. There was a time when the hunter killed only for his life and food, when wild animals were driven from one area into another instead of being shot or poisoned. Now there are few places left to drive the game. Only 50 years ago man had to be protected from the beasts; today the beasts must somehow be protected from man.

—Peter Beard,
The End of the Game, 1963

It's the morning of our first full day walking in Tsavo, and after breakfast Bongo calls a meeting to discuss safety.

"It's important we establish our walking order," he says, "so Mohamed will be in the lead, I will follow, and the rear party will be Lokiyor. The rest of you agree where you'd like to be, and stay in that position as much as possible."

"We should give each other space," Danny adds. "Each unarmed person needs to be aware of who has a gun, then in case of a spit-up get behind that gun as quickly as possible."

"We should also try and be very quiet," Iain says. "Walk carefully, step over things, talk in whispers."

We leave camp, wading the river where it widens over a shallow sandbar. The air is cool and perfect for walking. I stay behind Bongo, my camera ready. If an animal should charge us, Mohamed could probably stop it with his semiautomatic assault rifle, but Bongo, with the elephant gun, is our backstop if anything were to get past Mohamed. If we do get charged, the only animals we would be likely to have to shoot to kill, however, would be hippo or buffalo. "Elephants will nearly always turn if a shot is placed over their head," Danny had said earlier. "They're more intelligent that way."

Intelligent or not, I had already learned enough about elephant to respect the danger they represented to our foot safari. The day I arrived in Nairobi to prepare for our walk the headlines in the local papers reported that Peter Beard, the well-known wildlife and fashion photographer, had just been tusked by an enraged elephant. There was a photograph of him being loaded into the backseat of a Land Rover, clutching his thigh and writhing in pain.

"Just the kind of thing that always excites Peter when it happens to others," Danny had said in an amused tone.

Peter Beard was one of Bill Woodley's best friends, and also for Danny a kind of honorary godfather. Danny suggested we go to the hospital so I could interview Peter for our video. "We'll barge through the door," Danny said mischievously. "You poke the camera in his face, and I'll start asking him questions."

Peter has had a lifelong fascination with East Africa since Ruth Hales, later to become Ruth Woodley, organized one of his early safaris, in 1961; since then he has crossed and recrossed the remote bushlands in vehicles and on foot, often for months at a time, taking photographs and collecting all manner of flotsam and jetsam for his journals that are more collage than diary. He has published two celebrated books on Africa, *The End of the Game,* and *Eyelids of Morning: The Mingled Destinies of Crocodiles and Men.* The theme central to both works is that the logarithmic increase of *Homo sapiens* across Africa—what Beard refers to as the "galloping rot"—is placing impossible and irreconcilable pressure on the continent's game animals, and unless the human expansion somehow reverses, the game animals are doomed. Today when you graph the increase in human beings against the decrease in all game animals across Africa during the last forty years, Beard's position is self-evident, but when you consider that *The End of the Game* was published in 1963, you realize that he was all the time assessing his adopted home through eyes that saw matters much more perceptively than many of his elders as well as his contemporaries. When *The End of the*

Game was published, it created such a controversy in Africa that Daphne Sheldrick, wife of David Sheldrick, founding warden of Tsavo East National Park, is said to have hurled it across the room. If Peter today feels any vindication that most of his predictions have come to pass, it is a Pyrrhic victory because the sad facts only add fuel to his prophecies of doom. Indeed, even to his best friends and staunchest supporters, his pessimism is such a pervasive part of his personality that many of them can only handle Peter in limited doses.

Another part of Peter's personality that has added to his notoriety is his thrill of flaunting physical danger. His friend Alistair Graham, who has spent months and years on safari with Beard, says, "When Peter sees a dangerous situation, he has to get involved." When Alistair and Peter spent a year camped on the shores of Lake Turkana shooting crocodile in order to get a random sampling for a population study, Peter fired a steel-tipped .270 bullet into a twelve-footer on the shoreline only to have the animal crawl into the murky water. As the astonished locals watched, Beard then waded in, dove down, and felt along the bottom until he located the crocodile, then surfaced with the stunned animal in his arms.

Beard is also well known for his history of approaching dangerous animals on foot to get his photographs. Once in Nairobi National Park, while filming rhinoceros for an ABC Special, Beard and Terry Mathews, a Nairobi friend, were approaching on foot a mother and her infant when a vanload of tourists arrived and caused the rhinos to move in their direction. Peter turned and ran, but his friend wasn't as fast: The rhino impaled him under the left hip, and as she raised him her horn drove upward between his spleen and kidneys, breaking his ribs and driving them inward, one of which stopped less than an inch from his heart.

Jon Bowermaster, in his book *The Adventures and Misadventures of Peter Beard in Africa,* quotes Tony Archer, a well-known Nairobi big-game hunter and safari guide, as telling Peter that "the smart thing you did that day was wear good running shoes." Mathews didn't consider the matter as lightly and sued Beard, ABC, and the film's producer. The case divided the white Kenyans in Nairobi as to whether or not Beard was culpable, and the merits of the argument resurrected when Beard was tusked by the elephant. As we drove around Nairobi making last-minute preparations for our own foot safari, a former hunting guide named Dave Williams ran into Bongo and me on a Nairobi street and said, "Did you hear about Peter? Seems he finally got his comeuppance, now that he's a bit older and couldn't run as fast as the other chap."

It was the next day that Bongo, Danny, and I drove to Nairobi Hospital, video camera in hand, and went to Peter's room. A friend was posted at the door. "I know he would like to see you," the friend said. "But there's been too many press trying to get in, and Peter's in too much pain." We decided perhaps it wasn't the time for a prank, and we left.

I caught up with Peter a year later, however, at his house in Montauk, on the tip of Long Island. Despite multiple surgeries and metal pins in his hip, he walked without a limp, and the only indication of his injury was a moment of stiffness when he stood after sitting too long.

"I was down on the Tanzanian border with my good friend Calvin Cotter," he told me. "There'd been a lot of shooting down there, game department control, big-game hunters. When I look at the tape of the charge, I can see that elephant was fucked up—the whole herd was totally stressed. My mistake was, I didn't see that at the time."

Calvin and Peter had gotten out of the vehicle to approach the herd on foot, just as Peter had done dozens of times to get his photographs. One of the people who stayed in the car had a video camera, and when you look at the tape you can see the matriarch begin her charge, and Calvin and Peter turn and begin to retreat. The elephant's ears are out, her head is up, and she is trumpeting: all signs that it is a demonstration charge (hunters and field biologists call this a "demo"). Sure enough, the elephant stops and returns to the herd.

"Then she turned and came at us again," Peter said. "Now her head was down, which was unusual, and we started running. She was a long ways away, but when I looked over my shoulder, she was still coming. The third time I looked back I knew it wasn't a demo. Then we split, Cotter going one way, me another, so we each had a fifty-fifty chance. Then I felt her breathing down my neck, and she was right on me. I saw an anthill and dove for it.

"I never felt the tusk go through my leg, but when she crushed me with her head I felt the bones go, ribs snap, and pelvis crunch. The pressure was incredible, and then I went blind: I'm convinced it was from the blood being squeezed into my head. I couldn't see anything, but I could sense she was still there, and then the other elephants were there, too. I could hear their feet."

While Peter lay motionless the elephants milled around for a minute or less, then left. Cotter ran up, the car arrived, and Peter was loaded in the back and evacuated to Nairobi Hospital. On the way his sight returned, first one eye, then the other. The tusk had missed the main artery in his leg, but he was still bleeding badly, and by the time he reached the hospital his pulse was gone. He was given more than a half-dozen pints of blood, and the surgeon pinned his pelvis. After another operation he was transferred to New

York, and in a third operation that lasted nine hours, his hip was reconstructed with titanium plates and screws.

"It wouldn't have taken much effort on her part to kill me, if she'd wanted
to," Peter said. "It was a reminder of how tiny and pathetic humans are up
against the true force."

◈

It was one of the few times Peter had been on foot near elephants without either a gun or a vehicle close by. With a rifle, a shot over the elephant's head
would probably have deflected the charge; it would have been unlikely, even
as agitated as this elephant was, that they would have had to shoot to kill her.

Unfortunately that is not always the case with other large animals. Many
times a shot at a charging hippo is not enough to turn it. (Hippo are also the
most dangerous animal in Africa, killing more people each year than any
other large mammal.) In the span of ten years that Iain has walked the Tsavo,
his rangers have had to shoot six hippo. The only way we could have ensured on our walk that we wouldn't have to shoot an animal would have
been to walk unarmed. I had already given that some thought during the
planning stages of the trek, telling myself that if one of my goals on this trip
was to get a sense of what it is like to make a long journey on foot in the close
company of wild and potentially dangerous animals, wouldn't it then be appropriate to make the walk as natives would, carrying only spears?

I had actually made a journey like that once to the high Arctic with Doug
Peacock, the grizzly bear expert famous as the inspiration for Hayduke, the
militant environmentalist in Edward Abbey's *The Monkey Wrench Gang.*
Doug had been adamant that we give the polar bears—notoriously dangerous predators known to stalk and devour humans—an even chance, so we
went armed only with a ten-foot spear tipped with an iron head Doug had
modeled after an Anasazi point he had found in Arizona. Similar to stories of
how Masai spear lion by letting the animal impale himself as he makes his
final leap through the air, tales are told in the Arctic of how Inuit hunters
used to do the same thing to polar bears.

But using these stories as models for what we might do if we were carrying spears has two problems. First, if the stories of the incidents in both the
Arctic and the Serengeti of hunters impaling bear or lion at the last
nanosecond of a charge were not apocryphal, they were at a minimum
probably very rare. There is archival footage, for example, taken by Osa
Johnson, the writer and filmmaker of popular adventure stories in the
1920s and 1930s, that shows the way a lion was usually speared by Masai.

In the film several *morani* approach the lion each from different directions, and as the animal begins a charge at one, another hurls his spear, impaling the animal and making him spin, while another then runs in, throws his spear, and quickly retreats. By the time the lion goes down he has perhaps ten spears in him.

The other problem is that whether or not the stories of a single spear taking a lion are apocryphal, it is clear that if you walk among predators armed only with a spear, the only way you could possibly survive a charge would be if you were a consummate expert with that spear; if your father had given you your first toy spear when you were three years old and you had been practicing ever since.

What then if we hired a contingent of Masai armed with spears to accompany us? That brought to mind a story Iain had told of an incident with a group of tourists in the Masai Mara. Iain doesn't do walking safaris in the Mara, but he does set up wilderness camps where his clients relax after spending the day viewing game from four-wheel-drive vehicles, and he hires Masai tribesmen armed with spears to protect these camps from predators. One evening when everyone was gathered around the fire, a lioness suddenly stepped out of the bush not more than twenty feet away. Iain told the clients not to move while he stood and turned to wave the Masai into position. To his chagrin all of them had dropped their spears and were climbing a tree. Iain then had no choice but to step toward the lioness, clap his hands, and shout. The lioness ran into the bush and the clients, assuming this was common, congratulated Iain for his display of cool courage. Iain ordered a gin and tonic, chugged it down, and requested another. Trying to remain calm, he then walked to the Masai, some of whom hadn't yet come out of the tree, to inform them they were all fired.

When I remembered my own trip to the Arctic, and how naked I had felt hiking across open tundra thick with bear, behind Peacock who was carrying only his spear, it was clear to me that it only made sense to make our foot safari across Tsavo with the protection of firearms. Otherwise it was foolishly risky. Whether or not we were justified in placing the animals at risk so we could be safe was something else again. I didn't have a ready answer to that question, but I did resolve, in the course of our foot safari, to consider it further.

◈

We hike into the morning sun, and ahead I watch two giraffe, their necks fringed by backlight, lope with their peculiar slow-motion gait into the fever tree forest. In *Out of Africa,* Karen Blixen wrote, "I had time after time watched the progression across the plain of the giraffe, in their queer, inimitable, vegetative gracefulness, as if it were not a herd of animals but a family of rare, long-stemmed, speckled gigantic flowers slowly advancing."

When the first live giraffe arrived in Europe in 1827, an estimated ten thousand people crowded into Paris to see it. The giraffe is the tallest animal in the world, yet it lives an average of only ten years. It travels in mixed herds of males and females that number anywhere from a few individuals to as many as fifty animals. It is not uncommon to see two giraffe "necking," standing side by side facing the same direction, crossing and wrapping their necks; this is not a love ritual, but rather a kind of graceful sparring between rival males. Researchers have also discovered that giraffe, like bees, are important to the reproduction of trees in the acacia woodlands as they carry pollen on their lips and noses.

We pass an *Acacia mellifera* that has been torn and stripped by grazing elephant; then a grove of juvenile doum palms whose fronds have also been cropped short. Iain points out large wads of masticated fronds that the elephant have chewed and spit out, presumably to gain the nutritious juice.

"Elephant chewing gum," he says. Then a moment later he stops abruptly and points and whispers, "Over there!"

We look to our right, toward the river, and spot the gray backs of two elephant against a backdrop of mature doums lining the river. We stop and watch through binoculars. There is a large female, two juveniles, and two infants.

"There's probably at least one more mature female in the area," Iain says.

The animals are a little less than a hundred yards distant. Suddenly the matriarch raises her trunk like a periscope.

"She's smelled us."

"Let's move," Danny says.

We break into a trot, glancing over our shoulders as we go. The matriarch herds the others away from us, directing them into the doum grove. They all disappear behind the palms, and we slow to a fast walk. Suddenly we hear a trumpet, and turn to see the matriarch coming from behind the palms charging straight at us. Iain and I quickly fall behind Danny, Bongo, and Mohamed, who have their rifles raised, and the others gather in behind us. There is a good hundred yards between us and the elephant—about the same distance Peter Beard had when the elephant that crushed him had started her charge.

"Fall back!" Bongo orders.

We trot backward, heads turned to keep an eye on the matriarch, careful not to trip. Her ears are out, she's trumpeting and coming right at us, eighty yards . . . seventy yards . . . sixty yards.

"Shall we fire?" Bongo calls to Danny.

Fifty yards.

"Hold off!" Danny counters.

Then the elephant slows and stops. Bongo motions us to keep retreating. Bongo and Danny are on each side of Mohamed, who has been silent the whole while, but his eyes have remained glued on the elephant, his rifle across his chest, finger on the trigger. The matriarch trumpets again, but holds her position.

"They often do that," Danny says when we are far enough away to resume a walking pace. "Disappear, then suddenly come at you." He glances backward: The elephant has now turned back into the grove. "She was just making sure we were going to leave."

The river flows along the southern terminus of the Chyulu Hills. The Taita Hills are to our right, twenty miles away. We leave the riverbank to shortcut a bend, crossing a tongue of lava flowing out from the Chyulus that is from a recent eruption only two hundred years old. It's the type of lava rock that geologists call a'a, a Hawaiian word that I have always considered onomatopoeic after the sound you would make if you tried to walk on the stuff barefoot. I am in fact close to barefoot because, as an experiment against blisters, I have decided to go the day wearing my Teva sandals. They are very comfortable, although I have to watch my step so I don't stub my toes on the exposed rock.

Soon we encounter an elephant path crossing the lava that is as good as any trail in Hawaii's Volcano National Park: The elephant's comings and goings have crushed the coarse black rock into fine gray gravel, and the rubber soles of my sandals crunch with each step. We pass a pile of white bones lying on black basalt that Danny identifies as waterbuck.

It is hot. We leave the lava, dropping into a small *lugga* where a pair of bush shrikes scold like seagulls as we pass. The thick acacia opens to a spring-fed meadow framed by *Phoenix reclinata*, a handsome date palm native to tropical Africa that grows in swampy areas in dense clumps of slender trunks that tend to bend and recline, hence the name. We cross on an

emerald lawn of Bermuda grass cropped by grazing animals, passing the
skull of a Cape buffalo that Danny says would have been taken down by lion.

"This is a perfect setup for lion," Iain adds. "They lie in ambush in the tall
sedge over there, waiting for game that wouldn't be able to resist this grass,
even though they know the danger."

We leave the meadow following a game trail through thickets of *mellifera*
and wait-a-bit thorn, past quartz rocks with crystals that flash in the sun. In
another hour we gain a rough dirt road, cross the river on an old bridge built
in the First War in defense against troops entering from German East Africa,
then reach the confluence where Mzima Springs flows into the Tsavo.

Mzima Springs begins about five miles upriver, and it is one of the natural
wonders of the world. At the base of the Chyulu Hills, in a valley otherwise
dense with dun thornbush, it wells up in a sudden artesian gush of cool
water that flows at a rate of sixty million gallons a day, creating a river lined
with arching *reclinata* palms where you watch through ginclear water as
hippo walk the floor of pools twenty feet deep. This is where the celebrated
wildlife cinematographer Alan Root has made his film studies of hippo, and
it was here he was shooting underwater when one of the animals bit his leg,
removing a large hunk of flesh.

We stop to rest at the confluence where the clear water of Mzima flows
into the red water of the Tsavo. Danny sits on a log and lights a cigarette.

"I used to come here as a kid," he says, "and ride inner tubes down these
rapids. Until one day I saw a bloody great croc in this pool right here."

"Danny was down here all the time," Bongo adds, "with his girlfriends."

I am now familiar enough with their family history to know Bongo refers
to the period in their lives when their father was transferred to Kamboyo,
park headquarters for Tsavo West.

◈

A week before we started our trek, Bongo and I had made an aerial reconnaissance, in his small plane, of the upper Tsavo River, and on the way back
to Nairobi we landed in Kamboyo for a brief visit. As the warden was driving us back to the airstrip he had asked Bongo if he would like to stop by the
house where his parents had lived when his father was transferred back in
1978. Bongo's face brightened. It was a handsomely built house that commanded a view over the plains to the Chyulu Hills in the distance. As we
walked to the entrance an old African in a blue shirt stepped forward and
saluted. "It's Wangungu," Bongo said. "He was our cook." The old man, who

had stayed on by himself as the caretaker of the unoccupied house, grinned, revealing his two remaining teeth, and clasped Bongo's hand with both of his, shaking his head and saying over and over, "Oh, oh, oh."

Wangungu opened the door and we walked in. The furniture was still in place. It was very clean. In the living room Bongo ran his hand slowly across the dining table and said, "Rather nostalgic, this." We walked through Danny's bedroom and then into his parents' room with two beds that had nightstands on opposite sides and clearly were designed to be joined. "These beds push together . . ." Bongo said, stopping short, self-conscious of what I assumed was to him an indiscretion. Back in the living room we paused at a large black-and-white photograph of Mt. Kenya encrusted with snow. "Dad used to tell visitors this photograph was our air conditioning."

"I've heard Iain say your dad enjoyed visitors."

"The Woodley household was a popular place. Mom and Dad were very gregarious."

"Who were the guests?"

"All sorts. Wilfred Thesiger, George Adamson. And of course Peter Beard, who was always out here with his women, Iman and Cheryl Tiegs. He got on exceptionally well with Dad."

We walked back to the entrance, and old Wangungu was there, waiting, and again clasped Bongo's hands in both of his and held them, and this time I saw the moisture in the old man's eyes glinting in the equinoctial sun.

◈

When I had traveled to Montauk Point, New York, to look up Peter Beard, we rendezvoused at the Shagwonk Bar and Grill, where the local fishermen greeted him by first name. He was fifty-nine years old, and he still had his celebrated good looks; his hair, now beginning to gray, was cut in the same early Kennedy style that he wore in a photograph of himself published in *The End of the Game* that was taken in the 1960s while on safari. It was in the autumn and the weather was cooling, but instead of a jacket he wore four or five flannel shirts, one over the other, and open-toed leather sandals known in Kenya as Woodleys because they were designed by Bill for bush walking (they can still be purchased in downtown Nairobi where they are handcrafted by an old Indian shoemaker).

From what others had told me about him, including Bongo and Danny's middle brother, Benjamin, I felt I already knew Peter. "He's not really a photographer," Benjamin had explained. "He's a diarist. He records events in his diaries, collages of words, photographs, clippings, and scraps. I remember him sitting on the floor chatting with Mom and Dad as he cut snippets from stacks of newspapers and magazines, gluing things in his diary. Peter had this obsession with the macabre. There was a photo session with Danny after he'd blown his thumb off in a hunting accident, on the veranda, with the head of a dead cobra we'd chopped off: Peter had Danny hold the snake head next to the remains of his thumb. I have this potpourri of images, all mixed together: old Elui, Dad's Wakamba guide with his scars from leopard attacks and rhino gorings, Dad, with one squint eye, gaunt from his cancer, and Peter, in the middle of it all, pleased by the extremes.

"Dad was the one person Peter held as most special," Benjamin continued. "There was never a conflict between them. Two souls who understood each other. Dad saw through Peter's facade; it didn't matter if Peter was on mushrooms or acid, with his girlfriends or by himself; he was Peter, and he was always special in our household."

Peter Beard agrees with Benjamin, saying of himself that he is not a photographer (he disparages the medium as a pseudo-art at best and a potentially dangerous misrepresentation of reality at worst). But if he is not a photographer, then it is curious that his book *The End of the Game* has in it images that have emblematically lodged in my consciousness: the black-and-white portraits of native Africans, evocative of the best of Edward Curtis; an aerial of an elephant herd crossing the infinite bushland of Tsavo; three giraffe, suspended above a graphically stark plain that melts into a featureless sky, their slow-motion gait somehow brought to life, as though the black-and-white image was the progenitor of cinematography.

After several plates of clams at the Shagwonk, we drove to Peter's house, and the first thing you notice walking in is that it is a three-dimensional version of his collage diaries. Every square foot of every wall was covered with memorabilia. In the kitchen there was a black-and-white photograph of a gerunuk with its giraffe neck framed by a giraffe-necked tree, with dozens of snapshots of his daughter Zara inserted around the picture; several newsclippings; postcards; an old illustration of a red snapper fish surrounded by more snapshots of Zara; a contact print from a photo session with the German supermodel Franke; an eight-by-ten of the supermodel Danielle Luna, her impossibly lanky black body clothed only in a strip of leopard skin around her waist; an illustration from a nineteenth-century magazine of Lincoln's assassination; the dried shell of a horseshoe crab nailed in place; an old pen-and-ink of an elephant tied and trussed to huge groundstakes, like a circus tent; a crossbow and quiver of arrows; one dozen

Masai knobkerries; an empty Barnum and Bailey animal cracker box; a needlepoint illustration of a lion biting the leg off an antelope. All this was on one partition wall about four by eight foot in size, and it was representative of every square foot of every wall in the house.

Peter sat on a single bed that served as a couch in a small room open to the kitchen, and while I asked questions he spent three hours with pens and India inks in blue, red, and green drawing his trademark designs on the inside cover of a copy of The End of the Game, for a nineteenth-birthday present for a friend of a friend he had never met. "I don't do autographs," he explained.

"Did you hit it off right away with Bill when you first met him?" I asked.

"Nothing is ever that extreme. I met Bill on my third trip to Africa, in 1960, and we kept in touch. I sent him some photographs; he always appreciated photographs. He was an easy guy, that's the thing: He didn't need to always be proving he was an adult. If you consider the whole cast of characters [he was referring to the Kenya-born whites who worked as hunters, guides, and later as wardens], they had it made. Their lives were full of adventure, back when the place wasn't fucked up. But one way or another all of them fucked up as well. All but Bill, who managed to pull it off, with the least amount of ego, concocted theories, and know-it-all attitudes. He lived with an open mind; he was flexible. He also could see the whole picture; he had a holistic vision. And he learned all of this from the bush. That was the thing. For me, he was a living example of how to do it, how to live."

When Bill was transferred from Mountain Parks to Tsavo West, he was forty-nine years old. Less than a year later he was diagnosed with stomach cancer. He flew to England where his esophagus and part of his stomach were removed, and he was back in Tsavo two months later. "He couldn't sleep lying down," Danny told me. "He had to prop up in bed, and he was told he probably wouldn't have long to live."

"But he was a positive thinker," Bongo added. "Incredibly optimistic."

That positive thinking proved the doctors wrong. He beat the cancer. But he never recovered full health, and the next ten years was a series of maladies: a stroke, cerebral malaria, a broken leg, epilepsy. None of it, however, prevented Bill and Ruth from their love of seeing friends, meeting new people, and telling stories: The Woodley house in Tsavo West remained open to a continuous flow of ex-army buddies, park wardens, writers, field biologists, filmmakers, politicians, farmers, safari guides. The rich, the poor, the famous, the forgotten, the never known.

In addition to Peter Beard, I talked to a half dozen of Bill's old friends who still live in and around Nairobi. "Of all the wardens in Africa I have met over a forty-year period," one of them told me, "none showed a greater interest in people than Bill Woodley."

"He was full of fun," another said. "Everything was a joke."

"He was a great storyteller, a true raconteur."

"He just plain old loved people."

"If the devil walked in, Bill Woodley would buy him a drink."

"One time I was visiting Bill and Ruth," Iain Allan told me, "when a delegation from Austria was there for dinner: the ambassador, several other high-ranking officials. Bill and the guests were enjoying sundowners on the veranda and everyone was very merry when the houseboy came up and whispered something in Bill's ear. Apparently Elui had showed up at the back door, having walked across Tsavo East just to see Bill. That was it. Bill sat outside with Elui the rest of the evening, the two of them telling stories, and that was the last any of the other guests saw of Bill Woodley."

Bill was notoriously bad about keeping appointments. "He would be heading one place to meet someone, and then would run into someone else, and start telling stories, and the first person would be forgotten."

"It was called Woodley Time. Everyone knew about it, and accepted it as part of Bill."

"You had dinner there and you would never know when you would eat. Bill would start telling stories, and listening to stories, and Wangungu would peek in, frown, and go back to the kitchen to keep things warm as guests started sneaking in to get bites."

"It's because he had time for everybody," another said. "*That* was Woodley Time."

❖

"Bill's the reason we're on this trek," Iain told me.

"How's that?"

"Remember I told you how Bill had once taken me on a flight in his Cessna along the Tsavo? That was when he suggested I do walking safaris along the river. We did our first one in 1979, and it was very successful. Then on my third trip we were camped below Kichwa Tembo when this incredible storm struck. It poured for ten hours. In the morning it cleared,

and Mohamed, who was our main ranger even on those first safaris, said,
'We should go up the side of the hill and check back toward Kilimanjaro.'
We climbed for fifteen minutes and looked back. I'll never forget that sight
Kilimanjaro was covered in new snow—the snow line was four thousand
feet lower than normal—and I knew in an instant we were in trouble. We
ran back to camp and got out just before the flash flood hit.

"I didn't have the idea just then, but that's when it started, the realization
of how intimately connected Kilimanjaro is to the lowlands of Tsavo, how
the water threads it together. The idea germinated from that: to walk that
thread, starting on the summit of Kili, following its water all the way to the
ocean."

9

On foot, the pulse of Africa comes through your boot. You are an animal among others, chary of the shadowed places, of sudden quiet in the air.

—Peter Matthiessen
The Tree Where Man Was Born, 1972

We leave the confluence and follow a four-wheel track that parallels the river. It is mid-day and hot. The rhythm of walking—the one-two, one-two—combined with the heat is hypnotic, and either because he senses my daze, or because he shares it, Bongo says, "This is the time of day when we're not as alert, when our guard's down, and that's when it often happens, when you get charged."

I take deep breaths and open my eyes and force myself to stay more alert. We leave the road, entering thick bush that Danny calls "Young *Commifora.*" Sweat stains our shirts.

Iain says, "I think we need either to go back to the road or down to the river and follow hippo trails."

"The river winds and bends too much," Danny replies.

Iain doesn't respond, so Mohamed carries on through the bush as the rest of us follow. Even though he owns only a few words of English, Mohamed must have understood Iain's comment because I notice our course has altered subtly toward the river. I wonder what Mohamed is thinking, placed in this awk-

ward position: As a sergeant in the Kenya Wildlife Service he is outranked by
Danny and Bongo, yet he also works for Iain as his chief ranger when Iain con-
ducts his walking safaris in Tsavo. Mix into this the hierarchy of black versus
white, and I'm impressed that Mohamed has displayed such calm equanimity.

Mohamed, who is about fifty years old, has known Bongo since he was a
teenager and Danny since he was twelve years old. When Bill Woodley was
transferred to Tsavo West in 1978, Mohamed had already been there for
many years. He quickly caught Bill's eye. He was tough and uncomplaining.
He was a good shot, he was good in the bush, and he was a good walker. To
Bill, Mohamed seemed loyal and committed, and if the scar on his face that
ran from his lower ear to his chin was any indication, he had no sympathy for
Somali poachers.

The story is well known in KWS. Mohamed's patrol had a "contact" with
poachers and he had captured one and was sitting on his chest when another
tried to escape. Mohamed turned to see what was going on, and the poacher
he was sitting on pulled a knife that he had hidden and went for Mohamed's
throat. Mohamed saw it coming and quickly lowered his face to take the
knife on the cheek instead of the throat. It laid open the whole side of his
face, but he grabbed the poacher's hand, squeezed the knife out of it, then
calmly used it to slit the Somali's throat.

When Bill Woodley first suggested the idea of walking safaris to Iain, he
had also recommended Iain spend ten days walking the Tsavo River, to re-
connoiter the route and fix campsites. "You'll need an armed ranger to go
with you, and I've got just the man. His name's Mohamed."

At the time Iain was twenty-eight years old. He had spent his career as a
climber and guide on Mt. Kenya and Kilimanjaro, but he knew next to
nothing about walking through bushcountry in the company of wild animals. "I suddenly realized that although the idea of foot safaris sounded ex-
otic," Iain told me when I asked him about this first scouting walk, "there
was going to be another side to it which I hadn't thought about: It was dangerous. On the mountain everything was always controlled and calculated,
and I was in charge of my own actions. That's one of the reasons I sometimes
feel alarmed flying in airplanes—I'm not in charge of what's going on. So
here I was walking down the Tsavo River, hippos everywhere, behind this
big guy who looked impressive but was nevertheless a total unknown quan-
tity. I was the passenger and he was pilot."

Iain's apprehension lasted about thirty minutes. "I realized that just as a
rock climber can read the rock, Mohamed could read the bush. I could see it
in the way he held his rifle, in his concentration, in the way he flowed through

the bush, the silence that was around him. Then on the second day we had our first encounter with a massive hippo cow whom we later came to call Isabella. She always hung out below Kichwa Tembo, and she always charged. On that first safari, she came erupting out of the water like an explosion. Mohamed waved me behind him, and then he stood his ground. Isabella kept coming, then suddenly she stopped no more than ten feet away. Mohamed shouted at her and she turned back to the river. On our second safari the same thing happened. Then the third time she came too close and Mohamed let off a shot over her head. She raced back to the river, and Mohamed followed, yelling abusively, telling her next time she did that it would be her last."

Since then Mohamed has worked for Iain as the lead ranger on nearly all his foot safaris. "We've probably walked together over a thousand miles," he says. If Iain has complete trust in Mohamed's ability to protect his clients, however, Bongo and Danny, who have been in the bush or on patrol with Mohamed for nearly as many years, don't share the same unreserved confidence, especially when Mohamed's near towns or villages. "We'll have to watch him when we get to lower country where there's palm wine and *miraa*," Danny had told me, referring to the khat narcotic chewed in Somalia but also favored by Samburu and Turkana. "Otherwise he'll go on a piss-up and get out of control."

Danny has full confidence in Lokiyor, however, who is a Turkana from the vast desert country in northwestern Kenya near the Uganda and Sudan borders. Like the Masai, the Turkana are of Nilotic origin, and historically they were considered even more warlike. Today they retain many of their traditional customs and costumes. The women, for example, still wear beaded skirts and necklaces of ostrich egg beads and cowry shells, the fertility symbol among many tribes in Northern Kenya because of the shell's resemblance to a vagina. Like all these Hamitic-speaking peoples, including the Samburu, the Turkana are tall and lean—Lokiyor is six foot four inches. He is thirty years old, and his expression is even more hawklike than Mohamed's. He has the habit of narrowing his eyes, and when he is in conversation he will keep his head motionless while his eyes move from one person to the other, so that he looks at you sideways, and you have the feeling he can see you even when you stand behind him. He was recruited into KWS in 1989, when Richard Leakey was appointed director and cleaned out the older rangers and wardens who were incompetent, corrupt, or both, hiring any new blood that showed promise. Lokiyor was trained to fight poachers using the semiautomatic weapons that Leakey had procured. In 1992 he joined the Problem Animal Control unit, working under Danny, and he was sent to train with Joyce Poole, in Amboseli, to learn how to age and sex elephant so he could select from a marauding herd the individual most appropriate to kill.

"Mohamed is good." Danny had told me. "But Lokiyor is one of the best I've seen. In a spit-up with poachers, or facing a rogue elephant, he's the guy you want next to you."

◈

Mohamed has led us to the river, and Danny wants to cross in order to short-cut the next oxbow. Bongo, however, disagrees, and wants to stay on the side we are on.

"It's much easier on the other side," Danny replies.

"Danny, if we're going to discuss this, let's do it without insult," Bongo says firmly, although I fail to hear the insulting tone in Danny's voice that Bongo charges. Then again, there is history between these two, as there is between all brothers, that I can only guess, but I have had indications. The night before, for example, Danny began to tell a story about a close friend of their father's who had a very short temper. "His car had broken down, I think the wiring had gone bad, and he was very frustrated trying to fix it, so he ordered his men to start cutting sticks—"

"No, you've got it all wrong," Bongo had interrupted. "The wiring wasn't bad, he was stuck in a *lugga* and couldn't get out. So he ordered his men to begin cutting sticks, and when they had them in hand he then ordered them to give the vehicle a good thrashing." We had all laughed, even Danny, who, if he was perturbed by his brother's usurpation of his story, didn't show it.

Once again Danny makes no reply and we continue, now following hippo trails that parallel the river, and the going is much easier. Iain glances back at me with a knowing look. We cross a lateritic pan desiccated and cracked; to our left a grove of *reclinata* palms mark the water's edge. In the dried mud we transect an elephant trail, their prints cast in sufficient detail in the red dirt that I can distinguish the skin folds in their feet that create a pattern as distinct to each individual as a human's fingerprint.

Mohamed's hand goes up as he instantly raises his rifle to chest level. We stop. Through the bush we see a large black shape: Cape buffalo. It is close enough we can hear it breathing. We remain frozen, staring at its baleful eyes, waiting for its next move. The animal snorts loudly, dips its head, then turns and crashes through the bush—away from us. In a moment Mohamed and the others lower their rifles, and we continue.

Cape buffalo are notoriously bad tempered. Danny told me his father was once hiking along the river downstream of our present position when he heard hooves behind him and turned to see a buffalo bearing down. He had no time to react before the buffalo knocked him over, trampled him with its hooves, bashed him with its horns, and, as if that wasn't sufficient, pissed and shit on him. Fortunately Susie, Bill's dog, was along. She was half Rhodesian ridgeback and all the while was snapping at the buffalo's legs. This finally distracted the buffalo long enough for Bill to scramble to the nearest bush and escape with no more damage than some severe bruising. (Susie got away unscathed as well.)

I am very alert, and I stay that way. This is not like a backpacking trip to the High Sierras. It's not even like that hike I once made in the Bob Marshall Wilderness where I kept an eye open for grizzlies. There you might have a close encounter with a bear once a month, but here we are having close encounters with potentially dangerous animals several times a day, and these encounters are producing a tension that is forcing me to hike with all my senses honed.

As we walk I take a mental audit of my body: legs no longer sore, skin no longer burned. I am getting used to going through each day with no lunch and with only two liters of water. My feet continue to toughen. So far so good in the sandals: They are increasing my connection to this place one more notch as I notice out of my peripheral vision thorns and sticks and rocks that could injure my exposed toes if I'm not careful; but being careful is its own kind of pleasure.

I think to myself that I will have no problem walking like this for the two more weeks it will take to finish the trip; I feel I could go two months if that's what the task required. I'm enjoying the feel of earth kicking up on my sandaled feet, and the cooling on my torso when I lift my arms. I am liking the tension when we are in thick bush, the call to attention when we see a hippo or a buffalo. But mostly, I am enjoying the rhythm of walking through the hours of each day in a landscape that has held me over the years with a captivation that is like a pleasant addiction.

I was once a houseguest of Robert Halmi—a producer of television dramas who has shot many films in Africa—at his place near the base of Mt. Kenya, and we talked about this attraction that bewitches so many. "I first came here in the early fifties," he said, "and since then I come back and come back, with friends and movie people—hundreds of them—and I have watched it happen almost every time: They fall in love with this place because there is something here that they recognize."

In the final month before I left to begin this walk from the top of Kilimanjaro, I was working to do background research on the area when in a past issue of *National Geographic* I happened upon a photograph of the footprints in volcanic ash turned to rock that were discovered by Mary Leakey in the Laetoli Plains of Tanzania, to the south of the celebrated Olduvai Gorge. They were the prints of upright primates, two adults and one child, walking side by side, and they were made 3.6 million years ago, an age that places them at the dawn of our species's lineage.

Like Bob Halmi's guests, there was something in the photograph of these footprints that I recognized. It was as though the creatures that made these prints had stepped out of the millennial past to leave the casts of their steps frozen in stone, then disappeared again into the bushland, toward the horizon, and somewhere in time they were still out there, still walking.

Now as I walk I think again of those footprints in stone. I look down to avoid a low-lying wait-a-bit bush and see my feet leave prints in the red earth and I feel a connection that is palpable. My mind flicks through the generations like calendar pages in a period movie—twenty thousand, fifty thousand, one hundred thousand generations—and there is my ancestral family walking across this same thornbush land with the same savanna trees and only variations of the same animals, leaving their prints in the soft mud as they stride bipedally toward their destination.

More than any of the hominoid skulls that have been found in Africa that link us to our ancestors, these footprints allow me to see in my mind's eye who we once were, and what we did in the beginning of our age. Is this, then, the familiarity that so many feel when they see Africa? Is this, perhaps, the source of the yearning I hold for long walks across wide and open places? And if it is, does my urge to walk tap some deep, ancestral memory of our distant forebears walking across these same thornbush plains?

Who knows? The notion is too ephemeral for more than daydream musing, but as I follow my comrades along a game trail through this thornbush and back toward the river, I have one more thought—one more question, if you will—that I can't let go, and it is this:

Perhaps this longing I have to wander in wildness across open spaces is connected to some even deeper urge to follow the herds between their seasonal pastures.

I suspect these satisfactions of going on long walks is what made Joseph Thomson keep returning to Africa. On his second expedition to the continent, in 1883 (when he was trying to establish a direct route through Masai land to Lake Victoria), he had made that first attempt to traverse the country to the west of Kilimanjaro but was repulsed by bellicose Masai. That was when he retreated and joined the slave caravan that took a route to the east of the mountain, crossing the Mogoini River somewhere along the route we had walked down.

Before he had encountered the slave caravan, however, he left the majority of his expedition in Taveta, a town that today is just outside the southern boundary of Tsavo West, and continued with his ten best men to the coast, in order to resupply. He had been told that he would find water en route, so he left with only a small supply. By mid-day he had run out. By afternoon his men were placing stones in their mouths to keep them from drying. By sunset they reached a water hole, and the men cried out *"Allah, hakuna maji,"* "Lord, there is no water!" They had gone too far to turn back. They continued marching all night. At three A.M. "I staggered forward a short distance and literally flopped down in a pool of water; there I drank till I reached the bursting point." Thomson then slept a few hours, and by morning reported that he felt "nothing the worse for my exposure" and marched on.

He reached the coast in five days, covering an average of thirty-four miles a day. With new supplies and additional porters, he returned quickly to Taveta, ready to try again. This was when his fortune improved and he encountered the slave caravan about to depart for the east side of Kilimanjaro, and with them, he made it all the way to Uganda and in doing so established a British presence in East Africa that was the foundation of the colonial expansion that followed.

On a personal level, however, Thomson did not walk across the bushlands of Africa to plant the flag. The principal reason he did it, I am convinced, was simply that he loved to walk through wild country in the company of wild animals. This was the reason he returned to Africa, and returned again. After his expedition across Masai land, Thomson continued his walks across the Sudan, the Atlas Mountains, along the Zambesi. It was between these expeditions that in a letter to his brother he wrote, "I am not an empire builder, I am not a missionary, I am not truly a scientist. I merely want to return to Africa and continue my wanderings."

In this I feel common ground with Joseph Thomson, and if we had lived in the same era, I feel he is a person I could have sat down with over a gin and tonic and spread out the maps and talked about the places that were still blank. I could imagine his enthusiasm as he planned his next adventure, and the yearning he felt to get out of the city and back to the bush country, back to the wild. As I learned more about Bill Woodley, I came to feel the same about him. Of all the wardens and game rangers in East Africa, he was known as the one who loved to walk. There is a story how in the beginning days of the park Bill used to walk thirty-five miles across Tsavo East just to pick up his paycheck. But in Joseph Thomson, Bill Woodley would have met his match: Thomson describes walking seventy miles across the Taru Desert, without stopping, just to get water.

❖

An hour before sunset we arrive in what is so far our prettiest camp. Our dining tent is positioned overlooking a bend in the river, and the safari chairs are arranged in front so we can enjoy the grove of doum palms that line the opposite bank, and the ruddy cliffs of Ngulia that frame the background. Across the river a troop of baboon climb the palm trunks, picking and then throwing to the ground the palm's fruit that they then descend to eat. "I've tried those things," Danny says, "and they're sickeningly sweet. You watch the baboons take a few bites, then spit out the fiber."

It is common to hear stories of elephant in Tsavo eating fermented doum fruit and getting drunk (although I could find no one who could verify this), but these baboon seem to be acting like normal baboon. In addition to fruit, the bulk of a baboon's diet is young grass shoots and various parts of acacia trees including leaves, flowers, and seed pods. Baboon are omnivores, however, and adult males have been observed hunting birds, dik-dik, and even animals as large as impala. Two anthropologists, Sherwood Washburn and Irven DeVore, who spent years studying baboon behavior, described how an adult male dispatched a young Thomson's gazelle: "[the male] grabbed it, brought it above his head, and slammed it to the ground. He immediately tore into the stomach . . . and began eating. Two hours later only skin, teeth and large bones remained."

I pitch my tent beneath a large river acacia near the water's edge, and don't bother with the rainfly as the nightsky is cloudless. The gentle lapping against the mud bank lulls me asleep. About one A.M. I wake to the guttural roar of a lion, and it is close to camp. Very close.

10

And those that are hunted
Know this as their life,
Their reward: to walk
Under such trees in full knowledge
Of what is in glory above them,
And to feel no fear,
But acceptance, compliance.
Fulfilling themselves without pain.

—*James Dickey,*
from "The Heaven of Animals," 1967

I listen, then it is quiet. I'm about to fall back asleep when the lion roars again, a series of deep exhales that you know can only be made by a large, forceful animal. I am wide awake. I try to determine the lion's position. It roars again, and this time it seems to be more from behind our camp. It's circling us. Does that mean it's stalking? I stare at the nightsky through the insect netting that forms the top of my shelter. Would a lion even consider this tent a barrier? I'm certain it wouldn't even slow it down a half a heartbeat. The camp is quiet, but surely the others are as awake as I am.

It is still quiet and I try to put the lion out of mind so that I can go back to sleep, telling myself that if there is any danger Danny and Bongo and the rangers would be up, rifles ready. Then I remember a time several years ago when I was climbing Mt. Kenya with Iain. We were beginning the approach hike when word came down that a German climber in the party just in front of us had been grabbed the night before from his tent by a rogue lion. The climber screamed and his companions jumped out in time to see the lion dragging the climber by the leg toward the forest. There was another climbing party from South Africa in the same campground, and one of them, knowing immediately what was happening, grabbed a cooking pot and rushed the lion, clanking the pot as loudly as he could, shouting the whole time. The lion dropped the German and ran off, but the climber was mauled badly enough that he later lost his leg. At that time Bongo was already warden of Mt. Kenya National Park, and the next morning he showed up with the Rigby .416 and disappeared into the thick bamboo. He came back three days later with the dead lion.

Again I try to assure myself that the others must know whether or not there is any danger. I remember another story by Richard Meinertzhagen describing a safari he was on in 1902 when a lion dragged a porter out his tent and devoured him. Then I think of the most infamous story of all, the notorious maneaters of Tsavo, a pair of lions who, at the turn of the century, halted construction of the railway when they began attacking the Indian workers building a bridge over the Tsavo River, hitting a different tent each night, eventually killing a documented twenty-eight people, although many more were unaccounted for. Where I now lay in my tent is about a three-day walk from the Tsavo bridge.

I lay listening: The lion must have moved on. I remember a Masai saying, *the day is for people, but the night is for wild animals.* I drift into an unsettled sleep.

❖

In the morning I wake before dawn, then at first light go to the mess tent for coffee. When the others arrive I ask them if they heard the lion.

"Oh yes," Bongo says, "I love that sound, a lion roaring at night."

"The cooks say they found footprints at the edge of camp," Iain says.

"You don't think we were in danger?"

"You never know," Bongo says. "But it would have been very unusual for him to take someone from the camp."

I drink my coffee wondering what it was like for the German to be dragged out of his tent. Did he wake first, perhaps hear the lion before it ripped the tent with its claw? Or did the jaws crunch down on his leg when he was in a dead sleep? What would I do in that situation?

It is interesting that by strong anecdotal case histories it seems that once a predator like a lion—or a shark or a bear or a tiger—does grab you, and you sense that your situation is hopeless, a kind of painless distancing from reality takes place. This perhaps is the same mechanism seen in prey animals in Africa when they are taken by predators; there are countless stories of antelope and zebra that, once in the grips of a lion or lioness, will stand passively while the predator disembowels them, then starts eating them alive.

In "Missionary Travels" David Livingstone described what it was like when he was attacked by a lion, how it caused "a kind of dreaminess, in which there was no sense of pain nor feeling of terror. It was like what patients under chloroform describe who see all the operation but feel not the knife." An even more gripping account of a mauling was by a young field biologist named Joanna Greenfield, in a short personal history published in *The New Yorker* titled "Hyena." Greenfield had had a lifelong desire to work and study in Africa, but the closest she could get was a job at a reserve in Israel dedicated to biblical animals: wolves, foxes, a leopard, and a hyena.

There are two principal species of hyena. The spotted hyena occurs across most of Africa south of the Sahara, and the striped hyena overlaps the spotted's distribution in parts of Central and East Africa, then continues across a broad band of North Africa and the Middle East, all the way to India. Perhaps more than any other animal, the hyena evokes in humans a feeling of evil. It has wide jaws more powerful than a lion's, and it is the only predator adapted to chewing, swallowing, and digesting bone. Its back slopes into a thick neck that seems to hang down in the skulking pose of someone who has just committed a sinister misdeed. Hyena hunt in packs, and they are known to run alongside their prey, tearing bites of flesh out and swallowing them, continuing until the victim succumbs from loss of blood, or trips over its own entrails.

Among her jobs in the biblical animal reserve, Greenfield had to feed the hyena. "I unlatched the cage door and bent over to put the dish down, talking to him," she writes. "The mind, I found, is strange. It shut off during the attack, while my body continued to act, without thought or even sight. I don't remember him sinking his teeth into my arm, though I heard a little grating noise as his teeth chewed into the bone. . . . he moved up the arm, and all the time those black, blank eyes evaluated me, like a shark's, calm and almost friendly. By this time, my right arm was a mangled mess of flesh, pushed-out globs of fat, and flashes of bone two inches long, but my slow TV mind, watching, saw it as whole, just trapped in the hyena's mouth, in a tug-of-war like the one I used to play with my dogs—only it was my arm now instead of a sock. It didn't hurt. It never did."

The attack lasted what must have seemed to Greenfield an interminable time. She broke her arm loose, but the hyena went for her leg, causing severe damage by the time she pulled to the door and unlatched it and the hyena dropped her and ran out. At that point, her story would have been a riveting account of a mauling, but Greenfield then takes her experience to another level. She explains how five years later, with "three long dents around the arm and the leg, blurred with spider tracks of canine punctures," she traveled to Africa, and from her tent she looked across the fire at the eyes of the hyenas approaching her camp, "shining green and gold, low down to the ground." She felt neither fear nor horror, however, but instead an affinity to the land and to its animals including—and especially—the hyena. I realized that what she was describing was the strange alchemy of fear and fascination, the mix of attraction and repulsion, that combines to form the bond between predator and prey.

We begin the day's hike crossing the river at a ford adjacent to our campsite. As is usual on these crossings, foremost on our minds is the whereabouts of crocodile; as I enter the water my eyes scan up and downstream for any sign of movement. The water is cool and feels good on my sandaled feet. While crossing Danny loses his balance and gets his ammo belt wet and curses. On the far bank he dries the cartridges while the others sit and dry their feet and bandage blisters before putting on their walking shoes. Bongo and Iain continue to have large areas both on the tops and bottoms of their feet where blisters have bubbled and popped and left exposed flesh.

Mohamed leads off, then Bongo, then myself. I am carrying my video camera in one hand. The bush thickens and Mohamed lifts his gun and holds it across his chest, finger on the trigger, in what I call his "Number Two Position." I move the button on the camera to Standby and hear the whir of the advancing tape. Bongo lifts the old Rigby .416 so the butt rests on his hip as he walks, his hand across the grip and his thumb on the button that has on the end of it, engraved in gold, the word "Safe." We walk cautiously and alertly, weaving around the *mellifera* and wait-a-bit until it again opens to the point we can see around corners. Mohamed and Bongo then lower their guns, and I shut down the camera to save its batteries. (When Mohamed has his gun lowered to his "Number Three Position" he carries it casually along his side in one hand, with his enormous fingers wrapped comfortably around the magazine. "Number One Position" is when he holds the rifle at shoulder level with the barrel pointed into the bush. So far he has only done this twice, both times when we have sighted a buffalo at close quarters.)

Ahead of me I watch Mohamed stride easily, two water bottles in the hip pockets of his field vest. Most women find him compellingly handsome. (I know this because when my wife first met Mohamed she stared at him goggle-eyed, and had a hard time saying, "Nice to meet you.") Like most Samburu, his face bulbs out so his head has a slight pear shape, and it sits on a neck that is striated with muscle. From behind I watch his jaws continuously flex (I have noticed Lokiyor has the same habit), and I can see sky through the holes in the distended lower lobes of each of his ears.

The sky is overcast and the temperature is cool and pleasant. By the river I hear the solitary call of a bird I don't recognize, and I wonder if it has been alerted by us, or by something else. We pass a dik-dik midden, a pile of droppings that these elfin antelope, only slightly larger than a hare, use to mark their territory. The Waliangulu—like other East African tribes—believe the dik-dik build these pellet middens because one day the chief dik-dik stepped in a pile of elephant dung and got stuck, and to get even he ordered all dik-dik to start going in the same place, with the hope they could build a pile big enough that an elephant would come along and step in it and also get stuck. Dik-dik, capable of taking what water they need only from the moisture they gain from their browse, thrive in the dry thornbush of Tsavo. Iain says they are more plentiful since the poaching wars in the 1980s reduced the elephant herds that otherwise kept the density of the bush in check: With denser ground cover to hide under, the dik-dik is better protected from its predators, especially eagles.

In the next hour we flush two of these tiny antelope. One is a male with two small stub horns, and when he bolts from a bush just in front of us he is close enough that I can see in the corner of his doe eyes his pre-orbital glands. These small black spots secrete a sticky substance that dik-dik use to mark their territory by actually poking the ends of branches into the gland.

Dik-dik live in small family units—two parents and one or two offspring—that occupy well-defined territories several acres in size. From what research is known about these endearing animals, it appears that they may mate for life. One researcher observed a male who lost his companion, presumably to a predator, and remained a bachelor for the remainder of the study period even though it presumably would have been easy to attract another mate.

We once more cross the river and as we climb the opposite bank we glimpse the impossibly long tail feathers of the white paradise flycatcher, a white phase in the males of this fairylike bird found almost exclusively in the dry bush country of Tsavo. We walk another hour, then stop at a low evergreen with pencil-straight branches that Danny identifies as the *Mswaki*, the toothbrush tree. Mohamed cuts off a ten-inch section of branch, makes several short cuts on the end to create a brush that he then rubs against his teeth. The rest of us follow suit, and for several minutes we stand around having a mid-morning teeth clean. "You have to brush vigorously," Iain says. "Like Mohamed." We turn to look at Mohamed, who has worked up a froth around his mouth. We all laugh, and he smiles self-consciously, causing the foam to spread across his lips.

All morning we have followed only game trails, and I comment how wonderful it is that this part of the country is still wild. "I may actually have had a small part in that," Danny says. "In 1991 there was Japanese aid money available to build roads in the parks, and I was sent to Tsavo to complete a survey. I recommended that the north sides of both the Tsavo and Galana be left as they are, with no roads. It's very nice to come back here and see it just as it was when I was younger, when Iain and my father were here."

"Actually I have no memory of your father ever coming down to the river when I was here with my groups," Iain said. "I always assumed it was because he didn't want my clients to feel like there was an official presence, so they could have a more natural experience."

A half hour later the animal trail we have followed suddenly turns into a freshly bulldozed road cut through the bush alongside the river. It's a direct and untimely insult to Danny's proud claim that this place has remained undeveloped in part because of his report. We are all courteous enough not to say anything until Danny breaks the silence and says, "Bloody shortsighted of them."

"One has to wonder," Iain says empathetically, "why they put a road like this in because it's not going to assist them much in making extra revenue. Tsavo doesn't lend itself to making more revenue. The kind of parks that do are the ones where you can jump in a minivan, and without going into four-wheel drive go for twenty minutes and find lions sitting beneath a tree and take pictures of them. Tsavo will never allow that. It's too wild for that. People are never going to come to Tsavo because the animals are too hidden, too elusive. So they might as well leave it like it is."

We all wish it were so. But for now we follow the caterpillar tracks of the bulldozer that has pushed the thornbush into piles adjacent to the fresh cut

until the road finally angles away from the river, and we return to a hippo
trail that parallels the river.

❖

Mohamed jumps back, freezes, and waves us to stop; Bongo turns and puts
his finger to his lips mouthing "Quiet!" as he points. Ten yards to our side,
under a *mellifera* bush, is a dozing hippo. This is serious. The animal continues to sleep, and we breathe as silently as we can. It looks like a giant
sleeping dog with the weight of its head flattening its fleshy jowls. Mohamed, Danny, Bongo, Galogalo, Lokiyor, they are all in Number One Position: rifles to their shoulders, safeties off, fingers on triggers. Bongo motions
us to begin moving, pointing to the ground to indicate twigs. We move very
slowly sideways, eyes going from the ground to the hippo to the ground.
The animal continues to sleep. The end of our column still isn't past him. I
glance back at Lokiyor. His head is facing the direction we are moving, but
his eyes are sideways, locked onto the hippo like the crosshairs of a gun-
sight. I lift one foot, move it, then carefully weight it before lifting the next.
We keep moving this way, step by silent step.

When we are far enough away Bongo says in a low voice, "If he'd woken he
almost certainly would have charged, and we would have had to shoot him."

As we continue to walk in silence, I consider what my reaction might
have been had the hippo charged and had we shot it. Would we have been
justified killing an animal just so we could walk across part of wild Africa to
see it, as I told friends before leaving, like the early explorers did, on foot
and at eye level? I remember again Iain's statistic that in his ten years walking sections of this river he has had to shoot six hippo—which he doesn't
think is too bad considering the number of times he has come down here,
and it certainly pales, on a "per-visitor ratio," alongside the numbers of large
animals that big-game hunters shoot, even today, in the African countries
where hunting is still allowed.

The alternative is to view African wildlife from a vehicle, as nearly all visitors do, but this would mean building roads into this wilderness, and that, to
me, is not an attractive alternative. Simply closing the place off and leaving it
to the animals may not be an alternative, either, because there would be no
economic value in that, and it is argued by many that if these parks cannot
carry their own way economically, their future in Africa is very much in doubt.

So perhaps walking safaris are the best of the alternatives for a place like
Tsavo, even at the risk of shooting an animal. That's not to say there isn't

some risk to the trekkers, too. Even armed with semiautomatic rifles, foot safaris in Africa still involve risk. Several years ago, Iain had fourteen people walking this same stretch of river we are hiking. Without warning, a hippo charged from the bush so close that before the lead ranger could turn to get off a shot it knocked him down but somehow missed crushing him as it stepped over. The hippo then went to a middle-aged woman who was next in line, grabbed her by the thigh, and shook her like a rag doll. Meanwhile the ranger scrambled to his feet, picked up his rifle, and started shooting into the animal while the woman was still in its mouth. The hippo dropped her and ran into the river where it presumably died.

"The woman had a compound fracture of the femur," Iain told me, "a broken arm, and quite a large chunk out of her right buttock. My wife was along, who is a doctor, and by good fortune we also had two registered nurses in the party, so we quickly applied tourniquets, stabilized her, and went immediately for help. We had her in the Nairobi Hospital within five hours, which I thought was quite remarkable for out here. She's probably one of only a few people who have been in a hippo's mouth and lived to tell about it."

❖

We reach camp with two hours of daylight remaining. We wash our faces, relax in safari chairs in front of a fire Chui has made, and, as seems appropriate on a day of close encounters with potentially dangerous animals, we get on the subject of hunting.

"I remember your father was very proud of the day when you shot your first buffalo," Iain says to Danny. "I don't remember the details, but it was somewhere near here, wasn't it?"

"Yes, on the slopes of Kilimanjaro. I was thirteen years old at the time, and we went out to do control work on a sisal estate. It was about five thirty on a misty and drizzly morning when the night watchman knocked on our window and told Dad the buffalo was in the fields. I had a .30-06, and Dad had the .416. The deal was, Dad was going to shoot it in the chest area to give the animal one or two minutes before it actually dropped, and that would give me experience to get in a heart or a brain shot. So we went off with the night watchman and my father shot the buffalo behind the shoulder and it took off into thick bush. We could hear it breathing and groaning. He went one way and the watchman and I went another, and as I came around I saw it down on its brisket, its head on the ground, and I thought it was finished. Suddenly it got up and came. I turned around and got out of there, then heard a shot and turned to see Dad had shot it again, but once more in the side. It was still coming at me, so I shot it in the face. It went down, and as quick as I could reload it was up and coming, and I shot it again and it was still coming. I reloaded quickly and fired once more and this time it was finished. All this took place at maybe a ten-yard distance. All the locals on the estate then came around and were very happy, and I was blooded—blood was washed on my face—and the people told Dad he was getting old and slow and this was why it was good to have young blood. He was very pleased, and I was too because I hadn't known how I would react. I could have easily been on the receiving end that day."

As always near the equator, twilight is short and darkness comes quickly. I crawl in my tent, sit against my foldable backrest, and feel the cool air drift through the insect netting that forms the top and sides of my shelter. I turn on my headlamp and record in my journal Danny's story of shooting the buffalo.

I consider that Danny has more in common with his father than only his mischievous tendencies. He has told me the most important thing he learned from his father was to think and live like a hunter, and it is this, I realize, that most connects father and son. But it isn't the only thing, because both men also dedicated their lives to a career in the national parks, and through that to a career that at least in part involved conservation.

I turn off my headlamp. The only sounds are a few cicadas and the gentle lapping of the river against the mud bank. I think about this combination of hunting and conservation. It's a hard one to get ahold of, and I realize it will take more than one night's musing before I grasp it, if I do even then.

11

*He perceived more clearly the cruelty of Nature, to whom our refinement
and piety are but as bubbles, hurrying downwards on the turbid waters.
They break, and the stream continues.*

—*E. M. Forster,* The Longest Journey, *1907*

In the morning I wake before light, as is now my habit, and listen· the cicadas, the quiet lapping of water on the bank of the river, the tuba protest of
a lone hippo not far from camp. We have breakfast at first light, and leave
camp at seven thirty.

Ten minutes after we start Bongo spots a small hole in the ground with a
ring of freshly excavated earth circling it; he motions us to approach but to
step lightly. A small puff of dirt flies out of the hole. "Naked mole-rats,"
Bongo says. I chew on this creature's name one word a time, naked . . .
mole . . . rat, and decide that if names precolor your regard for an animal
then this one has a severe image problem.

Bongo comes to the creature's support. "They are the only mammals that
behave like insects," he says in a low voice as we watch more dirt fly out of
the hole. "They live in colonies that can number a hundred or more, with a
selected number of breeding males, maybe four or five. They have one
queen, as it were, who gives birth to up to thirty young at a time; they just
march out of her. They live on tubers, and their tunnel system can extend

over three kilometers. They never come above ground, and snakes are their main enemy."

We watch the puffs of dirt continue to fly out the hole. "Very interesting, these naked mole-rats," Bongo concludes.

We cross to the south bank of the river and follow hippo trails.

"The nearest road on this side is forty miles," Iain says.

We are quiet and alert. I decide to take a photograph and say, "Mohamed!" and he jumps around like a spring-loaded trap, rifle ready, and I feel badly I didn't call his name using a more innocuous tone of voice. A wood hoopoe flies into a nearby river acacia—a tall riverine tree with needle-sharp thorns three inches long. Farther ahead a congregation of red-billed hornbills chatter like barnyard chickens. We pass a pile of elephant dung that Danny says is "this morning, maybe fresher." Mohamed leads us away from the river, and Danny calls to him and points back, but Mohamed says in Swahili that the river takes a deep bend here, and this is a shortcut. Mohamed knows this country better than anyone in our group, and we follow him as he relaxes into Number Three Position.

A thermometer we carry indicates the temperature has climbed to 110 degrees. We rejoin the river and, thankfully, the welcome shade of the riverine trees. Sweat dries on our shirts, leaving deposits of salt. Ahead the lone seagull cry of an African fish eagle carries upriver, and behind me Danny imitates the bird until it appears overhead. It flaps twice, turns, and glides over us again, showing its white head and tawny body. A band of vervet monkeys scamper overhead and scold us as we encroach on the ground below their arboreal claim. We are watched by a gang of submerged hippo who show us only their beady eyes and ridiculously small ears that spin clownishly. Across the river we spot four more hippo sleeping under a tree, and we stop to watch until a very small one wakes and alerts the others, who get up and plod disgruntledly into the water.

As is our habit we walk through the mid-day and into the afternoon, skipping lunch because in this heat none of us has much of an appetite anyway, taking rest breaks only for water. By mid-afternoon we arrive at the location of our day's camp, a place called Maji Ya Chumvi, "Salty Water." The camp is across the river, next to a salt deposit that is popular with the local animals: There is a major game trail leading into the river at the only point where it is shallow enough to cross. We all gather, and everyone hesitates.

"The thing about crocodiles," Bongo says matter-of-factly, "is that they observe the habits of animals and then they lie in wait."

From the abundance of tracks around us, it is clear that a great number of animals in this neighborhood have the habit of frequently crossing the river right where we stand. We explore downriver and then up, but in both directions the water is continuously narrow and deep. We go back to the crossing and everyone removes their shoes, and Bongo speaks in Swahili to Mohamed and Lokiyor. "What did you say?" I ask. "I told them to keep an eye for bow wakes." We cross in the same order in which we have been walking, each one silent as he wades through the turbid water, each one carrying his own thoughts. On the other side, as though to express our collective sigh, Iain says, "Well, welcome to camp."

❖

It is too hot for anything but lounging under what little shade is available from the scrub *mellifera*. Maji Ya Chumvi is at the end of a dead-end spur of rough dirt track that leads back to a road that provides access to the Ngulia Safari Lodge—a tourist hotel nestled high on a craggy overlook behind Kichwa Tembo—and when it cools, Bongo and Danny suggest we drive there. "I believe we need to reinforce the beer supply," Bongo says mischievously, and Danny adds that we will also pass through the rhino sanctuary.

We stand in the roof opening that is common to all game-viewing vehicles in East Africa, and the cooling breeze as we speed down the road is welcome. We are traveling at only thirty to forty kilometers an hour, but after so many days of walking it seems like eighty. It is still too hot for game to be out, but this ride in vehicles is nostalgic of past trips to Africa, and although I wouldn't exchange it for our walk, I realize that in the context of the future of ecotourism on the continent, three-hundred-mile foot safaris through bush country where daily temperatures are 110 degree and higher may not be the most popular way that visitors choose to see Africa's wild animals.

At a T-junction we turn and follow a dirt road along an electrified fence that encloses the Ngulia Rhino Sanctuary. During our walk, while we have had to be concerned at every turn with the possibility of running into a hippo or buffalo, to give elephant a wide berth to avoid charges, to ford the river only at shallow sandbars to prevent crocodile attacks, to cross our fingers that the lion prowling our camps at night were not too hungry, we have not had to worry about being charged by rhinoceros. Because during the 1970s and 1980s the Somali poachers that swept across Tsavo succeeded in gunning down to the last individual every rhinoceros in the eight thousand square miles of the combined Tsavo parks, except for a handful of holdout animals who sequestered themselves in remote valleys in Tsavo West and were then captured and transferred into this reserve and guarded by well-armed rangers continuously patrolling the perimeter.

During the 1940s, the 1950s, and even into the 1960s, it would have taken a considerable amount of imagination to envision the Tsavo ecosystem without any rhinoceros. Now in the 1990s, as we made our walk through Tsavo without any rhinoceros, I was curious to do the reverse: to try to get a sense of what the land was like when this most prehistoric-looking of all of Africa's large mammals was prevalent. To do that, once we had finished our walk, and I started to write this book, I asked several of the old-timers involved in those early years to describe just how common rhinoceros were in those days:

"That country you walked through along the Tsavo River? I once counted sixty-four in a single morning between eight and noon."

"They were a nuisance. So many you couldn't do anything without getting run up a tree."

"Thick as fleas."

"A road hazard along the Mombasa Highway."

I studied the accounts of the African explorers who first entered Tsavo, and they too described rhinoceros as abundant. A big-game hunter in 1886 reported that "rhinoceros is particularly common in the plains to the east of Kilimanjaro." Reports such as these—and especially the account of Theodore Roosevelt's expedition—attracted more big-game hunters, including a genial Scotsman eponymously named J. A. Hunter who arguably was the most skilled hunter of them all. He arrived in the colony in 1911, and his skill soon earned him position among the hunting elite (Denys Finch Hatton frequently chose Hunter to help him with wealthy clients who requested large and complex safaris). Pete Jenkins (who was the other junior assistant warden chosen, along with Bill Woodley, to serve in the new Tsavo National Park, in 1949) told me that J.A. was "probably the greatest elephant hunter this country has ever seen. I hunted with him on quite a few occasions, and he could use a double barrel faster than anyone. I have seen him frontal brain two elephant bulls right and left, bang-bang. He used to get very close, and he is one of the few people who went through his entire hunting career without ever being knocked down by a wild animal."

During World War II Hunter received instruction from the Game Department to clear an area near Tsavo of rhinoceros in order to make room for a Wakamba settlement. With two other game scouts, he began the effort of shooting all the rhinoceros in the region. It took one year, and the total number of rhino shot was 996.

When I read this statistic, I tried to imagine what a thousand rhinoceros would look like if they were stacked in a heap like victims of a wildlife holocaust. But I was unable to form what I regarded as an accurate mental picture of how big the heap would be, so then I wondered what one thousand rhinos would look like if their bodies were arranged in a row head to tail. The *Collins Field Guide to Mammals of Africa* says the body length of a black rhinoceros is between 295 to 360 centimeters. If you take 335 centimeters as the average length, that would mean one thousand rhinos would create a line of carcasses approximately eleven thousand feet long. Back home in California, I drove along a country road where I sometimes go jogging, and measured out 2.1 miles against the odometer. I stopped the car, put on my running shoes, and then covered the distance on foot, imagining in my mind's eye as I ran down the road a continuous line of dead rhinos beside me, bloating in the equatorial sun. Finally, I had a sense of what it means to shoot one thousand rhinoceros.

❖

We arrive at the gate into the rhino sanctuary that is decorated—as all entrance gates are in Kenya's national park system—with a sheet-metal cutout of a rhinoceros. The guard salutes when he sees Danny and Bongo. We get out and walk to the electric fence. It's only about five feet high. "We've tried different designs over the years," Danny says, "and this one is both cost-effective and it works. It's low so other game can jump over, or crawl under. The ground wire runs here, and the live wire here. Touch the live wire and nothing much happens. See."

Danny touches the live wire, and I do the same, pulling my finger back when I feel a very strong tingle, but then realizing my reaction is more from caution than from electric shock. "Touch the live wire and then the ground, however, and you'll get between six thousand and eight thousand volts, and you'll end up back there," Danny says, pointing to the bush behind us.

"My father was put in charge of this rhino program in 1986," he continues. "There were just a few rhino left in isolated pockets around Tsavo West, and there were poacher tracks on top of the rhino tracks; we even found one animal still alive with an arrow through its lip. Everyone was discussing what to do about the situation, and whilst they were arguing, Dad just put up a fence, captured the few rhino that were left, and put them in it. For security, we have ground patrols, observation points, and aircraft assistance.

"Studies have shown that rhino eat about one hundred and twenty different plant species," he continues, "and an ideal area with good water can support up to two rhinos per square kilometer. Here in the sanctuary we have between eighty and ninety of those plants, so we figure the area can support about one-point-five rhinos per square kilometer. In the original reserve we had six rhino. The Somalis broke in and poached one, and one escaped. Then we expanded the reserve to twenty square kilometers, automatically enclosing the rhino that had escaped, caught two more, and then slowly those had calves. Meanwhile other rhinos have been transferred in from Amboseli, Nairobi, and the Solia Game Ranch. The sanctuary now is seventy-four square kilometers and has between twenty-seven and thirty-two animals in it—we don't know exactly because they're very hard to count.

"As the rhino population within the reserve has increased, animals have been transferred from here down to the Free Release site in Tsavo East, where there's no fence. That's the ultimate goal, not this sort of zoo within a national park we have here. But from a plan that started as an emergency response to a real crisis, to what we see here, to what we'll see in three days when we walk through the Free Release site, I would say my father's original idea has worked very well indeed."

◈

We continue driving along the outer perimeter of the fence, on our way to Ngulia Lodge, and although we study the bush very carefully, we don't see any rhino. The road switchbacks up a shoulder behind Kichwa Tembo, and when we arrive the lodge glows in late-afternoon light. From the veranda adjacent to the bar we can see north and east across Tsavo West, and beyond, toward the lands we will be crossing the next two weeks. In the opposite direction a high grass plain extends to the crest of the Chyulus, and in sunset light three elephant amble to a water hole just beyond the terrace, as apparently they do every evening, and the hotel guests gather, drinks in hand, to snap photographs. I watch the elephant take water into their trunks and then release it into their mouths, and I imagine the difference if I were watching this same scene and the lodge wasn't here, if I were on foot, hidden behind a bush, studying the wind direction, studying the animal's every nuance to make sure they didn't detect me, looking for available cover if they did.

We return to the bar and order another round. Bongo points to the end of the bar and says, "That's where Dad always sat. He had one bad eye, toward the end, and sitting there he could still watch everyone. He liked that, watching people."

There is a tour group in from Abercrombie and Kent, the prominent East African outfitting service. Their guide is an older gentlemen who knew Bill, and now he is very pleased to see both Bongo and Danny, and he greets them enthusiastically. He is also excited and impressed when he hears about our walk. When he turns back to the bar I can hear him in a quiet voice tell a friend he is with, "Just like the old man, those two. Good to see that.

———————————◈———————————

The full moon is over the thornbush plains as we drive back. Danny and I sit on top with our feet dangling in the roof hatches, beer bottles in hand. The cumulus are ghostly white against the nightsky, and the moonlight that falls between is a patchwork on the plains that spread to the distant dark hills. It's what it looks like at sea on a full moon night in the trade winds: the scintillating silver waves, the horizon with the dark outline of a volcano island. I remember when I was eighteen and I had my first big adventure sailing across the Pacific with five buddies. Now I look out over Tsavo, and I remember a full moon night in Papeete when across the channel the spire summits of Moorea stood in dark silhouette against the bright nightsky. I remember how the world felt like it was full of adventures that were there, on the horizon, waiting. Now somehow I have this same feeling, even all these years later, even as my hair is starting to gray. This vast thornbush country, glowing in the moonlight, is fresh and young, and it calls to me. I turn and there is Danny, and he somehow senses how I feel. He smiles, and I see his teeth in the moonlight as his hand sweeps across Tsavo, and he yells above the wind, "This, Rick. This is my life."

12

The Tsavo bushland is tough, and it hones the character of its animals until each one is the lean and pure essence of its form.

—Daphne Sheldrick,
from a personal interview, 1997

The next morning I put my best face on a bad hangover. Everyone else seems okay, and they tease me as I nibble slowly on a single piece of toast. After the others enjoy their breakfast and I drink as much water as I dare, we ford the river at the animal crossing and continue along the hippo and buffalo trails on the south bank. I am oh-so-thankful that the day is cloudy and even holds a promise of rain. We hear the busy call of the honey guide, a small and drab bird that eats bees' wax and bees' larvae and is very widely revered in Africa for its implausible habit of guiding honey hunters to bees' hives in order to feed on the wax and larvae after the honey has been gathered. The honey hunters are careful to leave some of the honeycomb for the honey guide in appreciation for the bird's services, for it is said that if you don't, next time the honey guide will lead you to a sleeping buffalo.

The river flows straight and fast. Doum palms line the banks and game trails make walking easy. Some sections are even covered with *Cynodon dactylon,* the Bermuda lawn grass that I remember from my California childhood as being less comfortable to play on than the common bluegrass,

but here in Africa it is favored graze for buffalo and even elephant, and along
the riverbank the close cropping of this grass by these animals creates a
lawn that provides cushioned relief for our feet. I continue to wear my sandals, and the others report their blisters are improving, or at least the blisters have reached an equilibrium, healing as fast as new ones appear.

We are in a zone thick with hippo and buffalo, and there is dung everywhere. "I've never seen so much shit in my life," Pete, our cameraman, says.
A Nubian woodpecker calls from a tree to our right, and Danny says this is
good luck. "Dad told us the Waliangulu used to say that when you are hunting elephant and you hear the woodpecker call on your left, that's very bad
and you should not continue the hunt. But if you hear it on your right, that's
a sign you'll get big ivory."

The Waliangulu were the long bow elephant hunters that Bill had told
Danny about when he was a young boy, the bow hunters whose fate Danny
was hoping to discover when we walked through the area where they used
to live.

"Did your dad speak their language?" I ask.

"They didn't really have a language of their own. They picked up the language of whatever groups they were living next to, the Orma or the Giriama.
So he spoke Swahili with them, but he also tried to learn as much as he
could about their culture," Danny adds. "He was the cat and they were the
mice, but he would visit their villages, trying to gather information, and sit
under a tree and drink palm wine with them, and that's how he got along.
They loved that about Dad. He even tried to smoke marijuana with them
once, but the chief cut him off when Dad got a little wild and threw his
ammo in the fire."

"Once a poacher was arrested they would invariably end up in court,"
Bongo explains. "Although Dad was the arresting officer, he would almost always defend them before the judge, indicating that historically the Waliangulu had always hunted, and now suddenly they were poachers, and
everything should be considered in perspective. Dad would guarantee their
good behavior if they were given light or even suspended sentences; then
he would try and get them jobs as gun bearers for professional hunters, or
he would hire them for his own hunts when he took out elephant licenses.
He would sometimes be gone weeks or months at a time, tracking a big
tusker. Just he and his Waliangulu porters and trackers."

As our trek continued, I learned more about Bill, and after our trek, when
I met many of his friends, I came to know Bill well enough to imagine one
of his hunts.

It has been five days since the last resupply, but the warden has walked nearly three hundred miles through this bush country since he started in the Lorian Swamp three months ago. Tracking elephant goes this way, like you were some kind of religious seeker wandering the desert looking for something that you know will elude you. He has seen good tuskers, though, including two that were hundred pounders, but he let them go, gambling that he will find something even bigger, and he will stay out five months if that's what it takes. He moves the Rigby to his other shoulder and that makes him think of Tiger and that this is the longest safari he's made since that trip to Portuguese East twelve years ago, back when he was just a kid.

But that was long ago and now things aren't going good with Daphne and old Mervyn Cowie knows what's going on and Mervyn arranged to have him transferred, hoping that would save the marriage although Mervyn never said it that way. He'll be leaving Tsavo, putting this bush country behind him and going to the mountains as a full warden and a fresh start but first this time off to sort things out. He thinks best when he's bush walking, and bush walking is best when it has a purpose, and his purpose now is big ivory.

Just ahead Abakuna is excited and he chatters to the other Waliangulu. Have they found prints of a big tusker? No, it is just a woodpecker that has called from a bush to their left and Abakuna tells him this is very bad, so he follows the wily tracker as they backtrack and detour around the woodpecker until they leave the bird on their right and now Abakuna smiles. Abakuna was one of the best of the bow hunters. Not as good as the great Galo-Galo, but probably a close second measured against all the Waliangulu aces. He doesn't know how many elephant he has taken with his bow and poisoned arrows, but the Waliangulu thinks it's between four hundred and six hundred, and the bones from his kills still lay in bleached heaps across Tsavo East. He once shot three ushos, the largest of the male elephant, with three arrows in a single morning, and the largest of these giants had tusks weighing each one 180 pounds, and it was the biggest elephant ever taken in the living memory of the tribe.

This Waliangulu was also one of the hardest of the bow hunters to capture. The warden spent months beating the bush chasing him, racking his wits while Abakuna racked his to stay ahead. Through it all neither lost their sense of humor about the other, and now that they've met again it's like *old friends who have been playing chess through the mail. Their friendship has survived Abakuna going to jail, and now that he is out, warden and poacher have gone elephant hunting together.*

Abakuna has found tracks. The warden walks between the Commifora *and stoops down next to the Waliangulu and examines the prints pressed into the fine red dirt and the elephant are three males but none carry big ivory. Still, there may be a big tusker in the area and they follow the tracks; in an hour they hear the bush crack and it is the sound of the elephant browsing. They move downwind and approach. The largest of the three elephant has ivory weighing ninety pounds each and this would be a good trophy if he were just a sportsman from America but he is not even tempted, and Abakuna smiles and they relax and the elephant sense them. One is outraged these humans have stalked so close and he charges. The warden and his trackers and porters scatter each in a different direction and as he runs the warden looks over his shoulder and there is Abakuna but he isn't running. He is standing steadfast and unflinching, allowing the elephant to come right for him and the only thing he has is a small ax in his hand. What is he doing? He'll be killed. The warden raises his rifle and just as the elephant is about to tusk him the Waliangulu throws his ax directly at the animal and at the same time makes a loud, sharp shout and the elephant is so shocked he skids and veers away not twenty feet in front of the former bow hunter. The warden has never seen anything like this, and the other Waliangulu, many of whom were also great hunters, are all amazed and they talk excitedly and say this will be a big story when they return to the village and Abakuna smiles because that is the whole point.*

They continue following up the three males and there is nothing more until they find a tree that has the bark along its base worn smooth. They investigate and find new tracks. Abakuna and the warden stoop to study them. They are smooth and the veining of the sole pad is worn as it can only be by a great male who is old. The bark on the tree has been polished at a point only inches above the ground where the elephant rubbed his tusks, and only long tusks reach that far. They follow the prints and soon find the animal's dung and pull it apart and see that it breaks easily and the browse is intact here and there and this happens in old males because their digestion doesn't work as well. The great elephant continues and then rests and here is the mark in the dirt where he also rests his tusks and only elephant with big ivory could ever do that.

The warden and the Waliangulu stand and nod to each other. They have found the one they search for. "You see," Abakuna says. "The woodpecker."

❖

Across the river a lone baobab stands on a rock outcrop, its great millennial mass skylighted in emblematic isolation. Baobabs live in the coastal belt of East Africa, occurring inland as much as two hundred miles, and now they are becoming more frequent. The Waliangulu consider baobabs the most sacred of trees, believing that they are the abode of spirits, and a very large baobab, with trunks whose girths span up to seventy-five feet, can live for three thousand years and more, making the oldest of these trees perhaps older than the Waliangulu culture itself.

The game trail we follow leads into a grove of thick juvenile doum, and as we weave around the dense fronds that confine our view, Mohamed raises his rifle to the Number One Position, and I turn the video camera to Standby. Mohamed moves slowly forward, craning his neck around each corner, finger on the trigger, and I consider how in a thicket this dense the distance between discovery and disaster has been reduced to something like a single second.

We all sigh in relief as we exit the palm grove and enter a zone of toothbrush bush. Mohamed relaxes into Number Two Position, but I notice his eyes still sweep right and left like radar. Ahead through the bush I hear the almost human call of a baboon—hey-ha! hey-ha!—alerting others that we are approaching. A martial eagle lands in a tree just ahead, and when we are closer I stop to film this great bird with its massive body and dark, hooded head. This eagle is one of the main predators of the little dik-dik, and now the bird sits on a branch and fixes its eye on me as I zoom in. Suddenly I hear Mohamed yelling, "Mamba! Mamba!"—Swahili for crocodile—and I quickly lower the camera and see Mohamed, Iain, Danny, and the others running through the bush alongside a seven-foot crocodile. I follow just in time to see the reptile slither into the river and disappear, as the others hoot and cry out in surprise.

"It was quite a long way from the river," Bongo says. "And it chose a very funny route back to the water. Kind of slow and sluggish, too."

"Maybe it was cold," Danny says.

"I don't know. Odd behavior. Very odd."

We walk away from the river toward the area where the others flushed the croc from the bush, and Bongo calls out, "Come, look here." We walk over to find Bongo stooped down studying the partially eaten carcass of a freshly killed dik-dik. Only its hindquarters remain. Danny and Bongo converse in Swahili with the rangers, then Bongo says to me, "It appears that the martial eagle you were photographing killed this dik-dik, then the crocodile crawled off the river and was about to steal the dik-dik from the eagle when we happened along."

In the approximately one hundred years of experience that Bongo, Danny, Iain, and the rangers have adding together all their time in Tsavo, no one has ever seen a crocodile steal a kill from an eagle, or even heard of this happening. "This is very unusual," Bongo says again.

◈

We continue through a mix of river acacia with the shorter wait-a-bit in the undergrowth and the large hydra-headed doums at river's edge. I hear the mournful call of the blue-naped mousebird, unseen in the overhead branches. I notice a flash of color at my foot and stoop to pick up a single wing feather from a kingfisher, and it is colored an electric blue so bright it appears to be internally illuminated. We drop toward a sand-bottom *lugga*. It is still cloudy and humid. Mohamed suddenly jumps back, waving his hand for everyone to freeze. He points excitedly toward the bottom of the gully, and for a second I don't see anything, but then I make out the tawny shape of a fully grown lion, asleep on the sand.

This is another very lucky encounter, and slowly and quietly we approach. The wind is in our favor. We inch forward, under a large river acacia, and get within twenty yards of the animal. He is still asleep. We stop and watch his great chest rise and lower, and we can see flies circling and landing. Iain is sniffing the air and whispers, "I think I can smell a kill. Either that, or somebody is letting go some very nasty farts."

Then the lion senses us. Has the wind shifted, or did he hear us whispering, or did a bird chirp differently? He raises up, looks at us, and for two seconds we have eye contact. His body is covered by hair so short he almost looks hairless. He is a large male, and like all mature male lions in Tsavo, he has no mane, only a crest of a hair about an inch long, and longer stubbles on his jowls. Then he jumps up and runs into the bush.

We walk over to his bed and Danny reaches down and feels the sand. "Happy full lion," he says. Mohamed follows the animal's tracks and a moment later calls to us. We walk over and see the tall Samburu standing over the carcass of a buffalo. It is gutted and the hindquarters have been eaten, but there is still a substantial amount of meat left. Fifty feet away we discover the guts buried in the sand, and Danny says this is common. There is a deep groove from here to the carcass, suggesting this burial site of the guts is also where the buffalo was killed.

"It was probably more than the one lion that got it," Bongo says. "It's very violent, a kill of a big buffalo. Not a pretty sight."

Of the big cats, lions are the most improvisatorial hunters. George Schaller, the well-known field researcher, studied lions in the Serengeti Plain for three years and counted eight different ways that lions hunt. The most effective is communal hunting, and this is almost always used in taking a big animal such as buffalo. Lions will usually grab the animal with their powerful forepaws, and as one tries to pull it down others go for its throat, to strangle it, or for its mouth, to suffocate it. In Tsavo, however, lions never form large prides as they do in the Serengeti, and when they do hunt together, they usually do it in pairs, which makes the kill of this buffalo even more impressive.

Individual lions (or pairs) will often acquire a favorite method of hunting, and of the various techniques they adopt perhaps the most fascinating to observe is the stalk. A lion is not a fast runner, and it must use every available cover to approach a prey. A stalk can take a half hour or more, but when the moment of the kill comes, it is, as Schaller described it, "a drama in which it [is] impossible not to participate emotionally, knowing that the death of a being [hangs] in the balance."

We stand around the remains of the buffalo. The smell is heavy and fecund, and the only sound is the drone of flies.

"It's quite appropriate," Bongo says, "that today of all days we should have this close encounter with a lion."

This evening we will be camping less than a mile upstream from Tsavo Bridge. Within an hour we will be walking through the same rocky defile where Lt. Colonel J. H. Patterson stalked the "Man-Eaters of Tsavo," the two rogue lions that in 1898 delayed construction of the Uganda Railway for months as they terrorized the Indian workers. With this thought I gaze down at the buffalo carcass and imagine instead that it is the remains of a human, its limbs partially devoured. I wonder if the two lions that terrorized the railroad also disemboweled their human victims and buried the guts nearby? Looking at the buffalo again, and at the buffalo guts, I find it all too easy to imagine what it was like for Patterson when he found the human victims of the lions; as Bongo said about the kill of a buffalo, it must have been a very violent thing to witness.

"He's probably watching us from the bush right now," Danny says.

Referring to the recent Hollywood film inspired by Patterson's story, Iain smiles and says, "I wonder if he is Ghost, or Darkness."

13

In the whole of my life I have never experienced anything more nerve-shaking than to hear the deep roars of these dreadful monsters growing gradually nearer and nearer, and to know that some one or other of us was doomed to be their victims before morning dawned.

—Lt. Col. J. H. Patterson,
Man-Eaters of Tsavo, *1907*

We walk around the terminus of a lumpy ridge of granite boulders that descends to river's edge, and enter a copse framed by rock outcrops where Patterson spent many days stalking the lions. "He was at it day and night," Iain says. Iain has followed the history of Tsavo as closely as any authority, and no element of the region's story fascinates him more than Patterson's mano-a-mano effort to bag the two man-eaters. "By night he would climb into blinds or trees and wait for them," Iain continues. "By day he would track them into the bush, following the blood spilled by their latest victim, and many of those forays led into this canyon, which was one of the man-eaters' favorite retreats."

The game trail we follow passes through the canyon, and we exit onto a broad plain that is bordered in the distance by the Yatta Plateau, a lava escarpment that originated in the geologically recent past from vents in the Central Highlands over a hundred miles away. Now the trail becomes a dirt vehicle track, and in an hour we can hear through the bush the inconsonant waul of passing trucks. In the planning stages of our trek Iain had said that during the roughly five hundred kilometers we would walk from Kiliman-jaro to the sea, we would cross only three tarmac roads: the one out of Loitokitok that circles Kilimanjaro, the coast highway that, in the area where we will cross it, runs a mile or so inland of the beach, and this one, the Mombasa Highway, the artery connecting the Mombasa seaport to Nairobi and the rest of interior Kenya.

In a few minutes we see the tops of the trucks float across the bush a hun-dred yards away, like that scene in *Lawrence of Arabia* where the tops of ships pass over the sand dunes as they transit the Suez Canal. We cross the highway and follow it back toward the modern highway bridge over the Tsavo River. Trucks brake and slow as they pass, and the passengers in the buses crowd to the windows to gawk at rangers and *mzungus* covered in red dust wearing clothes shredded by thornbush; and the whole lot very well armed.

We walk to the middle of the modern bridge and look downriver. Two hundred yards away is the railway that parallels the highway, and, where the tracks cross the river, Patterson's original bridge. It is today in as good a shape as it was when completed early in 1899, and in the nearly one hun-dred intervening years the bridge has held up to at least one flood of bibli-cal proportion and dozens of lesser ones, and it can count several trains a day passing over it as they transport freight and passengers between the coast and the inland cities. This bridge and the railroad have been faithful servants to the development of what in the beginning were the British East African Colonies, and later independent Kenya. Before the railroad was con-structed, however, there was a sharp division between those who foresaw the impact the line would have on the future of East Africa, and those who saw it as an example of British Imperialism taken to its foolish extreme, who called the railway the Lunatic Express.

❖

The Lunatic Express is also the name of a book by Charles Miller that de-scribes not only the construction of the railway but also the history of the ex-ploration of East Africa as well as the attendant political climate in Europe that preceded it. As Miller points out, when Joseph Thomson marched through Masai land in 1883, he did succeed in his ostensible goal of demon-strating a more direct route inland to the vast lakes region known as Uganda. Despite the fact he was himself motivated principally by his per-

THE SHADOW OF KILIMANJARO

sonal love of adventure and exploration, Thomson's efforts advanced the expansion of British hegemony into the heart of the Dark Continent. This expansion of British influence was a goal that was championed a few years later by the officially sanctioned Imperial British East Africa Company (IBEA) which, in 1890, hired another explorer, Frederick Lugard, to proceed inland from Mombasa to negotiate a treaty with Uganda's ruler, Mwanga, a notorious and unrepentant sadist who frequently had his foes quadriplegically dismembered and forced to watch their own arms and legs roast over a slow fire before their hapless torsos were also set on the coals.

In 1890 Britain had just signed a treaty ceding control over a small island in the North Sea to the Germans, who wanted it for a naval base, in exchange for Germany's recognition that Uganda and the region to the north known as Equatoria was to be considered under the "British sphere of influence." Now the British Foreign Office and the IBEA were anxious to consolidate their paper claim. As far the public knew, London's concern was a mix of interest in the commercial potential of the area and a desire to support the missionary projects in the interior that included eradication of the slave trade. Behind this, however, was a more convoluted fear that control of the Central African highlands was connected to control of the centerpiece of Britain's empire, India. The linking factor was the Suez Canal. A few key players in the Foreign Office, including Salisbury, the prime minister, were concerned that whoever controlled the upper Nile controlled access to the Suez, and whoever controlled the Suez controlled Britain's rule in India.

Lugard chose to march inland following the Sabaki River, the same route we would walk down once we entered Tsavo East. It was an expeditious route, and Lugard reached the Ugandan capital in four months. There he successfully negotiated the treaty with the king-sadist who was understandably concerned that he was giving up much in return for little more than Lugard's assurance he would now receive the protection of the British Empire. Lugard then spent the next year extending Britain's influence by helping converted Christians defeat their Muslim foes in the kingdom of Bunyoro in the headwater regions of the White Nile to the north and west of Lake Victoria, by sealing a blood pact with another local king in a region known as Ankole, and building a fort for the sympathetic king of Toro. It was a great surprise, then, when he returned to Uganda and opened his mailbag to find a letter from the IBEA director in Mombasa ordering him back to the coast.

The reason was simple: IBEA was nearly bankrupt. The company's directors believed that the only thing that could save the enterprise and give them any hope of a return on their investment would be the construction of a railroad from the coast to the interior, but that would require the support of Lord Salisbury's government. Then a letter of reprieve arrived: Enough money had been raised in London, principally by appealing to missionary aid groups and humanitarians, to extend Lugard's expedition. He stayed in Central Africa another seven months, now assisting converted Protestants to defeat converted Catholics (thereby raising the ire of the French, who themselves started to expansionistically rattle their sabers). Then he returned to the coast, and to England, to lobby for consolidating British control in East Africa, and, indirectly, for the future construction of the railway.

Lugard made a barnstorming tour of England in 1892, championing the battle cry "Save Uganda." Why turn backs on "coffee, wheat, cotton and gum," he wrote in a newspaper editorial, adding as well the question of what would happen to the security of the Suez if the upper Nile fell into the hands of the Germans or the French. Lugard was greeted by cheering crowds, and the petitions supporting Britain's consolidations of the East African colonies began pouring into the Foreign Office. By now the Salisbury government had folded, replaced by the aging but indefatigable Gladstone, who was returning to the prime ministry for the fourth time but who had little patience for this "Uganda business."

Meanwhile, even in the face of this political uncertainty, the IBEA had commissioned a survey to explore possible routes for the railway. This had occupied nearly four hundred people for nine months, and in the end the survey's report proposed that the railway follow the traditional slave caravan route inland from Mombasa, across the Taru Desert, and then into the Tsavo *nyika,* crossing the Tsavo River just upstream from the confluence with the Sabaki.

By the time the results of the survey reached London, the Uganda question was (other than the arguments for Irish Home Rule) the debate du jour. It was Imperialists against anti-Imperialists, and a cartoon in *Punch* titled "The White Elephant" showed a large, white pachyderm wearing a yoke labeled "Uganda" tied to a tree called "East Africa Company" with a parody of an African explorer telling a politician, "See here, Governor. He's a likely looking animal, but *I* can't manage him. If *you* won't take him, I must let him go." In a marathon writing session Lugard finished a book about his expedition titled *The Rise of Our East African Empire* even though there was as yet no empire. The reviews were positive, and the debate advanced. Finally the Gladstone government fell, Salisbury returned to power, and Parliament voted to have the government buy out the IBEA, thereby officially bringing

Pax Britannica to East Africa. Within a year the first funds were approved to begin initial stages of the construction of the railway.

From our position on the highway bridge, looking downstream, I take a photograph of Patterson's bridge, then we descend to the river and walk two hundred yards to the base of one of three rock towers that support the iron girders that span the river. Each tower, built on a solid masonry foundation, is about twenty-five feet long and fifteen feet wide and maybe sixty or more feet high. Each block of rock has been carefully chiseled and fitted into place alongside its neighbors. "The best of British," Iain says. In his book *Man-Eaters of Tsavo*, Patterson says he was despairing of ever finding in the area quarry rock suitable for construction until one day when he was out shooting guinea fowl to feed the workers he happened upon an outcrop of just the kind of rock he was looking for. The Indian workers had to build a spur line from the quarry to the bridge site to transport the blocks, but the fact this old bridge has withstood so admirably the ferocious flash floods that seem to sweep Tsavo every ten years or so is testament to the qualities of their labor and to Patterson's skill as an engineer.

If Patterson was an experienced engineer, he was not an experienced hunter. "My principal work was to erect a permanent [bridge]," he writes at the beginning of his story. "I accordingly made a survey of what had to be done, sent my requisition . . . and in a short time the noise of hammers and sledges, drilling and blasting, echoed merrily through the district. Unfortunately this happy state of affairs did not continue long, and our work was soon interrupted in a rude and startling manner. Two of the most voracious and insatiable man-eating lions appeared upon the scene, and for over nine months waged an intermittent warfare against the railway and all those connected with it in the vicinity of Tsavo."

I run my hand over the chiseled rock of the bridge tower. It feels cool. When I visit a historical site, I sometimes try to listen, to see if I can hear the ghosts. Now when I close my eyes I hear the swifts chirping as they fly in and out of their mud homes high on the underside of the bridge. I listen more carefully, until I can hear the hundreds of hammers hitting their chisels, the call of the Hindustani *jemadar* for more mortar, the echoing ring of the iron rails as they are lowered into position. I try to imagine the evening, the crackling of the large fires kept going through the night, the low, tense murmurs inside the tents, then, in the early morning hours, when most have

finally fallen asleep, the shouts of panic, the screams of terror, the moan
from the victim followed by the sound of crunching bone.

"The story really goes back to the early part of the last century," Iain says,
leaning against the stone tower. "This area on the Tsavo River right here became a big encampment of the Arab slave traders. There were a lot of slaves
who were too enfeebled or weak to bring much money at the coast, and
since there was no point in taking them further, they would toss them in the
bush. So this area frequently had slaves stumbling around half dead, and the
lions would eat them, and they grew quite fond of human flesh. Then when
the railway reached this point, there was all of a sudden something like four
thousand coolies, who had been imported from India to do the job, camped
all around here, and the predators just could not believe their luck. Here
were four thousand hamburgers, if you like, for the taking, and they didn't
hesitate."

The two lions began to attack nearly every night. Patterson would stake
out the location of the previous night's attack, only to have them choose a
different tent the next night. The Indians built thick thorn *bomas* around
their encampments, but the lions jumped them. They built a higher thorn
wall around the hospital, but they jumped that and made off with a patient.
Patterson relocated the hospital, but left the old one in place and staked it
out, hoping the lions would return.

"In the middle of my lonely vigil," he wrote, "I had the mortification of
hearing shrieks and cries coming from the direction of the new hospital,
telling me only too plainly that our dreaded foes had once more eluded me.
Hurrying to the place at daylight I found that one of the lions had jumped
over the newly erected fence and had carried off the hospital bhisti [water
carrier], and that several other coolies had been unwilling witnesses of the
terrible scene which took place within the circle of light given by the big
camp fire. The bhisti, it appears, had been lying on the floor, his feet nearly
touching the side. The lion managed to get its head in below the canvas,
seized him by the foot and pulled him out. In desperation the unfortunate
water-carrier clutched hold of a heavy box in a vain attempt to prevent himself being carried off, and dragged it with him until he was forced to let go
by its being stopped by the side of the tent. He then caught hold of a tent
rope, and clung tightly to it until it broke. As soon as the lion managed to get
him clear of the tent, he sprang at his throat and after a few vicious shakes
the poor bhisti's agonizing cries were silenced for ever. . . . [I was] easily
able to follow his track, and soon found the remains about four hundred
yards away. There was the usual horrible sight. Very little was left of the un-

fortunate bhisti—only the skull, jaws, a few larger bones and a portion of the palm with one or two fingers attached. On one of these was a silver ring that was sent to the man's widow in India."

For a revised edition of his book *The End of the Game*, Peter Beard located Patterson's original journal, and made photographs of the entries. The writing is in careful, straight sentences, and the concise prose does more to flesh out the terror of Patterson's challenge than even his book, which he wrote a few years later. "March 1st. One man killed by lion last night, & one badly mauled. Indian shot thro' temple by accident last night—fear he will die also. Have seen mauled Swahili in hospital, do not think he can possibly recover. March 17 (St. Patrick's Day). Am busy most of day writing up diary. Very hot day. Have a slight attack of fever. Wish I were back in Old Ireland. Go and visit surg. Capt. Haslam & see several of his animals dying of bite of Tetsee fly. I procure a goat and walk a mile to a tree where I sit all night in wait for lion—Lion takes man from Railway truck at Engomani (Ogilvie's servant). . . . Sit up all night for lion. Mosquitoes appear & are troublesome—Two more coolies taken by lions from Railhead. . . . Sat up all night. Lion turns up & tries to get one of my men out of tree. . . ."

With only occasional respite—when the lions wandered to other areas of the line, and Patterson received reports of their raids at different camps—the rogues laid siege to his workers for eight months. The Indians thought the lions were devils that were incapable of being killed, and Patterson began to wonder if they were not right. He built a trap that had two compartments separated by an interior grill, and his plan was to bait one side with several very reluctant Indians armed with rifles. The contraption worked. One of the lions entered, stepped on the trigger, and the door slammed shut. The armed guards started screaming and firing, and bullets flew everywhere, including one that hit the lock on the door allowing it to fly open. The lion ran out; not a single bullet had touched him.

On December 1, most of the workers gathered in front of Patterson's tent and told him they could no longer remain in Tsavo, saying, "they had come from India on an agreement to work for the Government, not to supply food for either lions or devils." Hundreds of them then stopped the next supply train by lying across the tracks and swarming on board. Patterson couldn't blame them, but now, more than ever, it was him against the lions.

"As I was leaving my boma soon after dawn on December 9, I saw a Swahili running excitedly towards me, shouting out "Simba! Simba!" (Lion! Lion!), and every now and again looking behind him as he ran." The lion had taken a donkey and was eating it, in broad daylight. Patterson grabbed his rifle and ran toward the man-eater, but as he approached one of his men stepped on a branch and the lion ran into the bush. Patterson then gathered several more men armed with pots, pans, and any other noisemakers they could find, and while he positioned himself on one side of the bush, they lined up on the opposite and started making as much noise as possible. "Almost immediately, to my intense joy, out in the open path stepped a huge maneless lion. It was the first occasion during all these trying months upon which I had had a chance at one of these brutes. . . . I pulled the trigger, and to my horror heard the dull snap that tells of a misfire." Patterson was so taken aback he forgot he had a double-barreled rifle. He was certain the lion was going to finish him, but the animal was so distracted by the noisemakers that he bounded toward the bush. Patterson remembered the other barrel and just as the animal was about to disappear, he fired. "An answering angry growl told me that he had been hit."

Hit, but apparently only stunned: The animal disappeared into the bush. Patterson inspected the donkey and saw the lion had only devoured a small part of it. He had a strong suspicion the lion would return to his kill, so he had his men construct a twelve-foot-high tower next to the carcass. As night fell he took up his position. He waited and was just dozing off when "suddenly I was startled by the snapping of a twig: and straining my ears for a further sound, I fancied I could hear the rustling of a large body forcing its way through the bush. 'The man-eater,' I thought." Then, to his horror, Patterson realized that instead of going for the donkey, the lion was stalking him. "For about two hours he horrified me by slowly creeping round and round my crazy structure, gradually edging his way nearer and nearer. If one of the rather flimsy poles should break, or if the lion could spring the twelve feet which separated me from the ground . . ." Patterson peered into the darkness and finally he was able to see the outline of the lion creeping stealthily for him. He took careful aim and fired. There was "a terrific roar, and then I could hear him leaping about in all directions. At length came a series of mighty groans, gradually subsiding into deep sighs, and finally ceasing." The first lion was dead.

The few Indian workers who had remained in camp poured out of their huts shouting in glee. They recovered the lion in the morning, and it measured nose to tail nine feet nine inches. For a few nights there was peace. But then the second lion showed up at a bungalow built for one of the railway inspectors and spent the night prowling around the veranda. In the morning Patterson inspected the area and noticed a nearby iron shed, and he made his plan. He had the workers bring a length of iron rail weighing about 250 pounds, place it in front of the opening of the shed, and then shackle to it three full-grown goats. His strategy was to hide in the shed and wait, hoping the lion would take one of the goats, and then when he tried to haul it off the rail would slow him enough to allow Patterson to get a clear shot.

At nightfall Patterson positioned himself inside the shed and waited. Again, his instincts were accurate: The lion showed up and began to stalk the goats, which were, predictably, increasingly nervous. The animal then attacked, leaping on one of the goats, but before Patterson could get a shot off the lion had loped off into the bush, with the goat, the goat's two companions, and the 250-pound rail.

A few nights later the lion tried to get at several Indians who had taken refuge in a tree. Patterson realized the lion was now repeating himself, so the next night he positioned himself in the tree and sure enough, the lion returned. "It was a most fascinating sight to watch this great brute stealing stealthily round us, taking advantage of every bit of cover as he came. His skill showed that he was an old hand at the terrible game of man-hunting. . . . I waited until he got quite close—about 20 yards away—and then fired my .303 at his chest." The bullet hit, the animal growled and bounded off. In the morning Patterson tracked the spoor of blood a quarter of a mile "when suddenly a fierce growl was heard right in front of us. Looking cautiously through the bushes, I could see the man-eater glaring out in our direction. I at once took careful aim and fired. Instantly he sprang out and made a most determined charge down on us. I fired again and knocked him over; but in a second he was up once more and coming for me as fast he could in his crippled condition. A third shot had no apparent effect."

Patterson put his hand back for his backup rifle, but turned to discover his gun bearer was running for the nearest tree. Patterson dropped his empty rifle and followed him, just making it to the tree as the lion caught up. He swung himself up, grabbed the other rifle from the gun bearer, and fired. The lion fell motionless. Patterson crawled down, approached the lion, and suddenly it jumped up and charged straight for him. Patterson fired again and once more the lion went down. This time it did not get up.

The second lion was dead. It had been almost ten months since the first Indian worker had disappeared. By his count Patterson had documented that the two lions had killed twenty-eight men. But because they had raided so widely up and down the railway, it was impossible to know exactly how many they had actually taken, and there were many workers who had sim-

118   RICK RIDGEWAY

ply disappeared without explanation. By some estimates, the two man-
eating lions of Tsavo had killed and devoured as many as 132 men.

◈

The two lions of Tsavo are arguably the most notorious man-eaters in modern history. There have been voracious man-eating tigers in India, and a
single lion pride in Tanzania is said to have killed fifteen hundred people,
but no other man-eaters can claim to have slowed the advance and development of the British into their empire, nor to have their efforts noted by
the prime minister in an address to Parliament ("The whole of the works,"
Salisbury stated in a speech to the House of Lords, ". . . were put to a
stop . . . because a party of man-eating lions . . ."). Patterson's book was a
best-seller, and the story was briefly resurrected with the release of the film
The Ghost and the Darkness. In none of this, however, was there ever an attempt to see the episode from the lions' point of view.

As Iain had explained to us, the site along the Tsavo River chosen for the
bridge was also the ford of the slave caravans coming out of the interior.
Tsavo was the last water before the traverse of the *nyika* desert, and the caravans normally rested at the river before making the difficult crossing. It
was never, however, a popular place. (The word "tsavo" means "place of
slaughter," and this probably referred to the fact that Masai raiding parties
would sometimes sweep across the region, killing everybody in their path.)
The Tsavo River crossing also was thought to be haunted by spirits. It was
well known that men who deserted the caravans at this point almost always
disappeared, and in all likelihood this was because the lions in the area
found them easy prey.

These slave caravans were still crossing Tsavo even as late as the early
1890s, so Iain's theory that the two lions had been preying on humans for
many years is entirely plausible. Tsavo lions are known to be more cunning
than other lions (this is thought to result from the extra effort they must
make to earn a living in the demanding thornbush country), and that they
were hunting as a pair is also typical.

The two lions were therefore acting very much the way Tsavo lions typically act, and building them into superpredators, or even into demons, is
only another example of our species's tendency to mythologize the great
beasts. The more I thought about it, however, the more I realized it wasn't
mythology to view these two lions, and the circumstances surrounding their
predation on the Indian workers, as a leitmotif of the major events that were
taking hold in East Africa one hundred years ago. It wasn't an exaggeration

to think of them as symbols of the relationship their kith and kin were to
have with their new European overlords, and not just lions, either, but all
the wild animals. Or to think of the train as a metaphor of the advance of the
empire and the subsequent colonization of the continent, and later the in
troduction of European technology and goods. Or the Indian workers as
representing the racial hierarchies that fueled the revolts and fights for independence in Africa later in the century, and still shape the politics of the
entire sub-Saharan continent.

Today I would wager there isn't one in a thousand travelers crossing the
modern bridge over the Tsavo River who glances downstream, where you
can see clearly Patterson's construction, and pays it any mind. Even a few
years after it was completed, people soon forgot about the bridge, even if
they recalled the story of the man-eaters. In *The Lunatic Express*, Charles
Miller recounts how seven years after finishing the bridge Patterson made
another visit to Kenya, and in the night, when the train approached the
Tsavo River, he woke his fellow passengers to point out his bridge, but they
seemed unimpressed. "Naturally I could not expect them, or anyone else, to
view the bridge quite from my point of view; I looked on it as a child of
mine, brought up through stress and danger and troubles of all kinds, but
the ordinary traveller of course knows nothing of this and doubtless thinks
it only a very commonplace and insignificant structure."

I suppose Patterson would have been pleased to know that one hundred
years later there was a group of trekkers gathered round his bridge who considered it far from commonplace or insignificant. We gave the old stone towers a final pat of our hands and left, walking back upriver to a place where
Iain had arranged to set up camp. There was a good trail at river's edge. As
I walked I thought of a time when I was ten years old and I had responded
to an ad in an outdoor magazine for a starter kit in taxidermy. My first victim
was a blackbird I killed with my pellet rifle. I then ordered out of the catalog of supplies that came with my kit a pair of small yellow glass eyes for my
blackbird.

This catalog also had a sidebar article about the great man-eating lions of
Tsavo. There was a picture of them that I remember today with great clarity,
and what puzzled me at the time was that the article said they were male lions,
yet the picture showed they had no manes, and in some way, to me, this made
them even more sinister. I remember the fear I felt as a young boy imagining
what it would be like to sleep in a tent when a lion was prowling outside.

I also remember the article said that the two lions had been mounted by
an expert taxidermist, and that they were on display at the Field Museum of
Natural History in Chicago.

❖

"They are much more popular now that the movie has come out," Bill Stanley, collection manager of mammals at the Field Museum, told me over the phone when I called after I had returned from our trek.

"How did they end up in Chicago?"

"Patterson came to Chicago in 1924 to give a lecture, and Stanley Field was in the audience. Apparently he asked Patterson what happened to the lion skins, and when Patterson told him he still had them, Field offered to buy them, and negotiated a deal for what was then the considerable sum of five thousand dollars. We assume the skins until then had been lying on Patterson's floor. When they arrived in Chicago the skins came with the original skulls. They were then prepared by our staff very carefully, but the taxidermist didn't have a lot to work with, and the end result is that the lions are smaller than their original size."

"What do people think when they see them?"

"They wonder why they don't have manes, and why they're so scruffy. But I'll tell you, when I first came to work here, I looked at those two lions and wondered about all the humans that had passed through their two mouths."

14

A continent ages quickly once we come to it.

—*Ernest Hemingway,*
Green Hills of Africa, *1935*

In the morning we follow the railway tracks for an hour, then cut cross-country through thornbush back toward the river. The decision to make this shortcut was made by Bongo and Danny the evening before. Neither Iain nor I was consulted on this, and Iain told me later in the evening he had wanted strongly to follow the Tsavo to the confluence of the Athi, then turn right and continue down the Galana (below this confluence the river is called the Galana, until farther downriver it is also known as the Sabaki); this was one section of the river he had never walked. As it is now, we are cutting the corner—making a more direct line for our day's campsite on the Galana—but thereby missing the confluence.

"I've been wondering why I'm being left out of the decision making on this trip," Iain had told me, "and I think it may have something to do with the different echelons of wildlife people here in Kenya. You've got people like Danny and Bongo who work for the parks for very little financial gain. The next rung down are the safari guides like me working in the parks but making a lot of money. The field biologists are even a rung lower, because they are dealing in theory.

"Remember too that for Bongo and Danny, Tsavo is their backyard," I said. "They see themselves as much more expert on the area, even though you've been down here a lot. They probably don't need any advice."

"I'm aware of that. On Mt. Kenya, Bongo doesn't hesitate to ask my advice, so perhaps they see my background there as a climber like their backgrounds here as hunters growing up in the bush."

As the hike continued I considered one other ingredient that perhaps contributed to Bongo and Danny's tendency to take charge and, in some cases, to make unilateral decisions. It was the fact that, because we were in potential danger each day, they felt a responsibility for our safety. In this I was reminded of situations I've sometimes encountered on mountaineering trips where more experienced climbers are teamed with novices. I was once on an expedition with the famed British mountaineer Chris Bonington, guiding two relative novices, when we decided to dig a snow cave because we feared a potentially dangerous windstorm was brewing. Considering that we had very strong tents with us, one of our clients questioned this, and Chris turned and said very slowly, "You have no idea how fast things can turn up here. I do." We all knew that over the years Chris had lost more close friends on his climbs than perhaps any other high-altitude mountaineer active today, and he made his reprimand with such an icy tone that our clients, without a reply, grabbed shovels and started digging. Remembering this incident, I realize how similar Bongo's demeanor is to Bonington's, and it occurs to me that the potential threat from avalanches and storms on a climbing expedition is not far removed from the potential danger of hippo and buffalo on a foot safari.

◈

The train bed is in good repair, and the gravel has been picked carefully off the surrounding dirt and placed back on the bed so that its edges are as straight as a surveyor's plumb. The steel sleepers are each imprinted with the date "1953," but Iain says the originals were Indian teak shipped across the Arabian Sea in steam transports that also brought the workers.

The sleepers are spaced too closely to single-step and too far to double-step, so I drop to the side and walk along the gravel bed. We hear an approaching train that appears around a bend only fifty yards ahead, and we stand aside as the morning freight from Mombasa lumbers by, the engineer sticking his head out his window as he passes and looking back with wide eyes.

"This train takes quite a toll on game," Danny says. "About twelve elephant just in the last three years. One young was caught and dragged, and as the train slowed the mum and her teenager tried to save it, and they were killed too."

The railroad has been a hazard for game animals since it was completed. In 1909, Theodore Roosevelt, in his book *African Game Trails,* wrote: "In the dusk we nearly ran over a hyena. A year or two previously the train actually did run over a lioness one night, and the conductor brought in her head in triumph. In fact, there have been continual mishaps, such as could only happen to a railroad in the Pleistocene Age! The very night we went up there was an interruption in the telegraph service, due to giraffes having knocked down some of the wires and a pole in crossing the track; and elephants have more than once performed the same feat. Two or three times at night giraffes have been run into and killed: once a rhinoceros was killed, the engine being damaged in the encounter, and on other occasions the rhino has only just left the track in time, once the beast being struck and a good deal hurt, the engine again being somewhat crippled. But the lions now offer and have always offered, the chief source of unpleasant excitement."

We have followed the train tracks for about three kilometers when Bongo says we are positioned to cut cross-country, and in only fifty yards after leaving the tracks we are swallowed into the *Commifora.* Since the railway tracks demarcate the boundary, we are now in Tsavo East National Park, the great thornbush wilderness that Mervyn Cowie first proposed as a national park because no one wanted it, no one lived in it (so he believed), and further, he thought someday he might be able to trade it for a smaller but more valuable tract of land.

When Bill Woodley and Pete Jenkins won their jobs as junior assistant wardens in the new park, Tsavo was at that time a single entity. It was April 1948, the season of the long rains, and it was pouring as the two young men left Nairobi in a new Ford pickup seriously overloaded with supplies. They arrived in the town of Mtito Andei, a stop on the Mombasa road where it enters the new park, and met the new warden Ronald Stevens, the Nairobi pharmacist whose knowledge of Tsavo was limited to looking out the train window whenever he had passed through on his way to the coast for holiday.

It was clear from the beginning to both Bill and Pete that they knew more about their jobs than their boss. Bill, of course, had already been on several safaris, including the big one with Tiger Marriott to Mozambique. Like Bill, Pete had also grown up spending time in the bush. Pete's great-grandparents arrived in Kenya in 1907, with horses and wagons, and with his parents Pete frequently went on safari to the Masai Mara. During the war Pete's father was commissioned to shoot game, mostly zebra and wildebeest, to feed the prisoners of war, and young Pete would accompany his father on these outings.

On my return trip to Africa after our trek was finished, I visited Pete
Jenkins. He was living in a small farmhouse an hour's drive east of Nairobi,
along the transition where the highlands drop into the thornbush country,
and from the veranda, on clear days during the wet season when the rains
clean the dust from the air, he can see in the distance Kilimanjaro with its
mantle of fresh snow. The house was neat and orderly, with photographs of
old friends and relatives on the mantle, and a black-and-white photograph
on a wall of a sand river with several elephant and rhinoceros standing
around, the latter with their heads inside water holes dug in the dry
streambed. The animals seemed to be waiting their turns at the water in a
kind of peaceful coexistence that was evocative of those dreamlike idylls you
see in a Rousseau painting: a paradisical world too perfect ever to have
really existed. Pete saw me studying the photograph and walked over.
"That's taken from a blind I made when we were building the first roads into
the Tiva," he explained. "The river had dried and the elephants had dug
down for water, and these other animals, including the rhinos, are getting a
drink after the elephants have finished." I continue to admire the photograph and Pete adds, "Right at that spot a rhino came charging straight out
and nearly floored me."

At sixty-seven years of age, Pete was a well-kept man, calm and medita-
tive. He was dressed in a safari-green wool pullover with a rhino embroi-
dered on the breast, a pinkish cotton shirt with its collar positioned just so
in the sweater's V-neck, and khaki twills that had been creased and pressed.
While we talked he sat in a rocker on his veranda and smoked his pipe.

"One of the first things we had to do was survey the area," Pete said.
"From Tsavo Station (a few hundred yards from Patterson's bridge) we
headed opposite directions: I went off upriver and Bill took off down,
toward the Athi junction. There were no roads, and the only way we com-
municated was by telegram when I walked out to Taveta and Bill to Icutha
(the direct-line distance between these two towns is one hundred miles).
We were left to our own devices, and for a year we mainly wandered around
discovering what was going on, seeing how many animals were in the area,
and getting the names of poachers."

They would return to Mtito Andei to resupply and also to report to
Stevens what they had learned. The gathering point in Mtito was Mac's Inn,
a popular watering hole for travelers between Nairobi and Mombasa operated by a baggy-trousered pukka sahib from the Indian army named C. G.
MacArthur. "Congenial sort of guy," Pete said. "An avid naturalist, not a
hunter, either. I don't think he ever shot an elephant." Working as a game

warden, MacArthur had spent many years patrolling Ukambani country (the homeland of the Wakamba people) and the adjacent Tsavo region, and his advice had been influential in establishing the boundaries of the park.

When Bill returned from one of these surveys, MacArthur listened to the nineteen-year-old's report that there was a considerable amount of elephant poaching going on in Tsavo, and not by any *mzungu* hunters, but by natives using bows and arrows. Stevens didn't think this was plausible, but MacArthur was well aware that the Wakambas could take down an elephant using poisoned arrows; he had arrested many of them when he was the game warden. Neither of them, however, believed Bill's report that he had found nineteen carcasses just in the area of the Tsavo and Athi confluence.

For the next few months Bill and Pete worked to extend roads from near Mtito Andei into their respective halves of the park and to continue their survey work. Bill knew that he was touching only a small part of his new domain, as the entire northern half of this section was still little known. The only *mzungus* who had been there were the big game hunters Bror Blixen and Denys Finch Hatton, and MacArthur, who had once cut a track along what was now the eastern boundary of the park. Still, wherever he went, Bill quizzed anyone he could find to learn more about the Wakamba bow hunters. He was gathering only bits and pieces, until one day his luck improved when one of his rangers reported that a Wakamba hunter was at the moment camped near the Tsavo railway station.

Bill hopped in his truck with the ranger and drove to the station, then walked up the track until he spotted the hunter's campfire. Bill was nearly on him before the hunter, finally realizing someone was approaching, stood up. His bow was against a tree, his arrows hanging in their quiver. He made no effort to escape; in fact he was friendly. The man said he was a Wakamba from Mutha, a small village to the north, and yes, he was a hunter. Bill asked his name and the man said he was known as Elui.

Bill explained that hunting within the national park was against the law, and he arrested him and took him back to Mtito. It was a house arrest if you could even call it that. Bill had no intention of prosecuting this Wakamba who was clearly respectful and even cordial. Bill could tell he was also very self-confident. He was of medium height, lean and well muscled. He was observant and alert, and his eyes moved quickly, taking everything in, perhaps compensating for what Bill soon realized was his near deafness (that was why Bill had been able to approach his camp so closely before the Wakamba had realized anyone was there). As the days went on, and the two had lengthy discussions, Bill put together the picture of a man who was a loner, preferring to hunt by himself, but was also a man with a deep regard for the land, the game, even the plants (he was very fond of flowers). Elui was forthcoming in explaining to Bill which Wakambas were hunting in the area, and how many elephant they were taking. Bill realized that Elui was a valuable informant, but more, he could be an even more valuable tutor. So their relationship started as teacher and student in one direction, officer and conscript in the other, but was to develop into a friendship that would last the rest of their lives.

◈

We now weave through thornbush that is only a few miles from where Bill would have first encountered Elui. It is not easy walking. The sandy soil grits between my soles and my sandals, and when I'm not careful the thorns prick my feet. There is a dark line of blood that runs from a hole in my ankle where I was stabbed by a big thorn earlier in the morning, and it feels like it has broken off inside. This is true *Commifora* country. I push the branches away, careful not to let them whip back on whoever is following. I understand Iain's complaint that we are making this cross-country shortcut, but in a way I am pleased we are hiking through the thornbush as it gives me a chance to feel what the country is like away from the rivers; in other words, a feel for far and away the majority of Tsavo.

"We are more or less entering the Rhino Free Release area," Danny says. "If we contour we'll get to the headquarters where the rhinos are kept in pens so they can acclimatize to the country a little before they're released." Danny looks at me and adds, "I thought you might enjoy seeing that."

I realize there was more to the decision to go cross-country than just shortening distance, and I am grateful to Danny for the consideration of including the Free Release area in our itinerary, but I understand Iain's disappointment that he doesn't have a voice in these decisions.

Danny then calls to Mohamed and tells him in Swahili that he thinks he is taking a line that contours too far toward the river to intercept the Free Release headquarters. Mohamed and Lokiyor climb a ten-foot termite hill and study the terrain ahead; standing on top, their hands shielding their eyes, they look heroic, like models in a Bruce Weber photograph. Mohamed lowers his hand and tells Danny he thinks we are still on the right heading, but I can see Danny is less than convinced.

We hike another half hour and Mohamed stops and points to the ground and says *kifaro*, Swahili for rhino. Bongo draws an outline around the print with a stick and says, "Good to see this again, especially here in Tsavo East."

"Rhinos are endangered, but people are not," Danny says, leaning on his rifle, his hands folded over the end of the barrel. "If one of them charges, it's every man for himself. We will not shoot it. Remember, they are quite blind animals, so if you do take off with one on you, just keep an eye on it, and a last-minute evasive action, diving under a bush or something, will normally save the day."

We weave through the dun-colored bush like puff adders, threading through one opening, then, without thinking, making for the next hole, lifting delicately a branch lined with two-inch thorns and easing it back so it doesn't slap and puncture the person behind. A black-bellied bustard wings away in its gooselike flight. It is now late September, nearing the farthest distance in the year from the rains, and the country feels like dried bone. Then under a thornbush, like a solitary torch, is an eight-inch plant with a single green stalk supporting a brilliant pink ball with orange-yellow stamen. "The fireball lily," Bongo says, then adding, from his impressive memory of detail, "*Scadoxus multiflores.*"

Danny points to a rock outcrop on the slope of the Yatta escarpment that is shaped like a "W" and says that when he is working in this area his rangers sometimes tell him they believe it is a "W" for "Woodley." "Do you think they are referring to father or to sons?" I ask Danny. "Probably to Dad," he answers. "He still has quite a reputation in this area."

In 1948, his first year in Tsavo, it would still be some time before Bill Woodley earned that reputation. With Elui as guide and teacher, however, the angle of his learning curve steepened dramatically. In September of that year, the warden Stevens asked Bill to organize a safari to the little-known northern area of the park, to survey any existing roads, signpost the boundaries, conduct an audit of the wildlife, investigate a report that Orma herders were grazing cattle within the park, and keep an eye for signs of poachers. Bill, of course, took Elui with him.

With eight additional rangers, they left in a three-ton Dodge truck loaded with food, water, and camp equipment. There was no direct road to their destination, so they had to drive around the park, entering from the north and west, through Wakamba country and Elui's own village of Mutha. Wherever they could, they pushed the Dodge down the remains of hunting tracks that had been cut years earlier by Bror Blixen or C. G. MacArthur, leaving signposts when they estimated they were crossing into the park.

Moving south they crossed the Tiva Drift, a sand river that in the wet seasons flows sometimes in raging floods, but even at those volumes eventually
absorbs into the dry bushland and never reaches the sea. (This area of the
Tiva Drift is where Pete Jenkins, a few years later, would take that black-
and-white photograph of the elephants digging for water that I had admired
in his living room.)

Here Bill and Elui discovered a band of Orma people who had dug
wells to find water for their cattle. The Orma are a Cushitic people with
lighter skin, wiry hair, and lean and slight features. Bill met with the
group's headman, who explained they had moved this way from their traditional grazing area to the north because of a water shortage there. Since
it was still several weeks before the short rains would break, Bill knew
they had to remain where they were, but he told them next season they
could not return to this area as it had been declared off limits for people.
(One year before Bill died, Ian Parker, a former game warden and a friend
of Bill's, would ask him how he felt telling these people to get off the lands
that they had occupied seasonally for untold generations, and Bill replied
that he did sense the Orma were being treated unjustly, but that he was
following his orders, and he assumed his superiors knew what they were
doing. As Parker said, that was excusable in a nineteen-year-old.)

Bill continued south sixty-five miles along a rough track just inside the
park boundary until he reached the Galana River. There he set up camp at a
spot we were to pass through in a few days on our own walk. He went to the
river's edge to bathe and discovered a gathering of vultures collected
around the carcass of an elephant. The tusks were gone, slabs of meat had
been cut away from the head, and stomach fat removed, all indications the
animal had been poached by African hunters. He then drove east along the
riverbank and discovered several more dead elephant.

That evening in camp Elui told him that at the end of the dry season,
when the elephant gather near permanent water, their carcasses could be
found everywhere up and down the Galana, even as far upriver as the junction of the Tsavo and Athi.

"There are hundreds," Elui said.

"Hundreds?"

Elui assured him he spoke the truth. Bill then asked him who these people
were who were killing so many elephant, and doing it with bows and arrows.
Elui paused, then answered that they were not Wakambas but rather a
people who hunted with very powerful bows much larger than those used
by any other tribe. "They are a people called the Waliangulu," he said.

When he returned to Mtito Andei, once again C. G. MacArthur pooh-poohed Bill's report of such extensive elephant poaching by hunters using only bows and arrows, no matter what size the bows. Stevens the warden sided with C.G., of course, and Bill was left wondering if Elui was right. But he had seen the carcasses himself, and he resolved to figure out what was going on. Little did he know he had just started a project that would take ten years to complete.

◈

We descend into a *lugga* carpeted with Bermuda grass that has in its bottom a standing pool of spring-fed water. Hundreds of hoofprints of all sizes have created a patternwork in the surrounding mud that is interrupted here and there by deep holes left by elephant. We leave this small oasis, climb the opposite bank, and immediately return to the ossified thornbush.

"Bloody Mohamed needs to chew on some more *miraa*," Danny says, critical of Mohamed's route finding. "He's contouring too low, and we'll miss the headquarters by three or four kilometers."

Mohamed changes course and Danny says, "The station's there, in that doum grove," but when we arrive at the grove there is no station, and he says, "Then it's the next *lugga*." To be fair, in the monotony of this thornbush, a mistake seems inevitable, but it also seems the allowance should go to Mohamed as much as to Danny. We approach the next *lugga* and there is the station. We *are* too low, but only by half a kilometer.

The headquarters of the Rhino Free Release Area is a cluster of three stone buildings with thatch roofs surrounded by shade trees. The resident rangers greet us and we are escorted into the largest building that opens through a wide veranda onto a small lagoon lined with green canebrake. The room is arranged around a large bar shaped from a slab of native hardwood that wraps around the log uprights supporting the thatch. "It looks like a resort," I say.

"That was the idea," Danny, who was in charge of construction, replies. "We wanted to make it comfortable, so it would be considered a good place to be on assignment, and that way attract the best people."

On the wall someone has affixed a paper that is headlined: KWS Mission Statement. "We hold in trust, for now and tomorrow, the responsibility for protection and conservation of Kenya's extraordinary wealth, as represented by its fauna, flora and natural beauty. KWS will manage these resources, which are of inestimable economic, socio-cultural, aesthetic and scientific

value. To fulfill this mission KWS will develop the required human resources, achieve financial self-sufficiency and encourage support and participation of the people of Kenya."

Earlier on our trek Danny had told me the unofficial motto of KWS: "We
the willing, led by the unknowing, are doing the impossible for the ungrate-
ful. We have done so much for so long with so little, we are now qualified to
do anything with nothing."

Next to the KWS Mission Statement there is a map of the Free Release
Area with pushpins marking the position of each rhino. I count twenty-
four pins.

"How do they know where they are?" I ask Bongo.

"Each rhino has a tiny radio transmitter surgically installed in its horn."

Danny explains that the rangers are taught to track each animal's position,
and that they make frequent roll calls. In addition, there are regular patrols
around the perimeter. Outside we visit the holding pens where the rhino are
housed until they have recovered from their transfers. There are no rhinoceros in the pens at the moment, but the corrals, made of heavy sheet metal
secured between ten-foot-high poles buried in the ground, are badly
dented. "They are a bit aggressive when they first arrive," Danny explains.
"But that's actually good because it keeps their systems working, gets them
exercising after their transport."

The rhino arrive from the Tsavo West sanctuary, and also from Nairobi
and Amboseli national parks. "The genetic base is pretty good," Danny says,
"and it's thought that when you have about thirty animals in an area, you
have a viable herd. Already we've had two calves born this year, and they've
both survived. As long as we continue to keep the poachers at bay, it looks
like the program will work."

❖

As we leave the headquarters, I ask the managing ranger, through Danny, if
there are any rhino roaming in the area we will walk through this afternoon.
"He says there are four, and three are quite close," Danny tells me.

"Keep an open eye for tick birds," Bongo says, referring to the oxpecker,
a medium-sized bird of the starling family that walks over the backs of animals, especially hippo and rhino, feeding symbiotically on ticks and blood-
sucking flies. The Swahili word for this bird translates as "rhino policeman,"
and seeing them above the bush almost always reveals the location of large
game. (I can't resist a small digression to describe my favorite Gary Larson

Far Side cartoon. From a view looking across the broad back of a rhino, you see, from behind, a grown-up oxpecker with one wing around a much smaller oxpecker and the other wing indicating the rhino's back. The caption says, "Someday, son, this will all be yours.")

I am thrilled. At last on our trek all the animals in the ecosystem of the thornbush *nyika* of East Africa are present. All the pieces are in place. I walk alert, eyes craning above the bush looking for oxpeckers, glancing at the ground looking for prints. I wonder what it would be like to be charged by a rhino, even *hoping* that we are charged by a rhino. I have been on foot around rhinoceros only twice, once hiking through jungle in southern Nepal, and once walking through a private game reserve near Mt. Kenya that had two rhino who were both very tame. Those encounters were enough, however, to allow me to suppose that being charged by a rhinoceros while on foot would be as close as you could come on our planet today to simulating what it would have been like to be chased by a dinosaur.

When we had finished our trek, and I returned to Africa to interview many of the old-timers such as Pete Jenkins and Ian Parker, they all had good rhino stories. It seemed like every outing in those days involved getting chased and often treed. It became a game, and the goal when you were chased up a tree was to reach down and touch the rhino's back, like a North American Indian scoring a coup.

"The funniest story I heard," Ian Parker told me, "was when Bill Woodley was with a chap named Cogs Pearson, buggering around in their old truck when a rhino charged them and got his horn stuck in the back. They got out and stood on the sides as this rhino bucked around trying to get loose—the truck lifting up and down—and they didn't know what to do so one of them said, 'Let's give him a beer, calm the bugger down,' so they poured a bottle of beer down the rhino's mouth, foam everywhere."

This story reminded me of another one that, although it involved a crocodile instead of a rhinoceros, suggested father and son shared a similar fun-loving mischievousness. When he was seventeen and living with his parents in Tsavo West, Danny was out one night with his friend Mark Jenkins (Pete's son), when they decided for amusement to drive to Lugard's Falls and catch a crocodile. They picked a big one, and blinding it with a flashlight one of them jumped on the animal's back while the other covered its head with a burlap. They then trussed the animal and loaded in their truck, drove to the tourist hotel in Voi, near the park headquarters of Tsavo East, and released it in the swimming pool. In the morning, an early-rising hotel guest, up for a swim, panicked and ran to the manager, who called Stephen Gichangi, the

warden of Tsavo East, who took just a moment to add up the evidence before calling Bill and reporting that his son Danny had been once again up to
his pranks.

Now the low afternoon light warms the rock on the escarpment of the
Yatta Plateau. Our track angles toward the river, and we will arrive in camp
within an hour. On the escarpment I again see the "W," and I think of Bill
walking this same bush country, wondering what he was going to do about
these mysterious people of the long bow, the Waliangulu. It would take Bill
ten years—from 1948 to 1958—to contain the Waliangulu bow hunters.
When he returned to Tsavo twenty years later, in 1978, it would be on the
eve of a new, and much more sinister, chapter in the history of elephant and
rhino poaching in East Africa. The Waliangulu and Wakamba bow hunters
would be gone, melted back into the bush, to be replaced by Somali *shifta*,
the fierce and very well armed bandits from the northern tribes. This next
wave of poaching would no longer be a gentlemanly skirmish, but real war
with real casualties, and it would not be won until shortly before Bill died.

That too is history. In the golden light we pass out of the territorial boundaries that the freely released rhino have established. We have not seen a
rhino, much less been charged by one. But they are here. As are the elephant, who have made a steady comeback in Tsavo these last six or seven
years. As though to validate this recovery, we hear a trumpet call that carries
over the top of the bush. We stop. Danny climbs a termitarium and points to
the north. "At least two," he says, and we angle toward them, picking up, as
we go, the dirt road that leads to the river just above Lugard's Falls. We spot
the elephant and stop to watch. There is a mature female, one juvenile, and
one infant that is only about four feet high.

The next three days of our walk will be the "elephant section," the area
along the Galana where the animals congregate at the end of the dry season.
Now, as I watch this elephant and her young through my binoculars, I hear
a vehicle and soon see a Land Cruiser crest a rise in the road and come
toward us, a contrail of dust rising in its wake.

"Look, it's Joyce," Iain says.

We had arranged two weeks before for Joyce Poole to join us on this day,
and from here to walk with us the next two days through this elephant section. That she should arrive while we are watching the first elephants we
have seen in several days is a coincidence almost too perfect, but I take it as
a sign that the next few days will prove very interesting.

15

In order to preserve the wildlife of the wilderness at all, some middle ground must be found between brutal and senseless slaughter and . . . unhealthy sentimentalism.

—*Theodore Roosevelt, 1905*

We cannot win this battle to save our species and environments without forging an emotional bond between ourselves and nature as well—for we will not fight to save what we do not love.

—*Stephen Jay Gould,
from an essay titled "This View of Life: Unenchanted Evening," 1991*

Joyce has brought her three-year-old daughter Selengei, and also the family *ayah,* a middle-aged African woman with a wide smile who helps Joyce with child care and household chores. "Look, Selei, there's elephants. Over there." Joyce climbs atop the car and lifts her daughter on her shoulders for a better view.

After reading Joyce's recent memoir *Coming of Age with Elephants,* Iain sent me a fax: "The book is currently tearing the East African wildlife circles apart. It's a great read, but very controversial—touching on stuff relating to Tsavo and the corruption of officials involved in poaching. You've got to read it, and then I think we should get hold of Joyce and invite her to join us for part of our trek. What do you think?"

I read the book and agreed with Iain. He arranged a meeting with Joyce and she agreed to join our trek. It's a privilege to have such an expert with us during these next stages of our walk, and I am looking forward to getting to know her. "We'll see you in camp," she says as she starts her vehicle and drives off, disappearing down the road.

We follow on foot, and in a half hour we are at our campsite, which has been positioned near a concrete causeway that David Sheldrick, the first warden of Tsavo East, built in the early days when the park was first divided; it is serviceable only in low water, and it also is the only vehicle crossing on the river between the coast and the first real bridge nearly two hundred miles inland. Our tents are pitched on a sandbar that will clearly be underwater when the rains come, and as the sky is cloudy we make a mental note to keep an eye on things. The river here is wide, and even in the dry season it carries the brick tint of the Tsavo laterites. We sit on a wide apron of exposed gneiss and enjoy the early evening cooldown.

"Look what I found," Joyce calls, and we turn to see her holding a dried elephant turd that is over one foot on the cross section. "It's the biggest one I've ever seen," she exclaims. I ask her to hold on while I fetch my camera, and in a moment I take a portrait of her all smiles as she holds the turd. She sets it down and calls Selengei over, then breaks it open and explains to her daughter what the elephant has been eating. They are both crouched over examining the specimen, and it is endearing to watch Joyce pass her enthusiasms to her little girl.

Joyce herself was six years old when her father took a job running the U.S. Peace Corps program in Malawi. He took the family on safari on every available holiday, and camping became one of Joyce's childhood pleasures. Her father was soon transferred to Kenya, and when Joyce was eleven she went to the National Museum in Nairobi to hear Jane Goodall deliver a lecture on her venerated studies of chimpanzees. That initiated what became in Joyce a lifelong passion to study African mammals, and when her family returned to the United States when she was thirteen, she focused her stateside studies on biology. After a year in college her father took another job in Nairobi, and it was agreed Joyce could take a year off and return with her parents, to see if she could get a job as a field research assistant.

By then Joyce had read about Iain Douglas-Hamilton's elephant study in Lake Manyara National Park, in Tanzania. Over a four-and-a-half-year period Douglas-Hamilton had learned to recognize nearly every one of the more than five hundred elephant that lived in Manyara, and this ability had allowed him to identify patterns in the matriarchal family structures of elephant that had never previously been understood, especially how some family units organized into larger social units that he had called kin groups.

Joyce's father arranged for her to meet Douglas-Hamilton, and later Joyce was able to visit Manyara. That experience confirmed her interest in elephant. Then at a party in Nairobi she met an American protégé of Douglas-Hamilton's who had first worked in Manyara but then had established her own research program studying the elephant population in Amboseli, a small national park just northwest of Kilimanjaro. Cynthia Moss must have detected the enthusiasm in the young Joyce Poole, who was then nineteen years old, because she invited Joyce to join her in the Amboseli study. It was 1975, and Joyce had found her mentor.

Cynthia began her Amboseli study by building a file of photographs that she used to recognize individual elephants, a technique she had learned from Douglas-Hamilton. She then used the files to identify which individuals belonged to what matriarchal family groups. Her intention was to learn all she could about how these groups worked both as families and as social units in the larger population. So the first thing Cynthia taught Joyce was how to tell one elephant from another.

At first they all looked the same, but after a while Joyce began to distinguish differences, especially in the ears and the tusks. Eventually she could see "there were small ears, big ears, smooth ears, ragged ears, round ears, flop ears, curtain ears and crumpled ears . . . long tusks, short tusks, splayed tusks, asymmetrical tusks, convergent and crossed tusks . . . one left tusk, one right tusk or no tusks." Another trick Cynthia taught Joyce was to apply names to individuals as another way to remember them. Cynthia gave names to individual animals in the same family that began with the same letter—further aiding her to recall who was part of what group. So Teresa was the matriarchal head of the family that included Tristen and Tolstoy, Tina and Tim. Sometimes elephant received names because that was simply who they were. Split Ear, Bad Bull, and one of the favorites, Beachball, because he was so round.

Joyce learned that elephant families ranged from just two individuals to as many as thirty, and that often two families would join into what Cynthia called a bond group (she didn't like Douglas-Hamilton's term "kin group" as some were known not to be relatives or kin). Sometimes during the wet season several families would travel in groups of one hundred or more. She also learned that male elephant leave their mother's family by the time they are teenagers, and they aren't nearly as social, sometimes forming and then dissolving a group, or often wandering on their own. Cynthia said she would be grateful if Joyce could spend some time sorting out the males, since her focus was on the female family structures. "The males are boring," Cynthia had said with a laugh.

The males were just fine with Joyce. Most important, they gave her a study subject she could call her own, and she pursued it, as well as subsequent studies on elephant communication, with tenacious enthusiasm for the next fifteen years.

❖

My small travel alarm beeps at five A.M., and I sit up in my sleeping bag and by headlamp write in my journal. I note it is September 30, and that there is a light rain that sent all of us scurrying out during the night to clip the rainflies over our tents. This is the first rain since we ascended the windward slopes of Kilimanjaro two weeks before, and I wonder if perhaps it's the start of the short rains, also known as the grass rains, that in a normal year begin in early October and end in November. These rains coincide with a northeast monsoon, and in the days of sail the trading dhows used this wind to cross the Arabian Sea where they bartered their wares up and down the African coast, then waited for the next season's southeast wind to carry them back to Arabia.

As the sky lightens I look to the east and see a thin orange band that suggests clear skies toward the coast, and also provides a painterly rim of color behind the doum palms that line the river. As I get out of the tent I notice my ankle is stiff and swollen where the large thorn entered yesterday (I had tried to get it out last night, but it was buried too deep). In the mess tent I pour a large cup of steaming milk tea and wrap my fingers around it, and after a few sips I feel ready for the day's march.

Joyce arranges to have Selengei and the *ayah* stay with the camp staff, who will be driving the vehicles about fifteen miles along a dirt road that parallels the Galana on the south bank before setting up our next camp. Meanwhile we will cross the river and walk the north bank, which has no road and, in fact, is wild country all the way to the park's northern boundary nearly eighty miles away.

We cross on the concrete causeway, then scout up and down a braidwork of side channels looking for safe places to jump. These kind of channels are prime crocodile habitat, but one channel is too wide to jump and we have no choice but to wade; as I cross I think to myself that this must be what it is like in a war, walking on patrol through forest country you know contains the enemy, but you have no idea when or if he will strike.

We jump the last channel and climb onto bedrock scoured clean by seasonal floods. To our right we can hear the falls, and we head in that direction. Lugard's Falls is not a waterfall but a deep and narrow gorge cut into a riverbed of red sedimentary rock here and there striped with dark gray bands. It is, of course, the namesake of Frederick Lugard, the explorer who first came this way in 1890 on his march following the Sabaki River inland toward Uganda. When he reached the falls, Lugard noted in his journal only that "all along here the river bed is bare rock and boulders [and] is confined in a deep gorge only a few feet broad and very deep." This laconic description of what is arguably the most dramatic natural wonder on the entire river probably speaks more of Lugard's character than do the laundry lists of his accomplishments, and I suspect had Joseph Thomson passed this way, we may have enjoyed reading a more picturesque description.

We approach the edge of the gorge and look in. It is fifty or sixty feet down, and the entire river is flowing in a maelstrom of whitewater through a space in places only thirty feet wide. The sides of the chasm are a tortured sculpture of fins, bowls, and bulges all rounded and polished by the water. The narrows continue for a quarter mile, and to say anything to one another we have to shout above the roar. As we walk the edge of the precipice we continue to stop and gawk into the whitewater, and I know that everyone is thinking the same thing: If I slip and fall, I'm dead.

That's just what happened to three tourists who came to view the narrows the year before. One of them was taking a picture of his wife when she backed up and slipped on the smooth rock. He dove in to save her and a third member of the party did the same, but they were all swept down the falls. They were never found, and it is presumed that their bodies flushed into a deep pool at the end of the gorge that is inhabited by several very large crocodile.

Below the falls the river flows smooth and wide, and we stop to watch four hippo lounging on a sandbar.

"Look, there's a crocodile," Bongo says.

It's on the sandbar just downstream of the hippo, and when it senses our presence it turns toward us, lifts on its front legs, and opens its maw, exposing four rows of conical bone-white teeth.

"He's just waiting for something to flush down," I say.

"Or *someone* to flush down," Iain replies, referring to the tourists.

"It was just downstream from here I once had a nasty encounter with a crocodile," Bongo says. "In 1981. I was nineteen years old, and on safari with my girlfriend. We had started in Mzima Springs with the plan to walk down the Tsavo, then the Galana. We decided to cross the river at a place where it braids through a channel filled with rocks. We commenced to cross, jumping rock to rock, and in about mid-stream Ann jumped to a rock where it was then too wide to jump again, so she sat down to fish for a foothold in the river. At that moment I jumped to the same rock, and as I was standing above her, she suddenly screamed and was immediately pulled off the rock.

"Without thinking I grabbed her under the arms, and as I struggled to pull her back on the rock the crocodile came to the surface with her entire foot in its mouth. Ann was screaming, I was tugging and pulling, and shouting to the rangers to shoot. The crocodile was lashing left to right, its tail thrashing violently. The rangers then began firing from the hip, and I thought we were going to be hit. Suddenly the crocodile let go, and with the release of pressure I flew back into the river with Ann in my arms. I was then very keen to clamber out in case the crocodile came in for a second attack.

"We didn't see the croc again, however, so I attended to Ann's injuries, which were fairly serious. She had very deep holes on the sole of her foot. The big toe was torn badly, and from her ankle down the flesh had been literally ripped away, her tendons and white bone exposed. I washed the wound with fresh water, stitched up the cuts, then we crossed the river where we had a vehicle with a radio on the other side. My father flew down and evacuated her.

"Thus ended our safari," Bongo concludes. He pauses, looks across the river, then adds, "And the relationship as well."

◈

On the south side eight large and stout animals with taupe-colored fur graze on the emerald grass that grows on a seasonal sandbar; I recognize them at a glance as waterbuck, and think to myself that, thanks to tutoring from Iain, Bongo, and Danny, I am getting better at identifying game at distance, and at quick glance. We stop and examine the bleached bones of a rhinoceros, and Bongo finds what looks like a bullet hole through the jawbone. "The bad old days," he says. In a few more minutes, however, we discover the recent track of a live rhino, and it can only be an animal from the Free Release program. It is very encouraging to see them crossing the river and expanding their territorial claims. "It means the program is a success," Bongo says with a smile.

My ankle is sore, but I imagine that to my predecessors who spent months and years of their lives walking this thornbush country, from Joseph

Thomson right through to Bill Woodley, a thorn in the foot was just that, and nothing even to mention. As Bongo said one day when he was doctoring his blisters "They say in the army that pain is a sensation, and sensations are to be enjoyed."

The sky is overcast and threatens rain, but the effect of increased humidity has eased in the face of a slight but welcome breeze from the east. We follow a game trail that parallels the saltbush that grows in a band along the river's edge. We flush a group of impala that, with lyrate horns and tawny fur, are arguably the most elegantly beautiful of the one hundred species of antelope that occur in Africa. This group pronks in graceful leaps across the trail in front of us. This behavior is thought to be a response to a high-level alarm, and it is a pleasure to watch: All four hooves strike the ground at once, and then, as though each landing spring-loads the animal's legs, it bounces up again. In a few more minutes we spot a herd of Peter's gazelle, a subspecies found only in this thornbush region of Southeast Kenya that is distinguished from the common Grant's gazelle by a tawny brown mark along the antelope's croup that reaches the tail.

The cloud cover is starting to break into small puffs of fair-weather cumulus that have the look of trade wind clouds, and the headwind cools my skin. When we originally planned this expedition, we had the choice either to start on the beach and march upriver, or climb the mountain first and then walk to the coast. One factor suggesting the summit-to-sea route was the wind: In addition to providing a cooling headwind, walking into the prevailing wind also places us downwind of game, and this fact has aided us considerably in approaching animals such as these Peter's gazelle; had we been walking in the opposite direction we may never have seen them, and this downwind advantage is even more important with elephant, who have an extraordinarily acute sense of smell.

So far this morning, however, we haven't seen any elephant, and I wonder if Bongo's decision to follow this game trail that is about two hundred yards away from the river is at the cost of seeing the one animal that I hope to observe while we are in Joyce's company. I am hiking behind her, and she assures me that Bongo has made the right call and that we are well placed to see elephant. "As it heats up they will be coming down to the river for water." Then in timely validation of her opinion, and of Bongo's choice of routes, a few minutes later I hear the cracking of fronds in a doum grove to our right.

I see that Joyce hears it too but that the others, including Mohamed, don't. "I think there's an elephant over there," Joyce says, and in a few more yards we spot its gray back over the juvenile palms. She studies the animal through her binoculars, then adds, "It's a young male. Probably about nineteen or twenty years old."

"How can you tell?"

"Older males have much more massive heads. See the line from his eyes down to where his tusks erupt? It's very straight, and as a male gets older it becomes an hourglass shape so that by the time he's thirty-five it is broad at the forehead and eyes, then it comes out, then in, then out again, as the tusks thicken."

Still unaware of our presence the elephant steps toward us, it ears swaying as it walks, its great legs lifting massively yet gently, even delicately, and I remember once watching a very large Hawaiian woman dance the hula with the same kind of slow-motion grace.

Six months after she had arrived in Amboseli, and Cynthia Moss had given her the assignment of studying the male elephants in the park, Joyce was watching a huge male elephant—the biggest she had ever seen in the area—when she noticed that he was dribbling urine, and the sheath around his penis was green, as though it were infected. She estimated the elephant was fifty years old, and her first thought was that perhaps elephants become incontinent. A few weeks later she noticed another big male with the same malady. Both bulls also had secretions flowing from their temporal glands located behind their ears, and Joyce noticed that they were both walking with their heads held in an almost stately pose, and they were following the females around.

After she had worked in Amboseli nearly a year, Joyce returned to the United States to continue her studies at Smith College. Cynthia wrote that she was observing more males with what they then called Green Penis Disease, and when Joyce returned to Amboseli, in 1977, Cynthia warned her that any males with the suspected disease were also very aggressive, and it was best to stay clear of them. When Joyce went out to study them, however, she found that at least three of the individuals who Cynthia had said in her letters had green penis were now normal, and moreover not only were they no longer aggressive, they seemed completely disinterested in sex even though they were in close proximity to females. Could it be that Green Penis Disease was not really a disease at all, but had something to do with sexual cycles in male elephants?

She mentioned this idea to Cynthia, who replied that many people had by then studied African elephant, and no one had ever found any evidence to support this. Joyce then returned to Smith, but was back briefly in Amboseli during Christmas break where she noticed additional males who had what she and Cynthia now called Green Penis Syndrome, since it didn't appear to be a disease at all. Then, on her way home, a friend in Nairobi showed her a paper on Asian elephant describing a periodic condition in males known as musth, an Urdu word meaning "intoxicated."

Musth had long been described in Asian elephant, and elephant researchers had long looked for the same musth condition in African elephant, but because no one had ever observed it, it was assumed that for some reason it was a condition found only in Asia. Joyce flipped through the paper and saw a picture of a domesticated Asian male elephant in musth with arrows pointing to "some discharge from the temporal glands behind the eye, and a dribble of urine from the penis."

Joyce knew immediately that they had made an exciting discovery. She returned to Smith and wrote her honors thesis on musth in African elephant, then presented her paper at an international meeting of mammologists where she was frustrated to find several eminent scientists who ignored her conclusions. She entered a graduate program at Cambridge and designed an observation and testing program that she felt would settle the question once and for all. She returned to Amboseli in 1980, where, in addition to behavior observations documenting increased aggression and sexual activity among male elephant in musth, she collected urine samples from several musth males by following them around and siphoning up their urine before it soaked into the ground. Analysis of these samples showed conclusively that when in the musth condition, African male elephant have extremely high levels of testosterone. Her hypothesis was proved.

◈

"Are these Tsavo elephants any different from the ones in Amboseli?" I ask Joyce as we follow a bank that rises about fifty feet above the river.

"They are very noticeably larger," she replies. "Around Amboseli the elephants tend to be short-legged, very fat, and with big ears. The Kilimanjaro elephants have shorter bodies but relatively longer legs, small triangular ears with a very particular veination pattern, and no or very little hair on their tails."

"Why is that?"

"They step on each other's tails coming down the mountain."

"Oh come on."

"Well, it's the best theory we can come up with."

We stop to watch a gathering of hippo sunbathing on a sandbar, until they hear us and rush into the river making waves that carry across the water. We flush a group of gerunuk, with long giraffelike necks and lithesome bodies, that spring away in tall leaps as though they were on another planet with less gravity. The river is wide and slow and begins to oxbow. The sky is open and broad, and ahead the land is flat save for the trapezoidal shape of a distant, flat-topped escarpment. There is a feeling of transition into a great flatland, with the promise of ocean on the far horizon, and from the bank above a bend in the river we look back and see in the blue distance the Chyulu Hills.

I walk behind Joyce. She is wearing cream-white shorts, a slate-blue shirt, and a brimmed hat. She has dangling earrings that hold on their ends a blue bead the same color as her shirt. Her neck-length brown hair has a touch of red, and she wears a very light lipstick. I walk alongside and ask her to tell me why she thinks all of us are so captivated by elephant. She considers the question, then says, "Part of it is the way they look, with funny trunks and big ears. But after you spend as much time as I have with them—fourteen years now—you learn they have so many qualities we like best about ourselves, dignity and loyalty, even a sense of humor. They have a family structure very similar to ours—okay, there are no males within the families—but there are very tight bonds—grandmothers, daughters, sisters, cousins—that last a lifetime. Then when you see members of a family separated for half a day, or even an hour, and they meet again, they go through this incredible ceremony as if to celebrate their reunion. They trumpet, scream, rumble, spin around, urinate, defecate. I know as a scientist you're suppose to say, 'Well, you know, animals don't have these sorts of feelings,' but you can't watch them and not think it's anything but a celebration of being happy that they're back together."

One of Joyce's strengths, in my opinion, is that she doesn't hesitate to cross the scientific taboo against applying anthropomorphic interpretations to her study subjects. Some may argue this is not good science, but I believe we have as much to learn about animal behavior from approaching them emotionally—from relating to them as one animal to another—as we do from quantified scientific observation.

The person with perhaps the most hands-on knowledge about the emotional lives of wild animals in East Africa is Daphne Sheldrick, who founded a celebrated animal orphanage in Voi, headquarters for Tsavo East, and has raised fourteen infant elephant, fifteen elephant three years or older, twenty-three buffalo, ten rhino, and "just about every other bloody thing," she told me when I interviewed her after our trek. "I also know every single one of them, from a tiny tree squirrel to an elephant, were individuals with their own sets of feelings and emotions, just as much as you and I are individuals with our feelings."

In her book *Tsavo Story*, Daphne describes experiences at the animal orphanage that allow you a view into the personalities of wild animals that you might never acquire watching them in the wild. One of my favorites was the story of Rufus the Rhino.

"Rufus loved his stable, his mud wallow, his food, his daily routine. He loved affection . . . having his tummy scratched, lying down with legs outstretched and eyes tight closed in bliss and contentment. He loved children and allowed them to clamber all over him, or ride him like a horse . . . who would suspect this side to a rhino's nature?"

Daphne also had views on the emotional lives of elephant that corroborated Joyce's opinions. "How can we gauge the depth of an elephant's intelligence," she wrote. "What goes on in that massive head when, coming across the carcass of a fallen comrade, they will deliberately pull the tusks from the sockets and carry them away and sometimes smash them to pieces? And what, I wonder, was going through the minds of a herd of elephants in Uganda, who stood outside the store that housed the feet of hundreds of their cropped companions, and shoveled earth into it through a narrow opening until the feet were partially covered with soil? What motive was behind the two elephants in Tanzania, who are reported to have supported and guided an aged blind buffalo for some two days?"

"There's always been a mental block in the scientific world about thinking of animals in a human sense," Daphne told me. "But those girls who have become scientists themselves, Cynthia and Joyce, have ignored that. I admire them for that, for the risk of being labeled by their profession a 'bunny hugger.' "

One of Joyce's favorite aspects of elephant behavior is their sense of fun, and she has several stories of elephant playing games. My favorite tells about a day she spent observing an elephant family she was very familiar with when, mostly out of boredom, she tossed her flip-flop at the teenage male member of the group. He smelled it, stepped on it, then, when he figured it was harmless, picked it up with his trunk and tossed it back to Joyce. She picked it up and tossed it back to him, and so began a good game of toss. It went on for a while, and finally Joyce decided she'd had enough of the game so she put her sandal back on and turned away, and suddenly a small piece of wildebeest bone thunked her on the head. "It seemed clear to me that [the young elephant] understood and was amused by our game," Joyce wrote in her book. "There we were, two species out on the plains, playing catch."

Joyce's most poignant story describes an occasion in Amboseli when she observed one of her study animals named Tonie give birth to a stillborn calf. Tonie nudged her newborn, trying to get it to move. She stood over it, refusing to abandon the baby. When the vultures approached, she chased them off. Joyce returned the next day, and Tonie was still at her vigil. Now there were over a dozen vultures and a jackal. She charged and scattered them. Joyce noted that everything about Tonie, from the expression on her face to the way she carried her body, spelled grief.

It was the dry season and very hot. Tonie had now been standing in the sun for twenty-four hours, and Joyce said to herself, "That's enough." She returned to camp, loaded a jerry can with water, and went back to the elephant. She knew that scientifically she wasn't supposed to interact with her study animals, but she didn't care. She climbed out of her vehicle, placed a basin on the ground, and filled it. Tonie walked over, paused, then drank it all in two trunkfuls. Joyce filled the basin again and the elephant emptied it. She drove back to camp, got another container, and returned; she filled the basin and Tonie drank that. Joyce got back in her car to go get more water when Tonie walked up to her car and stood next to it. Joyce was motionless as the elephant then reached in through the window and gently placed her trunk on Joyce's chest and arm.

◈

In addition to her realization that male African elephant go into musth, Joyce has made one other discovery that has significantly expanded our knowledge of the lives of elephant. It was a discovery inspired by a growing awareness that she was developing an almost extrasensory ability to know when elephant were in the neighborhood.

"I can't explain it, but I can tell," she says as we walk. "A couple of months ago, for example, I was driving around Amboseli with an Imax film crew trying to find elephants, and I just had this feeling there were no elephants in the area, and we drove and drove and searched and indeed there were no elephants. Why did I feel that way? And then when they are around, I know it. When I was doing my studies in Amboseli, as soon as I would leave camp in my Land Rover I would open the window, even when it was really cold, because I couldn't seem to find elephants as easily with the windows up."

Joyce and Cynthia began to suspect that elephant were emitting some kind of sound frequency outside of the normal range of human hearing, but at a level that she nevertheless was learning to sense. She also noticed that elephant often acted in ways that corroborated her suspicion. One day she noticed a solitary male elephant, for example, suddenly lift its head, extend its ears, then walk with determination in the direction he had been listening. About this time Joyce transferred to Princeton to continue her graduate studies, and there she learned of another researcher named Kathrine Payne, who had experience recording whale communications, and was now interested in elephant vocalizations. Joyce contacted her, and Payne was very excited about Joyce's suspicions, because she herself had come to the same conclusions with Asian elephant, adding something that Joyce hadn't realized: If elephant were communicating with one another using infrasound frequencies, then there was good chance they were doing it over distances of up to several kilometers because sound at that wavelength carries much farther.

After Joyce had returned to Amboseli, Payne arrived with all her recording equipment. They set to work, and the initial results were exciting. In one short recording session, Joyce heard with her own ears thirty-four elephant rumbles, a kind of low vocalization that is the most varied of elephant calls and sounds something like an elephant with digestive problems. When they played the tape back at high speed, however, they counted over one hundred rumbles: Some two-thirds of all the calls had been below the range of human hearing.

Eventually Joyce was able to understand the meaning of over thirty calls. She and Payne then began to play back these calls to the elephant using a speaker system. In perhaps the most dramatic corroboration of their discovery, Kathrine Payne and some other researchers staked out a water hole where several male elephant had congregated, while another part of the team drove out two kilometers and positioned a powerful speaker in the direction of the water hole, and then played over it the infrasound call of an estrous female. The male elephant at the water hole immediately raised their heads, then left, and in a half hour they had arrived at the speaker.

Up ahead, on the other side of the river, smoke is rising over the bush, and as we approach we see several workers feeding brush into a bonfire. Other workers are clearing an area along the river's edge. We cross the river to investigate, and we learn they are working for a Malindi hotel that has received permission to set up a tented camp for tourists.

"Better this than some permanent structure," Bongo says.

Bongo's point is true, but all of us, Bongo included, would rather it stay just like it is. Then again, there already is a dirt road along this side of the river, built by David Sheldrick in the early days of the park in the hope of attracting visitors. We are in the off-season, so we don't encounter any vehicles as we walk the road toward our own camp, but if we were here in August, or in December, there would be a string of game viewing minibuses moving up and down this track.

Mohamed slows and points to our right. About seventy-five meters off the road there is a group of eight elephants, two large females, several teenagers, and one infant. The wind is in our favor, and we walk slowly forward, then stop and watch as the animals continue to browse on the small acacia and scrub terminalia. One of the large females turns in our direction, fans her ears (thereby cooling the blood in the surface veins), then continues to browse. That the elephant has very poor eyesight but good hearing and an extraordinary sense of smell really isn't surprising if you look at them: Their eyes are very small, their ears are large, and their noses are huge. I watch the large female strip leaves and bark from the acacia using the two fingerlike tips on the end of her trunk to pinch the browse like pliers. An elephant's trunk has about 150,000 muscles in it, and it is incredibly strong, able to kill an animal as large as a Cape buffalo in a single swipe, if it wants to. The trunk is used to scratch eyes, to greet strangers, to comfort infants, to smell the ground for signs of musth males or estrous females. The trunk can suck up to twelve liters of water in a single gulp, when it is then squirted into the mouth. The trunk is also used to suck mud that is then fired with high accuracy over the animal's body. (It's the lateritic mud that has given the elephants of Tsavo their acclaimed brick red color.)

"Do you want to have a closer look?" Danny whispers, pointing to my video camera.

"Sure."

Mohamed, Lokiyor, Danny, Bongo, and I then creep forward. I turn and notice Joyce and Iain stay behind. We get within thirty meters of the animals and stand quietly behind a bush acacia. With the wind favorable the elephant are still unaware of our presence. We rejoin the others and continue along the road. I ask Joyce why she stayed back.

"Elephants can detect the outline of a human shape," she says.

"And if they had, and charged, we are armed."

"That's what really bothered me," she admits. "Although they may not have charged. Who can say. They are certainly more relaxed than when I was lost here."

❖

Joyce refers to a period in 1989 when she was in Tsavo conducting a survey to gauge the impact of poaching on the family structure of elephants. This was follow-up to a larger survey that Iain Douglas-Hamilton had conducted the year before that Joyce also had worked on.

"We were flying these blocks, back and forth, back and forth, marking each elephant carcass on a map," Joyce said, "then in the evening overlaying it onto another map that had the roads on it. I remember thinking, This is strange, and calling to Patrick [Patrick Hamilton, former warden of Tsavo East who was then a pilot assisting in the survey] and Iain and saying, 'Look at this map, all the carcasses are in a row, along the road,' and they looking at each other as if to say, Just what we expected. I thought, What am I missing here? Then I went out in the field with Barbara Tyack [a friend also working on the survey], and I mentioned this to her and she said knowingly, 'Yes, it's odd, isn't it? And all the elephants are afraid of green Toyota Land Cruisers, too.' And then I put it together, that the rangers (who drove in green Land Cruisers), the national park people, were shooting the elephants. They were in cahoots with the poachers."

"That was 1988, the year before Richard Leakey took over?" I ask.

"Yes," she answers. "When it was poised right on the brink."

16

Elephant social organization has recently been shown to be remarkably similar to that of man; in fact, the entire ecology of the elephant is now seen to be more similar to that of man than to any other animal. It is therefore not remarkable that man and the elephant are having to face similar and simultaneous crises—like survival.

—Dr. Richard Laws,
quoted in the revised edition of Peter Beard's The End of the Game, *1988*

We are camped on a sandbank covered with Bermuda grass adjacent to an enormous sausage tree whose namesake fruits, weighing up to twenty pounds each, hang from long stems like huge ornaments. This is one of Iain's favorite camps when bringing clients on his foot safaris, and as he discovered the place himself, he holds it in a certain proprietary regard, and makes sure his staff covers their vehicle tracks when they drive off the road and through the bush to get here.

We have a fire going in front of the tents, and we sit in our camp chairs as the last light of day reflects off the river (we are careful not to sit in the sand as there is a species of small scorpion that burrows in it, and its bite is extremely painful). I pick up the conversation about the level of poaching in the late 1980s, asking Joyce about the results from her follow-up work a year after she assisted on the aerial survey.

Mt. Kilimanjaro. View from the Tanzanian side. (*Rick Ridgeway*)

Iain Allan and Bongo Woodley on the summit icefield, Mt. Kilimanjaro. Mawenzi rises in background. (*Rick Ridgeway*)

Only 250 miles to go . . .(left to right) Iain, Bongo, Rick, and Danny on the summit. (*Rick Ridgeway*)

Iain Allan. (*Rick Ridgeway*)

Mohamed Hamisi.
(*Rick Ridgeway*)

Bongo Woodley.
(*Rick Ridgeway*)

David Lokiyor.
(*Rick Ridgeway*)

Rick Ridgeway in camp. (*Peter Fuszard*)

"We cross on an emerald lawn of Bermuda grass cropped by grazing animals, passing the skull of a Cape buffalo that Danny says would have been taken down by lion." Tsavo West. (*Rick Ridgeway*)

Danny Woodley. (*Rick Ridgeway*)

Bill Woodley, Portuguese East Africa, 1947. (*Woodley Collection*)

On the back of the above photo, Bill writes: "To Daph—I shot the lion, I ran over the porcupine. For lunch that day Daph—I had porcupine steak fried in lion fat, boy was it good, it was a change to the normal diet of elephant meat. Fondest love, Bill." (*Woodley Collection*)

Bill Woodley with two of his three sons—Bongo and Benj—Lake Turkana, 1975. (*Peter Beard, Woodley Collection*)

Peter Beard at Hog Ranch. Behind him is Denis Fynch Hatton's binocular case. (*Mark Greenberg*/Visions)

Fording the Tsavo River. "We always looked for a place that was wide and shallow." (*Rick Ridgeway*)

Peter Beard and Karen Blixen, 1962. "It would seem likely that the parallel interest [in wildlife photography between Denis Fynch Hatton and Peter Beard] is why Karen Blixen late in her life came out of her seclusion to see the young and handsome photographer." (*Peter Beard*)

"Watching elephants on foot is altogether different. On foot you study the direction of the wind, you watch each animal's movement to make certain they don't detect you. You hear their breathing, the sound of their ears flapping, and their stomachs rumbling." (*Rick Ridgeway*)

"I had time after time," Karen Blixen wrote, "watched the progression across the plain of the giraffe, in their queer, inimitable, vegetative gracefulness. . ." (*Peter Beard*)

Bill Woodley holding Patterson's original diary below Tsavo Bridge. (*Peter Beard, Woodley Collection*)

"In the whole of my life I have never experienced anything more nerve-shaking than . . . to know that some one or other of us was doomed to be their victim before morning dawned." Lt. Col. J. H. Patterson with first man-eating lion. (*The Field Museum neg#293658*)

Joyce Poole, elephant researcher. " 'I admire [Joyce] for that, for the risk of being labeled by her profession a "bunny hugger," ' Daphne Sheldrick said." (*Rick Ridgeway*)

Richard Leakey with new ranger recruits at training camp. Tsavo West, 1992. (*Kenya Wildlife Service*)

"Being charged by a rhinoceros while on foot would be as close as you could come on our planet today to simulate what it would have been like to be chased by a dinosaur." (*Clive Ward*)

Cape buffalo, "the most aggressively temperamental of Africa's megafauna." (*Peter Beard*)

Pete Jenkins's photo of the Tiva River, 1957. "The animals seemed to be waiting their turns at the water in a kind of peaceful coexistence. . . ."

Southern California twenty thousand years ago. "The Los Angeles Basin, most of the western United States. . . [was] once another Africa." Illustration: *Trapped in Time,* by Mark Hallett

The Waliangulu elephant hunter Abakuna Tise drawing a longbow. (*Mohamed Amin*)

Abakuna Gumundi. (*Ian Parker*)

Galo-galo Kafonde. (*Ian Parker*)

David Sheldrick booking Waliangulu prisoners at the end of the Anti-Poaching Campaign. Tsavo East, 1959. (*The David Sheldrick Wildlife Trust*)

Waliangulu poachers celebrating a big kill, 1957. (*Mohamed Amin*)

In the shadow of Mt. Kilimanjaro, 1988. (*Peter Beard*)

THE SHADOW OF KILIMANJARO

"In 1989 I spent three weeks in Tsavo, trying to measure the effect of poaching on family structures, and the results were fairly grim. Here in Tsavo East there were hardly any elephants over forty years old, and only a third of the family groups I surveyed were still intact. I found groups that were composed entirely of orphans. In Tsavo West it was even worse."

"It was open season," Iain adds. "Three elephants a day in greater Tsavo. I was told I had to stop my walking safaris because National Parks could no longer guarantee my safety. Personally, I think it had more to do with the fact we might have seen more than we should have."

"What about Bill?" I ask. "Wasn't he still warden in Tsavo West?"

"By '81 he'd been made an adviser for both parks," Danny says. "After that he made efforts to capture poachers, but he had no real authority, no law enforcement to back him. As for the corruption, all he could do was file reports."

To understand how poaching escalated to these levels it is necessary to go back thirty years earlier and examine what happened to the elephant populations in the greater Tsavo ecosystem in the intervening years. Less than a year after it was chartered, the Tsavo National Park was divided into two separate but contiguous sections: Tsavo West and Tsavo East. The pharmacist who had been the initial warden returned to Nairobi, and each of the two new parks received its own warden. A very bush-seasoned former hunting guide, David Sheldrick, became the first warden of Tsavo East, and the young Bill Woodley was promoted to be Sheldrick's assistant warden.

Other than two years that Bill was away in the army, he and Sheldrick spent the next ten years pursuing the native bow-hunting poachers, and this effort culminated in what became known as the Anti-Poaching Campaign that started in 1955 and finished in 1958, by which time the majority of the bow hunters had been arrested and jailed. As soon as the bow hunters were contained, the elephant began to move back into Tsavo, and in 1957 Sheldrick noticed that the elephant were beginning to uproot the *Commifora* that was then the dominant bush in the park. There was a drought in 1960 and 1961 that killed hundreds of rhinoceros in Tsavo, and left the elephant emaciated, but it didn't slow their destruction of the *Commifora* woodland, and the lack of water left only dry naked ground between the bare dead branches of the uprooted bushes.

Even more perplexing, the elephant would commonly knock the *Commifora* over without bothering even to eat it. It was as though they had some other agenda pushing them to alter their landscape. (If this were the case, no one then, or now, understands what motivated them to do this; it is also interesting to note that elephant and people are perhaps the only two animals on the planet with this capacity to alter so substantially their environment.) Sheldrick, alarmed by these changes in the Tsavo habitat, welcomed scientists and veterinarians who came to study the problem. Everyone agreed that if Tsavo were to be saved from becoming a bleak dustbowl, the number of elephant in the park would have to reduced. Sheldrick then embraced a plan to cull the herds: to reduce the elephant population by shooting them. (Daphne noted in *Tsavo Story* that David was chagrined by the irony that he, Bill, and the others had made such an effort to prevent the bow hunters from shooting elephant, only to end up ordering "professional hunters" to do the same thing.)

Before the culling plan could be realized, however, the rains returned to Tsavo with such force that the Galana broke its bank and swept away much of the riverine foliage. At first Sheldrick was afraid this was yet another cataclysm in what was becoming an apocalyptic string of disasters, but then the rains broke and suddenly Tsavo transformed. "Being faced with the possibility of a desert," Daphne wrote in *Tsavo Story,* "he [Sheldrick] had pressed for urgent measures to reduce the elephant population at the time of drought, but he now harbored serious doubts about the wisdom of such a step in view of the vegetational trends that had followed the floods. Instead of desert, he [saw] the amazing recovery of those formerly devastated areas, with large parts of former bushcountry colonized by perennial grasses."

As Tsavo blossomed with grasses that had never previously grown there in any abundance, Sheldrick began to wonder if perhaps the elephant's destruction of the *Commifora* was part of a natural cycle that no one understood. If that was the case, then it followed that the wiser policy was to let nature run it course. Sheldrick reversed his position on culling, but instead of being the end of the controversy, it was only the beginning.

The elephant population continued to increase. A census in 1961 estimated the population to be six thousand; a census in 1968 estimated it was forty thousand. Even though a substantial part of this increase was likely due to improved census techniques, there was no doubt the elephant were increasing rapidly. Not only were the elephant continuing to uproot the *Commifora,* they were now gouging out and destroying baobab trees, some of which were hundreds if not thousands of years old.

In 1966 the Ford Foundation funded a study to research the problem and propose a solution. A National Parks committee recommended culling three hundred elephant from an area in Tsavo East along the Galana River, and to conduct postmortems in order to establish baseline measurements for a complete survey of the overall elephant population. Ian Parker, the former game warden, was hired to carry out the culling, and Dr. Richard Laws, a well-respected large-mammal ecologist, was hired to analyze the data, which revealed information about the elephant's population structure with an accuracy that would have been very difficult to obtain by observation alone. When the scientists finished their measurements, the meat was dried for sale, the feet converted to stools or wastebaskets, the skin for handbags, and the ivory sold to coastal merchants.

As the study progressed Laws reported that he had identified between eight and ten different population groups of elephant in Tsavo East, and that if the committee wanted his scientific survey to extend the baseline measurements to cover the entire Tsavo elephant population, they would have to cull an additional twenty-one hundred elephant. This gave the trustees that administered the national parks reason to pause, and it also was the beginning of differences between Dick Laws and David Sheldrick that soon broke into open feud.

Whatever goodwill the two men initially enjoyed now vaporized. "They clashed on a number of issues," Ian Parker wrote in his book *Ivory Crisis,* "the most fundamental of which, to my mind, was that Tsavo East had no clear-cut management plan Hitherto its direction and goals had largely come from David's head, very much by intuition. This had worked adequately up to that point, but was no longer possible if worthwhile long-term research plans were to be laid." Sheldrick's very strong intuition was that culling was wrong, and Laws's position was that the national park was an artificial, man-made creation that had to be man-managed. What became known as the Tsavo Controversy captured the headlines of the Nairobi press, and worldwide it became one of the most heated and contentious arguments in the history of wildlife conservation. "In the heat of the feelings that were generated," Parker wrote, "many things were said that I am sure both sides later regretted. However, when it was suggested that Dick Laws advocated cropping in order to put business my way, in return for handsome kick-backs for doing so, I dropped all attempts to mend fences . . . and the affair ended unsatisfactorily with Dick resigning."

Meanwhile the elephant continued to increase, and Tsavo continued to convert from woodland to open savanna. "The Tsavo elephant problem is a classic example of indecision, vacillation, and mismanagement," Laws wrote after he resigned. "We can expect a series of dry years shortly, when the Tsavo problem will again assume manifest crises proportions." In this he was presciently accurate because two years later, in 1971, the drought hit and the die-off began.

Only two inches fell during the normal season of the long rains in the first half of 1970. By the end of the year the first elephant calves, unable to keep up with their parents, began to die or were taken by lion as they straggled behind the herd. There was a temporary reprieve when the short rains appeared at the end of the year, but in 1971 the long rains again failed, and now entire matriarchal groups lay under the skimpy shade of a single tree, unable to stand, until, one by one, they died.

In a drought elephant don't die of thirst but rather of malnutrition. There is too little protein in what browse and grass is available to support them. It is also the females and young elephant that die first; the males, unencumbered with young to care for, range more widely and find more food. "Family units disintegrated," Daphne Sheldrick wrote. "Cows took to wandering alone, abandoned and orphaned calves shuffled aimlessly about, making no attempt to join up with other elephants, but standing instead listlessly under trees." Daphne found one emaciated youngster "standing disconsolately beside the body of her mother" that was rescued and taken to her orphanage in Voi. "Happily, this little elephant, called Sobo after the place where she was found, was one of those that had a happy ending."

Saving a few individuals, of course, wasn't enough to change the course of the famine. There were also many "I told you so's" directed at David Sheldrick from those who had supported Dick Laws's position; if the culling had been carried out as proposed, they said, there wouldn't have been a die-off. Finger pointing did nothing, however, to save the elephant. Sheldrick estimated that nine thousand died in the drought; another biologist estimated the number was forty thousand. Ian Parker thinks that in the greater Tsavo ecosystem the number was about fifteen thousand.

Trying to imagine fifteen thousand dead elephant is much more difficult than the challenge I had imagining the one thousand rhinoceros that J. A. Hunter had once shot. How large a mound, or in this case a hill or even a mountain, would fifteen thousand elephant carcasses make? Trying to visualize the true reality of these elephant deaths—the bodies actually lying scattered across the Tsavo landscape—is made easier by examining the 1988 edition of *The End of the Game* because Peter Beard, who made several aerial flights over Tsavo during the drought to photograph the dead elephants (even though Sheldrick had ordered him not to), has reproduced 161 of them in a row, some arranged twelve to a page, some full page, and some as double-page spreads. "You could smell the rotting carcasses from two thousand feet," Beard says in *The Adventures and Misadventures of Peter Beard in Africa*. "Some were still dying."

❖

Elephants and rhinoceros weren't the only animals dying. To the north and west of the park, the Wakambas lost their cattle and their goats, as well as their crops, and they began to venture into the park to hunt game with their bows and arrows. What they found other than meat, however, was a treasure trove of ivory from the tusks of elephants that had died in the drought.

Word spread, and a kind of gold rush for windfall ivory started, drawing in scavengers from other tribes as well. In 1973, David Sheldrick arrested the first Somalis found within the park. They were only collecting ivory off dead carcasses, but Sheldrick still had a sense of foreboding that, it turned out, was justified. Within a year the ivory available to scavengers was gone, but the native peoples had a taste for it, and it was only a small step to go from gathering ivory off dead elephants to shooting live ones. It wasn't long before the Somalis returned, only now they came armed with AK-47s purchased across the border for as little as fifteen dollars.

David Sheldrick, however, was to miss this episode in the history of Tsavo East. In 1976 he received a surprise notice that he was being transferred to Nairobi. He had been warden of Tsavo East for twenty-seven years, and he had given the job everything he had. Some complained he ran the park as his fiefdom, but if he was a dictator, he was a ruler whose love and loyalty belonged to Tsavo. "At its height it was a show-piece park with everything meticulously kept—roads, buildings, records," Ian Parker wrote. "In a very special way it was his park not just in his eyes, but in the public's as well and to many the names Sheldrick and Tsavo were virtually synonymous."

The worst years for Tsavo were yet to come, but David Sheldrick did not witness them, even from the vantage of his new position in Nairobi. Within a year of leaving Tsavo, he was dead from heart failure. He had a family history of heart problems, but Daphne thought his death was due as well to stress from the bitter debates over culling, and also to the bitter disappointment he felt when, in the year he was transferred, the national park system was amalgamated into the country's general ministerial bureaucracy. David predicted that would be the beginning of major difficulties, and his suspicions were confirmed when, shortly after he left Tsavo, officials from the government arrived at park headquarters to retrieve the deadfall ivory he and his staff had been collecting. They carried it off, eight truckloads worth, and neither David Sheldrick nor anyone else ever learned what happened to it.

❖

In the year that he was to be transferred to Nairobi, Sheldrick estimated there were thirteen hundred poachers stealing across the border of Tsavo East to poach elephant, and nearly all of them were Somalis. (The term "Somalis" is used by Kenyans to refer to all people from the ethnic Somali tribes, many of whom actually live inside Kenya, in the block of wild country between the Tana River and the Somali border. Whether from Kenya or Somalia, they are fiercely independent and hold no allegiance either to nation or to their larger ethnic group; they are loyal only to their families and their kin groups.) The tales of these bandits' brutality are sometimes stupefying. One evening Bongo told a story about the manager of a tourist lodge on Lake Rudolf, which is far to the north and within the range that Somali bandits—the *shifta*—were known to operate.

"Dad happened to visit this lodge and he had his gun with him when he came to dinner," Bongo related. "The manager laughed and told him they had no problems with *shifta*. Only a week later the camp was raided, and the Somalis captured the manager and made him drive them away in his own vehicle, but when they ran out of fuel the bandits were furious and they skinned the poor bastard alive and rolled him in hot sand."

"Another common thing is gouging out eyes of opposing clans, and also castrating and making snuff bags for their tobacco from the scrotums."

There are of course two sides to any controversy, and in her memoir Joyce Poole has a story of a Somali poacher that at least allows a view of the world through his eyes. His name was Arrghas, and one day he shot a female elephant with a one-day-old baby, and the mother fell on the infant, killing it too. Two days later he received news that on the same day he shot the elephant, his wife and children had died when the boat they were in capsized while crossing the Tana River. He was convinced the death of the elephants and his family's tragedy were connected, and in a combination of surrender and atonement he walked across Tsavo to a town on the park boundary and turned himself in. To Joyce, Arrghas was a human face behind the other side of the war against poachers. He was also a marked man. Most of Arrghas's gang were subsequently killed by security forces in the weeks that followed his surrender, and the survivors knew that he had talked. "After our meeting," Joyce wrote in her book, "I never saw Arrghas again."

◈

Before Arrghas disappeared, he also told the authorities that in the late 1970s it had been easier to shoot elephant because some of the park authorities were assisting the poachers by sending the security forces to areas away from where the poachers were operating, and the officials would also provide vehicles to the poachers so they could transport their ivory. In exchange, the Somalis would cut the park personnel in on part of the profits.

The corruption started in 1976 when the administration of the national parks was merged with the corrupt game department and placed under the equally corrupt Ministry of Tourism. It was shortly afterward the Ministry transferred David Sheldrick to Nairobi. Daphne Sheldrick says, "David was transferred because he was too effective, and they wanted him out of the way. They gave him a nice house in Nairobi to keep him happy, and also to keep him inside the service, because they thought he was more dangerous outside."

Sheldrick wasn't the only one transferred. Two years later Bill Woodley received notice he was to go from Mountain Parks to Tsavo West. The Ministry stated the reason for the shift was that poaching was advanced in Tsavo, and that they needed someone there who could do something about it. In fact, by then, there were few elephant left in Tsavo, but in the Aberdares, where Bill still held the reins tightly, there were large numbers of rhino with large horns. Within a few years of Bill's departure, however, most of the rhino were gone, too.

Bill arrived in Kamboyo in April 1978. Bongo and his middle brother Benjamin were in boarding school in England, and Danny, who was then nine years old, was going to school in Nairobi. The family would reunite in Tsavo during school holidays, and the boys would sit in the back of the Cessna when Bill made his reconnaissance flights over the park. "We started to make a game of who could count the most carcasses," Danny recalled. "On one flight we got nineteen dead elephant and three dead rhino. We saw one elephant still alive, crawling in a circle that left a big, round mark in the ground. We saw vehicle tracks going up to several animals, their tusks chopped out."

Bill radioed his rangers, but by the time they arrived any poachers in the area were long gone. He filed a report and sent it to headquarters, in Nairobi, but he never heard back. Then he fell ill, went to London to have his esophagus and part of his stomach removed, and although he was back in Tsavo by early 1979, it was the beginning of his long string of illnesses. When a detached retina affected his eyesight and grounded him, however, he was still resolved to continue his antipoaching efforts, so he conscripted Patrick Hamilton, then an assistant warden, to fly him on his patrols.

"On many of these flights we would discover poached elephants near roads, with vehicle tracks leading to them," Patrick told me. "Tracks show very clearly from the air."

When I met him a few months after our walk, Patrick was head of investigations at Kenya Wildlife Service. He was a slightly built *mzungu* in his fifties, dressed in green trousers and a khaki shirt, and his hair was combed carefully over his pate. He spoke in pauses, and my impression was he chose his words slowly not to hide anything, but more because by speaking carefully he could relive the old days more vividly. There was nostalgia in his voice, as well as fatigue and even resignation.

"Bill and I would go back on the ground," he continued, "with a metal detector. The bullets were always British .303's. The Somalis were nearly all using semiautomatics; the only armed people in the area with .303's worked for what was then known as the Wildlife Conservation and Management Department."

Bill's efforts to do anything further were exacerbated when his payroll switched from the Kenya government to a British aid fund. Officially he was no longer a warden, but an adviser to both Tsavo West and East. While this significantly increased his salary—important to him with all three boys in boarding schools—it meant his reports to Nairobi had even less influence. Still, he was getting pointed messages from higher up that he should cease writing his reports or face deportation (he still carried a British passport).

That's not to say there were not occasional successes. During this period Bill managed to establish the rhino reserve at Ngulia and later, as the herd increased, the Free Release Area in Tsavo East. There were also several successful encounters with poachers, known to wardens and rangers as "contacts," and one of the most colorful was what Ian Parker in *The Tyranny of Freedom* described as the "Battle of Wounded Foot."

In 1981 Bill received word that a Somali gang had attacked a railway maintenance crew near the Tsavo bridge. Bill mobilized his rangers and took off in his Piper Cub to spot the gang, but by the time he arrived they were gone. Bill and the rangers tracked them for a week, but the only shot fired was when an assistant warden accidentally shot himself in the foot. Then the Somalis raided again, this time near Mtito Andei, and again from the air Bill followed their tracks to the Athi River where he spotted a group of tourists viewing wildlife. He dropped them a note out the plane's window ordering them to leave the area immediately. Meanwhile another plane, flown by a very competent African warden named Joe Kioko, joined the search, and he reported spotting the gang on the Yatta Plateau. There were thirteen of them, and they were armed.

Bill next flew low over the gang and dropped a message ordering them to surrender. The response was a volley of rifle fire. Bill circled, came back in low, and this time instead of a message he dropped a hand grenade. It missed. He circled again, adjusting his timing, and released another grenade and watched it detonate in front of the leading man, who then staggered into the bush. That was his last grenade, so he came back again firing his rifle, no easy task when you have to fly at the same time. The gang returned the fire. Bill's plane was hit twice, but Bill wounded another Somali, hitting him in the foot.

Meanwhile the rangers were closing in. They caught up and exchanged fire, but by then it was dark. The next day they again took up the chase, but the rangers and the warden leading them only caught one man, a seventeen-year-old kid who had fallen behind, and they failed to follow up on Bill's efforts to direct an ambush of the remaining gang members at a point where he knew they would cross a road in the north part of the park. The warden's response was that the Somalis were too dangerous to tangle with. (The poacher with the wounded foot was also eventually caught, but he eluded his pursuers for sixty-eight days, crawling from one hiding place to another, with no food beyond what bits of bark and roots he presumably foraged.)

The problem Bill had on this particular contact was representative of a larger malaise that had spread throughout the national park system. With the exception of Joe Kioko, most of the rangers involved in the Battle of Wounded Foot had turned in very mediocre performances. No doubt there was disenchantment in the ranks, because the rangers who were still honest knew that many of their brethren and their bosses were not. Why bother risking your life against an enemy as dangerous as the Somalis when your superiors were in cahoots with them anyway?

There were a few loyalists in the ranks. Joe Kioko was committed. Mohamed was working under Bill in these years, and he too willingly accompanied Bill on many of his antipoaching flights. But surely, I thought to myself as I learned more about these efforts, there must have been others coming up through the ranks who could carry the mantle of a Bill Woodley.

One day during our walk I asked Bongo if there any wardens now in KWS who were from the same mold as his father.

"Most definitely," he replied. "His name is Stephen Gichangi."

I fell back to join Danny so I could ask him the same question. "That would be Stephen Gichangi," Danny said. I asked Iain and he too said, "Stephen Gichangi."

I already knew the name Stephen Gichangi. At the time when we began to organize our trek Stephen was warden of Tsavo East, and Iain invited him to accompany us on that stage of our walk. The warden immediately accepted the offer, but then only three weeks before we began up Kilimanjaro, Gichangi was promoted to one of eight regional wardens in the country, and transferred to the Meru–Mt. Kenya district. This made him only three ranks down on the KWS's bureaucratic ladder from the top job of executive director, but it also precluded any time off to join us.

After our trek, when I returned to Kenya, I arranged to meet Stephen at the Naro Moru River Lodge, launching point for most climbing parties ascending Mt. Kenya. We sat on the lawn next to the trout stream that flows off the western slope of the mountain. He smiled as he talked, moving his arms and stabbing the air with a finger to make a point. His eyes were quick, and they had that sparkle common to people who enjoy what they do. He was forty-eight years old, had close-cropped salt-and-pepper hair and a gray mustache, yet he looked youthful and athletic. He was one of those people who had a need to move, and I could tell looking at him he was what the old-timers would call "a good field man."

"I grew up in this area," he said, moving his arm to indicate the country surrounding Mt. Kenya. "I had just come out of high school and one of the British teachers had told me I was too hot-tempered and pushy to become a teacher, and I needed to go into either wildlife or ranch management. He mentioned he knew Bill Woodley who was back then warden at Mountain Parks—just down the road here—and this teacher arranged to have me meet him. When I walked into his office, Bill was behind a desk scribbling a letter, and he asked me what I wanted.

" 'I want a job!'

" 'What do mean, you want a job?'

" 'Yeah, I want the sort of job you are doing.'

"So we sat down and talked and within a week I had a job helping the accountant. After another week I went back to Bill and said, 'This isn't the sort of job I want.'

" 'Well, you have to wait.'

" 'I don't want to wait.'

"So he arranged for me to work on field patrols. I came back from that and said, 'I want to be an assistant warden. I want to go to college.'

"Bill told me again I had to wait, so I wrote to the director [of Wildlife Conservation and Management] and told him I wanted to go to college. He wrote back to Bill and said, 'Who is this guy?' Bill called me back into his office and with the letter in his hand he shouted at me and said this isn't the way you do it. Then he calmed down and said he would see what he could do. Within nine months after I started to work for Bill, I was in wildlife college. Whatever I am today, it is because of Bill Woodley."

We have a sip of beer, and Stephen continues, "So I came back after two years in college and Bill says, 'Okay, now what do you want?'

" 'Now I want your job!' "

Stephen says this with an endearing mischievousness that I suspect is a characteristic that also attracted Bill Woodley. Bill was then transferred to Tsavo West, but two years later, in 1981, Stephen was promoted to assistant warden and also transferred to Tsavo West. When he arrived in Kamboyo, he greeted Bill and said, "I still want your job!" It became a running joke.

Bill was now very much Gichangi's mentor. "He was a fellow who could advise you," Stephen said. "He could see what I was, what I wanted to do, what I had to do to get there, to get his job."

Stephen laughs at himself and says, "Yeah, sure" as he waves his arm.

Then came the bad years, but Stephen had learned how to remain above the corruption that festered around him. It was not easy, however, to remain optimistic when, by 1989, three elephant a day were being taken out of Tsavo. Finally, when the Somali poachers had grown so bold they were attacking and murdering tourists (and Kenya's main source of foreign income began to wither), President Moi was forced to act. He appointed Richard Leakey director of Wildlife Conservation and Management, and the first thing Leakey did was to fire anyone on any level suspected of corruption. He called Bill up to Nairobi and told him he was now head of security for all of Tsavo. He also asked Bill who he would recommend as a new warden for Tsavo East. That was easy. Without pausing Bill said, "Stephen Gichangi."

Bill and Leakey then flew to Voi and called Gichangi into the office. Leakey handed him a letter appointing him the new warden of Tsavo East National Park. Stephen read it, looked at Bill with a big grin, and said, "So. I got your job!"

17

Poaching is not the cause of wildlife's decline, even if it is sometimes the means of it. The cause is quite simply the human population explosion which must inevitably displace wild animals.

—Alistair Graham,
Gardeners of Eden, 1973

Kenya Wildlife Service rangers attend a boot camp patterned after the training regimen that Kenya's special forces receive. They drill, learn to break down and field repair weapons, to interrogate prisoners, to survive in the desert, jungle, and mountains. They learn to shoot their weapons using live ammunition firing at targets shaped like people. They receive this training in large part because of the influence of one man, Richard Leakey.

The trajectory of Leakey's career has been, in some ways, Churchillian. Like Churchill, Leakey's moment in history was the result of a confluence of needs of the times matching the abilities of the man, and like Churchill, Leakey rose to the challenge with unbridled relish.

Leakey is a white Kenyan citizen who considers himself as African as any of his black countrymen. He was born at the close of the Second World War, and split his youth between a British-style Nairobi boarding school and the field camps of his famous parents—physical anthropologists Louis and Mary Leakey—looking for fossil remains of early man. "He never did things young people do," his brother told a journalist writing a profile for *Outside* magazine on Richard. "At seventeen he was an old man, smoking his pipe."

By the late 1960s, with a grant from *National Geographic,* Leakey was organizing his own excavations, and soon he made his first major discovery, a nearly two-million-year-old hominid skull. Seven books followed, international lecture tours, and, in 1977, the cover of *Time.*

In the 1980s Leakey ran Kenya's National Museum and, more importantly for his future, he was also chairman of the nonprofit and highly regarded East African Wildlife Society. Because of its international esteem, EAWS was perhaps the only organization capable of blowing the horn on the internal corruption within the Wildlife Conservation and Management Department that by the mid-1980s was becoming more and more evident to the mavens of African conservation. Curiously, and seemingly out of character, Leakey hesitated to roil the waters. Another key player in EAWS, a white Tanzanian-born field biologist named David Western, quit the organization in protest. Finally, in September of 1988, Leakey made a move, challenging the minister of Tourism and Wildlife, George Muhoho, to expose the truth. "Tell us how, last week, people in Tsavo were cutting off elephant heads with mechanized chain saws and loading the tusks into a car and driving across the park that has gates all around it?" Leakey said in a press interview. Muhoho countered that Leakey's attitude was "cheeky white mentality."

That was a mistake, and Muhoho incurred the indignation of whites and blacks alike. It also brought the flap to the attention of Moi, whose patience with the public airing of official collusion with ivory poachers was wearing thin, and whose concern with Somali poachers, who were becoming a threat to national security, was increasing. A month later Moi issued a directive to the Wildlife Department, as well as to the army, to shoot to kill anyone caught in the act of poaching. The army sent a special unit to Tsavo and the neighboring Galana Ranch. But Leakey kept up his assault in the press.

At that point Moi was fed up with the tirades and decided if Richard Leakey had such loud opinions, he may as well make him the director. Leakey took over the Wildlife Conservation and Management Department in April 1989, and in an early press conference said, "It'd be my hope that in the coming weeks the press will not ask to film dead elephants, but will have the opportunity to film dead poachers." He met with the senior staff of the Wildlife Department and told them, "I know seventy-five percent of you are crooks and poachers. You are all going." In addition to sacking the corrupt element, Leakey realized that to remain legitimate the management of national parks and game lands needed to be returned to its earlier status as a quasi-independent organization. With Moi's support he rechartered the department as the Kenya Wildlife Service, run by its own board, and most important, its own budget. Leakey next went shopping for international support, and soon won a World Bank grant, followed by pledges from several major Western nations, and additional millions from private donations. Leakey had the money, the authority, the power, and things changed fast. New recruits were trained, salaries were paid on time, new uniforms were issued. Most important, Leakey procured large numbers of modern semiautomatic assault rifles, the latest night-vision goggles, and for Tsavo, two Hughes 500 helicopter gunships each capable of firing two thousand rounds a minute. The war was on.

◈

In Tsavo East Stephen Gichangi cleaned house. "It was a critical time," he told me. "I had an idea who I could trust and who I couldn't, and I knew I had Leakey and Bill behind me. I told the ones I could not trust, 'Go on, get out of here. You are not Tsavo material.' To the ones I could trust I said, 'If you want to be Tsavo material, you are on your job twenty-four hours. Any time of day or night, you are ready. If you're not, you're out.' "

Both Patrick Hamilton and Joe Kioko were shifted to flying antipoaching patrols in their small planes. Bongo, who had been working as a safari guide for Ker and Downy, was also a pilot, and he was recruited to fly as well.

"Bongo was in the northern area," Hamilton told me, "when he spotted a whole bandit camp, guys in their cots covered with mosquito netting, morning fire going, they had their pants down. I arrived a short while later with Danny in the back spotting for me. We circled, keeping an eye on them, until the helicopter gunships arrived."

"There were fifteen, maybe twenty poachers," Danny said, when he told me this story. "Patrick and I would come in with our Super Cub at two hundred to three hundred feet, and circle, me keeping an eye out for any movement, calling in the gunships when I spotted something and they would fire their two thousand rounds. The poachers would lie as still as possible, but the gunships reloaded and came in three times. There were eight thousand rounds fired, and then two sections of ground troops arrived. We came in very low, and behind a bush I saw two poachers come out and aim at us and fire. We directed the ground troops in, and as we came around again I saw them scatter, then one slump down, and I said to Patrick, 'He's been hit.' "

The remaining poachers fled, carrying their wounded. The toll: one ranger killed, five poachers dead, and an unknown number injured, some of whom, they learned from informants, died later. "The next day Leakey was in Voi," Hamilton said, "and flew in by helicopter to the scene of the contact. That became a pattern: He was there after nearly every contact, sometimes within two hours, and the effect on our morale was amazing. Finally we had someone who cared."

They also had someone who knew the value of the press. Four months after he was appointed director, Leakey staged a made-for-the-press event when, standing at the president's side, and with video cameras humming, he watched Moi set fire to a stack of confiscated elephant tusks eighteen feet high, a mountain of ivory that represented eighteen hundred dead animals and dramatized very visually what was at stake in the war on poaching. Leakey also got lucky: Three months later the Convention on International Trade in Endangered Species (CITES) issued a worldwide ban on the sale and trade of ivory. While Leakey had certainly advanced the effort to win the ban by popularizing in the press Kenya's anti-ivory position—most dramatically when he and Moi burned the ivory—the ban was arguably more the culmination of a long struggle by international conservationists and some of Kenya's wildlife experts, including David Western, who felt Leakey nevertheless enjoyed more credit for the ban than was his due. Regardless of who deserved the accolades, the ban had an enormous impact on the antipoaching war as the price of ivory went from six thousand dollars a kilo in 1988 to ten dollars a kilo by the end of 1993.

By the end of 1993 the number of elephant poached in Kenya had dropped from over three thousand a year in the late 1980s to perhaps forty or fifty animals a year. Equally important, gate receipts tripled in the more popular national parks. The elephant population in Tsavo stabilized and started to climb from the low point of less than five thousand animals, although because of the eighteen-month gestation for elephants, and the three- to four-year-long weaning period, the population could grow at only about four percent per year. Still, it was a remarkable turn-around in only four years from the low point in 1988 when experts predicted, at the rate of decline the elephant of Kenya as well as other countries in Africa then suffered, the population would pass beyond the point of recovery by 1995, and would be extinct throughout the continent by 2015.

The war was won, but Leakey had not achieved victory without incurring enemies. His foremost nemesis was a Masai politician, William Ntimama, who had risen to power as chairman of the Narok County Council, a position that would have been obscure if it hadn't included oversight of gate receipts at the Masai Mara reserve, the vast acacia-studded grassland that is the Kenyan extension of the Serengeti, as well as one of the most popular tourist destinations in the country. Because it occupies the heartland of the Masai nation, the Mara was never included in the national park system—which would not have allowed any human occupation—and was instead set aside as a national game reserve. That meant gate receipts went to the county council and to Ntimama, who used a portion of the money to fund a web of underlings and cronies in a system of favoritism common in African politics. (While the Narok County Council doesn't release figures, it is possible to estimate how much they pull in. In 1994 there were 227,000 visitors to the Masai Mara, and most of them stayed at least two or three days, if not longer, and the Council charges visitors twenty-seven dollars a day.) Ntimama had even won from Moi, mindful himself of the need to patronize Kenya's varied tribes, a cabinet position as minister of Local Government.

Assuming he had Moi's support, Leakey, soon after taking office, began lobbying to have KWS take over management of the Masai Mara. Predictably, this did not go down well with Ntimama. According to the *Outside* profile, at a public appearance with Moi, when Leakey found himself standing next to Ntimama, he repeated his intentions. Ntimama leaned over and told Leakey, "The British couldn't control the Mara, and it won't happen now." Leakey replied, "Bill, if you don't agree, I'm going to ask the President to sack you."

Leakey was playing with fire. Kenya politics, like that in most of the African continent, or any place in the world controlled by influence, money, patronage, and power, is potentially very dangerous. In 1990 Kenya's foreign minister, who had threatened to go public with evidence of corruption, was found murdered. A year later, the opposition candidate for president was detained until his health gave out, and although he survived he is now permanently disabled, his spirit is broken, and he remains retired from public life.

◈

Today Richard Leakey lives on a fifty-acre estate in the Ngong Hills, on the outskirts of Nairobi, overlooking the Rift Valley. He has bushy V-eyebrows,

and a widow's peak splits his receding hairline. He favors khaki shirts with
shoulder lapels like the ones worn by safari guides. He likes to walk around
his property, where he finds solace from his work in town helping organize
a new political party that is in opposition to Moi's government (as I finished
this book, he had just won a seat in Parliament). But today he walks with a
noticeable waddle, the result of having both legs amputated below the
knees following the crash of his small plane shortly after takeoff, in June
1993. While it appeared to be an accident, there was immediate speculation
in the press as to why his engine had suddenly quit.

"If you are going to make allegations of foul play," he told me by tele-
phone, "you have to have some evidence. Although there were, clearly,
people gunning for me, and assassination was well within their powers, I
have nothing to this date that is concrete. You can either take the position
there was fifty percent chance it was sabotage, or fifty percent chance it
wasn't. Looking back on it now, however, I am slightly less sanguine than I
was that there was no interference. But I don't want to start a witch hunt,
and I don't want to set myself up as a martyr."

"Knowing what was going on, the crash certainly didn't surprise me,"
Joyce Poole said when I asked what she thought. "I know Richard has tried
to convince himself it was an accident, but I also know he can't live his life
thinking that someone purposefully was trying to maim or kill him. Still, if it
was an accident, then why did the attacks on him start even before he recovered?"

Joyce referred to a series of press releases Ntimama circulated while
Leakey was recovering that claimed, among other charges, Leakey cared
more for wild animals than he did for people. Ntimama also cajoled leaders
of other county councils to lobby Moi to withdraw support for Leakey, and
then he arranged the initiation of an official investigation of KWS's policies
and practices. Leakey tried to fight back. He returned from London in a
wheelchair in October, had to go back to London for further treatment, then
was home again in November "on my walking sticks," he said. For a while
Leakey thought he had Moi's support. The president honored his request to
be freed from fiscal oversight by the Ministry of Tourism. Then suddenly
Moi reversed himself, then later ordered Leakey to turn over KWS's armed
rangers to administration under the Kenya police. Leakey knew this was the
end, and in March 1994, he resigned. A week later Moi appointed the new
director, David Western.

❖ 18 ❖

Everybody loves conservation and wilderness—but just try to save some
of it—really save it! Unanimity vanishes.

—David Brower,
For Earth's Sake, 1990

Today we decide to stay on the south bank so that at eleven o'clock we can
be on the road when one of Iain's vehicles is scheduled to pick us up and
take us to the dirt airstrip at Sala, the eastern gate of the park, where we plan
to rendezvous at noon with David Western, the present director of KWS,
who is arriving in his small Cessna so that I can interview him for this video
we are making. We leave the road to shortcut a bend. I'm behind Joyce who
began the morning with a noticeable limp, but now I see she has walked it
out. There are a number of sizable blisters on her feet, acquired yesterday
when she walked thirty kilometers in triple-digit temperatures with no pre-
conditioning. She hasn't complained, however, nor did she accept our offer
this morning to ride with the vehicles to our next campsite.

The sky holds the usual assortment of fair-weather cumulus as well as the
promise of 110 degree temperatures by mid-afternoon. I see a gray-headed
kingfisher land on the amputated terminus of a dead doum trunk, and I stop
to view him through my binoculars. With its chestnut breast and scintillating blue wings and tail, this kingfisher is common in the riparian habitats of
the *Commifora* thornbush zone, and we have seen it several times on our
trek. There are eleven species of kingfishers found in Kenya, and most of

them are brilliantly colored; the same is true for the variety of kingfishers found across Asia. In the Americas, however, we only have six of the eighty-seven species known worldwide, four of which are distributed widely from the jungles of Mexico south through the Amazon, while the other two are found in more temperate areas. The belted kingfisher is the one we see most frequently across the United States, while the ringed kingfisher, with similar markings but larger in size, can be seen from southern Texas all the way to the southern extreme of Tierra del Fuego.

One of the joys I take from watching birds is the increase in the awareness it brings me of whatever landscape or habitat I am traveling in. My interest in bird-watching started when my mother gave me an Audubon's bird identification book for my twenty-seventh birthday. I lived in a tiny studio in the hills above Malibu, and there was a honeysuckle vine out the window in front of my desk that was frequented by what I identified, using the book, as Anna's hummingbird. "When displaying the male climbs high in the air and plummets rapidly earthward, giving an explosive 'peep!' as he levels off just above the ground," the book told me. "This sound issues from the specialized narrow tail feathers spread out during descent."

A few days later I was out working on my old rusted pea-green Fiat when I looked up to wipe my brow and my eye went to a hummingbird flying straight up. At the apogee of its ascent it paused, weightless, then began its dive, straight down, gaining speed until it swept up in a tight arc and made a loud "peep!" It was just how my book had described it. That wasn't, however, what turned me into a bird-watcher. I put my head back under the hood of my car, and a few seconds later I heard another "explosive peep." I looked up, but there was no hummingbird in sight: This peep had come from somewhere down the street. I listened carefully. Across the barranca there was another peep, up the road another. Over the chaparral hills above Malibu, male Anna's hummingbirds were making their mating peeps, and they had been making them all spring, and all that time their peeps had been falling on my ears which, until then, had been very deaf.

One more reason I enjoy watching birds is because they invoke memories. When I see a ringed kingfisher, for example, I recall a sea kayaking and climbing trip in the archipelago of islands and fiords just north of the Straits of Magellan, when we were pinned on an uninhabited peninsula for a week by a storm, and a ringed kingfisher visited us every hour or two for the entire week, always landing on the same stump of a dead beech tree, always looking at us like a cocky politician with a puffed chest who should have been smoking a cigar.

Now I watch the gray-headed kingfisher perched atop the doum stump, and I recall the first time I saw this bird. I was in this same area, on that trip with my wife and our three children as well as Iain's kids and another family of friends. Together in the group we had five girls and four boys, and we were on a foot safari that our kids recall frequently as the greatest adventure of their lives. (In the last presidential election, as the television newscaster announced which states Clinton had just won, our youngest son asked, "Has he won Africa yet?")

The kingfisher grows increasingly nervous because I have been standing here for so long watching him, and he flies off. Lokiyor has stayed with me, to make sure I am with someone who is armed. I lower my binoculars and jogtrot to catch the others while Lokiyor, making one walking stride for every two of my running hops, follows.

❖

We are walking on the edge of the saltbush that parallels the river and ahead we can see a group of elephant. We alter course to give them room, but they sense us and run through the bush toward the river. "We're still downwind," I say. "Do you think they smelled us?"

"They probably sensed our footsteps," Joyce says, spreading her hands behind her ears to imitate their sense of hearing. "But they could have smelled us. One time I was out with a film crew and I couldn't understand why the elephants were so nervous around us. I asked the crew if by chance they had recently had any Masai in the car, and they said yes, the day before. In Amboseli the elephants have only one predator to fear, the Masai with spears."

A Masai *morani* will spear an elephant most commonly as a right of passage to prove his manhood. More and more, however, as the Masai continue to convert from pastoralism to agriculture, they are spearing elephant who invade their fields, both to chase off the animals and as a form of protest to the government, who they expect to control these animals.

Problem Animal Control was historically the responsibility of the Game Department, which had jurisdiction over wildlife outside the national parks where the conflicts between people and animals occurred. In 1976, when the Game Department was merged with National Parks to form the Wildlife Conservation and Management Department, the Problem Animal Control unit suffered the same inefficiencies as the rest of wildlife management. When Richard Leakey took over in 1989, one of his early efforts was not only to improve the efficiency of the PAC unit, but to remake it into a program whose policies were based on scientific knowledge. In particular he needed someone who knew elephants, and he turned to Joyce Poole.

Joyce accepted the position, but with apprehension. She told Leakey she had never worked for anyone before, and he laughed and said he hadn't either. He needed someone not only who knew elephants, he told her, but who knew Kenya and who could inspire young Kenyans. Joyce quickly learned she had to see issues from people's points of view as well as elephants'. This meant hard decisions had to be made. Very hard decisions.

In the late 1980s, the elephants had been too terrorized to venture beyond whatever safe havens they could find. By 1992, however, Joyce was receiving messages from every end of the country about elephants raiding *shambas,* destroying houses, and trampling people to death. There was an uproar in the press with cries that something had to be done. Why weren't more elephants being shot? The reason was that the elephants had been so brutally shot down throughout the 1980s that in 1990 and 1991 KWS wardens and rangers were loath to resume shooting them unless absolutely necessary. But by 1992 more had to be done. At first Joyce's group tried to build electric fences. But the elephants snapped the wires with their tusks, or picked up logs and threw them across. There was only one other recourse.

Rogue elephants had, of course, been shot for years, but Joyce concluded that in far too many cases the wrong elephants were shot, and they were being shot by people who didn't know what they were doing. "I started gathering information," Joyce told me, "such as how many bullets it was taking to shoot an elephant. It was pretty grim. In one case there were twenty-four shots into an animal that thirteen hours later was still alive. So I wanted somebody who could work with a team of men first of all to teach them how to shoot an elephant. Secondly, they would go with me to Amboseli to learn how to sex and age an elephant. I would also teach them about the social structure of elephants, and teach them which animal might be the best one to shoot when you had a group that was raiding. The man I picked to head this up was Danny."

"It must have been hard on you to order killed the one animal you have spent your adult life trying to understand and protect."

"That's what everyone assumes. But what really bothered me," she answered, "was the futility of it. It was stopgap. You shoot elephants, they run into the parks, you try to fence them in, they get too crowded, then you have to cull them. Where does it all lead?"

If Joyce had frustrations in her job, there were also rewards. One was hiring and training bright young talent for her elephant research team, and seeing them blossom. Another was her growing friendship with Leakey, who more than anything taught her, when she was faced with difficult decisions, to step back and see things in overview. But it wasn't to last. When Leakey ultimately was forced to tender his resignation, Joyce felt duty bound to honor the man who had brought her in and resign with him. It didn't make the matter any easier to take, either, when she learned that David Western was being appointed to take Leakey's place.

It is hot, there are sweat stains on our shirts, but I can feel the first breath of a breeze cooling my skin. In front of us—to the east—there is a squall line in the far distance that seems to be approaching, while behind—to the west—the gibbous moon is setting over the terminus of the great Yatta lava flow. "When the moon goes down, the clouds will advance," Danny says.

Last night at camp, when Joyce learned that today we are to rendezvous with David Western, her first reaction was to tell us she was going home today—one day early. Iain then suggested that when his vehicles picked us up at the appointed hour to take us to Sala Gate, where we are scheduled to meet Western, we could first drop Joyce off at camp, and she could spend the afternoon playing with Selengei while we conducted our interview.

That seemed to mollify Joyce, and now she is hiking with us until Iain's vehicles arrive. We make sure we stay close to the dirt road so we don't miss the rendezvous. Joyce has no trouble maintaining our fast pace, and if she has any pain from her blisters, she doesn't show it. Considering her personal history with Western, and her allegiance to Leakey, her reaction when she learned we were meeting Western today didn't come as a surprise. Her differences with him began in early 1988 when several groups of wildlife conservationists, field biologists, and political strategists were working to win approval of an ivory ban, and in other ways reverse the epidemic of poaching that was sweeping across East Africa. Neither Joyce nor Cynthia were invited to join, and they both felt snubbed. Joyce voiced her indignation, accusing the committees of being sexist, which she later regretted and realized was inappropriate, but when David Western, who was a key member of one of the most influential of these groups, came down to Amboseli to discuss the matter, she was really incensed when he told her the reason she wasn't invited to join was that her work was not relevant to elephant conservation.

Joyce vowed to show that her work was relevant to elephant conservation. A month later Joyce was invited to speak at a meeting of the East African

Wildlife Society on the innocuous subject of elephant feeding ecology. Instead she decided she would speak about her demographic calculations regarding elephants' ability to survive into the future against the current level of poaching. The timing was perfect as the row between Richard Leakey and George Muhoho had just erupted in the press. Joyce's talk was quoted in the most prominent English-language weekly in Kenya, and it brought her to the attention of Leakey, which subsequently led to her appointment to KWS, and which made her work very relevant to elephant conservation.

If Joyce had long-standing differences with Western, there was also an enmity between Leakey and Western that dated to the mid-1980s when Leakey was head of the East African Wildlife Society and Western was criticizing him for not taking a more active stance against poaching and corruption. At the time Leakey took over the old Wildlife Conservation and Management Department, Western had for years enjoyed a fair amount of influence in government policy and decisions. At first Leakey listened to him, but when he failed to follow his advice, Western was subsequently left out in the conservation cold for the next four years that Leakey ran KWS.

❖

It is now eleven A.M., the appointed hour for Iain's vehicles to show up, but there is no sign of them. We approach a group of impala, and we are very nearly on top of them when they detect us and prance away, two of them pronking in high leaps as they go. On our right we scare up a huge male waterbuck who runs and stops to look back, then continues, then stops again and stares at us. We flush from the bush next to the road a dark cinnamon dove that flies off with the speed and shape of a bullet. "The Namaqua dove," Bongo says.

It is eleven fifteen and still no vehicle. Our interview with Western is scheduled at noon, and it is nearly an hour's drive from here to Sala Gate. "It would appear that Iain's men are not very good timekeepers," Bongo says.

"Look," Iain replies, "they've a lot to do today."

"Then they should have been given priorities."

"Well, I'm sorry."

"Not to worry. It's only the director."

I'm beginning to worry myself, and Danny is also agitated. We are discussing the merits of two of us shedding our day packs, rifles, and cameras and jogging ahead to Iain's camp, probably another five or six miles, when we see a dust cloud ahead and in a moment the vehicle arrives. We load in and speed off, dropping Joyce at the new campsite, and we make it to Sala Gate at twelve oh-five. At twelve twenty-five we spot Western's plane lining up for a landing.

When he has taxied to a stop Western steps out and Mohamed clicks his boots, straightens all six feet seven inches of his lean, muscled frame, shoulders his weapon, and presents a very snappy salute. Western seems uncomfortable and returns the salute with a phlegmatic wave of his hand, and Mohamed snaps his hand down to his side. It appears that Western would not make a very good general, at least not the part that requires a military bearing. He is a handsome man, however, with sharp features, a thin mouth, and a tanned face that reflects his years in the field as a wildlife biologist. His high forehead gives him an intellectual appearance, and he wears a light blue shirt with those shoulder epaulets that are so commonly favored by people who have spent time in the bush. He is fifty-two years old and is known to acquaintances and friends by his lifelong nickname, Jonah.

Like Leakey, Western is a white African whose parents spent much of their lives in the field (his father, who ran a small business in Tanzania, was also a hunting enthusiast and volunteer game control officer), but unlike Leakey, he is a professional conservationist with a doctorate degree in zoology and ecology from the University of Nairobi, and he has spent his professional life studying relationships between wildlife and surrounding human communities. He seems to be somewhat shy, and after a round of perfunctory greetings, when it appears he is not sure what to do or say next, I suggest we drive to the river's edge, where Iain's staff is setting up lunch, and where we intend to videotape our interview.

When we reach our riverside picnic it is apparent that Kahin the cook has outperformed himself once again. This time there is a grilled eggplant ratatouille, vine ripened tomatoes with fresh basil, mozzarella, and marinated fennel in the French style.

"Where did you get this one?" I ask Kahin.

"*Gourmet* magazine. The American edition."

We move to sit on a rock outcrop at water's edge under a large river acacia that is clearly favored by the local baboons, and Bongo apologizes that the rock is covered with baboon excrement. "That's okay," Jonah says. "I've studied baboons." He sits down on some dried shit, and the rest of us follow. On first impression I am liking Dr. Western.

One of the most public differences in conservation policy between Richard Leakey and David Western has been over the issues that fall under the heading of people versus wildlife. In the early days of Leakey's tenure at

KWS, Western criticized him for what he considered a naive disregard for the needs of people who live in the wildlife areas surrounding national parks. The needs of those people is one of the first questions we address.

"Wilderness is not an African concept," Jonah says. "Where I grew up in southern Tanzania, it was more remote even than Tsavo, but there were always a few people there, no matter how vast the land, and the people never understood the concept of pure wilderness. To them, nature and people go together. So I believe we have to be compatible."

"But how can you accommodate people and wildlife when there are so many people?" I ask.

"Certainly that's a great problem. There are five times more people in Kenya now than there were at the turn of the century. But don't forget in the areas where elephants and rhinos were poached there were few if any people. To me, an even greater danger than the number of people is the attitude that wildlife is the enemy, because then it will disappear, no matter how many or how few people there are. Don't forget that in the Pleistocene period in North America only a relative handful of Amerindians knocked off the very largest mammals, and the same thing happened in Europe. On the other hand, if wildlife is seen as having a value, then I think you can have high density populations living side by side with wildlife."

Jonah added that tourism is an obvious way to create that value, and he would like to see more of Kenya's parks opened up to more types of tourism. "Kenya is getting the reputation with tourists of being crowded, but roughly six of our national parks account for ninety percent of the tourism, and if you go to Amboseli, ninety percent of the tourists are in only ten percent of the park. I would like to see more kinds of tourism, more than just riding around in minivans. You are undertaking one of the sorts of safaris which I feel we would like to encourage, but to do that we need to preserve areas for people like you who want to get back to nature, whether in a raft or on foot or on camels. Here in Tsavo that means preserving the vast area north of the Galana and limiting it only to small camps."

"And the area south of the river?"

"Who would have ever believed twenty years ago that Tsavo would have as many visitors as it does today?" (Tsavo now has approximately two hundred thousand visitors a year, but nearly all of them are tourists from the coastal resorts of Malindi and Mombasa who come during the two dry seasons for day visits, driving the road from Voi to the Galana River; the rest of the eight thousand square miles is comparatively empty.) "So we have to manage that, because Tsavo does not lend itself to high density tourism, and the real threat is 'touristifying' the place. The only way we can prevent that is by allocating different parts of the park for different uses. As a conservationist that is not the way I'd prefer to go, but realistically I think it's the only alternative.

"The other problem I see is containing the encroachment of agriculture in the fertile areas on the south side of the park [this would include the area around Rombo, where we visited the farm fields damaged by marauding elephant]. I think someday we're going to have a hard-edge boundary between settlement and park, including fencing. I would like to confine that to the south, and leave the northern and eastern plains open."

This is so the elephant can continue their seasonal migrations, and I now ask Jonah what he thinks will happen in Tsavo if the elephant continue to increase.

"Tsavo for the next ten or fifteen years shouldn't have a problem. The elephant population is now back up to about eight thousand, so there's still room, particularly north of the Galana, and the elephant there are just beginning to resume their migrations. So we have time. Time in which to look for alternatives. In the long run I don't know what those solutions might be; I don't suppose anyone does. But it will probably reach a point where we'll have to limit the population. Whether it's through fertility control, whether it's through relocation, as we've begun to do [in other parks and adjoining areas], it doesn't matter. But you have to find a balance."

"Do you foresee culling in the future?" Iain asks.

"I would prefer to avoid culling. On the other hand, you have to ask how these elephant are going to regulate their numbers? In the past there was always some human interference [he is referring to the native bow hunters], and what worries me about the parks is that, to a great extent, we have separated the humans from the wild animals and I think we are just beginning to realize the consequences of that."

❖

We finish the interview, thank Jonah, and he takes off in his Cessna. Back in camp I walk down to the river to bathe, first throwing a rock to scare away crocodile. I lie back in the water and relax, but not too relaxed, as I still find myself scanning for any bow waves. Then I join Joyce and Selengei, who sit in camp chairs overlooking the river in front of a fire the staff has kindled. Afternoon light reflects off the water in crepuscular hues, and from the opposite bank I hear the plaintive call of the spotted thick-knee, a solitary wader whose voice is heard at sunset and at night.

"So how did it go with Jonah?" she asks.

"It was okay. I avoided the hot topics about the feuds with Leakey."

Since the interview I have been considering these contentions between Western and so many others of Kenya's conservationists. My own impression of Jonah Western is that he is a very capable and dedicated conservationist, but he's awkward around people. Also, according to many in Nairobi, he has a secretive manner that leads people to conclude he has ulterior motives. Whether or not this is true, I did learn, when I returned to Africa and interviewed several local conservationists, that Western has earned very mixed reviews:

"He has a problem building up trust."

"He's compassionate, but embroiled in an impossible situation."

"You never quite know what he's up to when he's playing politics."

"He's got a higher IQ than most of us."

"He's a scientist and he thinks like a scientist and that's the problem."

"Known Jonah for years, but don't really know him at all."

No doubt differences in style and personality have added to the feuds between Western and other conservationists, including Leakey. In some ways, Western and Leakey seem to be two mature bull elephant locking tusks in a fight over the same turf. There is substance, however, to their differing opinions on Western's focus of incorporating marginalized people into wildlife and wildland schemes. This is called Community Based Conservation (CBC to the cognoscenti), and it is motivated by the fact that national parks and other protected areas compromise only about four percent of the Earth's land surface. David Western, and other advocates of CBC, believe that to have any expectation of preserving the Earth's biodiversity, policies must be developed that address the other ninety-six percent, and the only realistic way to do that, they argue, is to include participation of local communities in conservation policies that bring them economic benefit. A recent convening of scientists, tribal leaders, government officials, and activists from twenty-one different countries, who all shared the CBC philosophy, agreed as a platform position that most parks and protected areas that have been chartered in the last hundred years have been exclusionary of local people and therefore "implicitly misanthropic"; they further agreed as a group that they had two overarching objectives: "the conservation of biological diversity and the alleviation of human poverty in rural landscapes."

David Western is regarded as one of the worldwide leaders—if not *the* worldwide leader—of this movement, and since taking over KWS he has worked to implement his ideas into real-life policies. Since much of his research in his early years was spent in Amboseli, where he came to know the

Masai cattle herders nearly as well as the animals he was studying, he has worked there to include the Masai tribes that live outside the park's boundaries in some of its policies, and (theoretically) its benefits.

"It is all very well to share revenue of a park with its neighbors when the income is good," Richard Leakey said in a speech in the United States a year after he resigned, "but what happens if there is an outbreak of typhoid, or civil war, or any of the other things which keeps the tourists away? The animals will still be there. Their neighbors will still be there. But the money won't be coming in."

Leakey (and many of Kenya's other conservationists) also takes exception to David Western's claim that seventy percent of Kenya's wildlife lives (permanently or part time) outside of the national parks. "The statistic is twenty years old," Leakey told me. "Personally I think now it's more the reverse— seventy percent in the parks and thirty outside—in particular when you consider only the animals that tourists come to see." It is Leakey's position that the national parks are more important for the long-term survival of those animals than the surrounding lands, and this is where his views separate most sharply from Western's. Describing his differences with Western when he ran KWS, Leakey said, "It was clear to me that the national parks, which existed in law and were respected in the country as impenetrable boundaries, should be our first priority. I did not see them, as I've been accused, as ecological islands, either, but as legal entities that could, with proper management, be retained for the public interest indefinitely, and because tourism in those areas could be made ultimately to pay for the parks, the parks could have ensured the survival of most of Kenya's biodiversity, at least on a species-count basis.

"Jonah's view was that the parks were relatively unimportant," Leakey continued, "and what was most important was the people around the parks, and that they needed to be made beneficiaries of their own wildlife outside the parks, so he created this concept of parks beyond parks. The problem with parks beyond parks is that you are then talking not about eight percent of the country [the percentage of Kenya set aside as parks or reserves], but about the ninety-two percent that belongs to the people, and what those people want from those areas is money, and what they don't want is to commit that money to conservation."

Jonah argues back that these people and communities will commit that money if they can see a return from that commitment, either through revenue sharing of gate receipts and lodge earnings, or returns from the so-called consumptive use of wildlife that includes sale of meat, hides, and ivory, and also licenses and fees paid by hunters. To support his arguments, Western and other advocates of CBC cite a successful program in Zimbabwe called CAMPFIRE where local peoples manage the wildlife on their tribal lands, and earn income not only from tourism but also big-game hunting. Such talk has, not surprisingly, loosed an outpouring of criticism among Kenya's conservationists. During my return visit six months after our trek, Daphne Sheldrick had just released a newsletter from the David Sheldrick Trust critical of Western's performance at KWS.

"A distinct bias towards 'the community,'" the newsletter read, "often compromising the interests of wildlife, seemed a contradiction. . . . 'Parks beyond Parks' . . . also seemed a contradiction, interpreted by many as ending up with 'No Parks at All.'"

A few days after the newsletter mailed, Pete Jenkins was at Daphne's house (positioned within the boundaries of Nairobi National Park, next to the animal orphanage she founded), and he told her that while he agreed with most of her points, he felt her attack on Western was personal, unnecessarily confrontational, and consequently counterproductive. She fired back that she was the only one with the guts to stand up and speak out, and further, by doing so, she was putting her house at jeopardy. She told Pete that if he didn't agree he should resign his position on the board of the trust. Pete said he would do just that, and left.

Daphne walked to her daughter Jill's house, which is in the same compound, and told her what happened. Daphne is a strong woman, but she couldn't hold back her tears. These arguments over both policy and philosophy between Kenya's conservationists are as passionate as they are bitter, and because they are also between a group of people who have relationships often going back to childhood, they are often painful. In this case Daphne was crying on the shoulder of Jill, who was her daughter by her first marriage to Bill Woodley, over the defection of Pete, who not only was one of her first husband's close friends, but also her brother.

"I wish Bill were still around," Daphne said, wiping a tear. "He's the only one who could see things clearly."

◈

During my return visit there was another controversy that had cracked into a widening schism in the always-shifting plate tectonics of Kenya conservation. Kuki Gallman, owner of the extensive and high-profile Ol Ari Nyiro game ranch on West Laikipia, and other big upcountry landowners, had come out publicly, under the banner of wildlife paying its own way, for the renewal of big-game hunting. They argued that before the ban was imposed in 1977, big-game hunting had been a major source of foreign revenue for the country. (Hunting brought in twenty million dollars in 1977, according to government statistics—close to eighty million in today's dollars—and about fifteen percent of that had been retained by private landowners where most of the hunting was staged.)

David Western announced in the press his support of the proposal. The controversy flared hotter when someone then leaked information to the newspapers that Gallman and the others, to win approval, had gone around Parliament and directly to the president. The antihunting contingent let go with all guns blasting.

"The current push to reintroduce hunting is entirely initiated by 'well-connected' wealthy whites."

"The likelihood of communities benefiting from hunting is doubtful."

"In a state of bad governance, none of the required regulations are applied in favor of the resource but rather in favor of the quick buck."

"The Kenyan hunting debate is characterized by two things," an article in the Kenya wildlife and conservation publication *Swara* said, "its importance to Kenya's declining wildlife populations and the acrimony it engenders between people who ostensibly share a common goal. With so many other ecological debates, it has become an issue of personality, of widespread mistrust and bitter accusations."

The debate grew so heated the ranchers had to back down, but no one in Nairobi's conservation circles believed the topic had gone away for very long. As I followed this debate I started comparing it to other issues that had divided conservationists in the past, like the arguments over culling. I started to see that flowing like a deep current under these issues was the greater question of whether or not we humans have a moral right to take the lives of these animals, especially elephant. ("Shooting an elephant is not the same as shooting a buffalo," Richard Leakey had said.) I also recognized this same current had flowed thirty years earlier under the arguments of whether or not the elephants in Tsavo should be culled. ("Killing animals to lessen densities is like poking a finger into the sub-conscious hive of sentimentalism," Alistair Graham had written.) It was there ninety years earlier when Theodore Roosevelt wrote that "in order to preserve the wildlife of the wilderness at all, some middle ground must be found between brutal and senseless slaughter and the unhealthy sentimentalism which would just as surely defeat its own end."

Roosevelt's sentimentalists are the ones labeled today as "bunny huggers" by those who argue that emotional regard for individual animals
should not cloud decisions or options, such as culling and hunting, that
otherwise may favor the long-term survival of a species. At a recent CITES
debate that considered, among other issues, the repeal of the ivory ban so
the profits from elephant hunting could be returned to both the national
and community coffers in Zimbabwe, Namibia, and Botswana, Richard
Leakey made it clear what side of the fence he was on when, as he stood to
make his speech, he pulled out of his pocket a stuffed bunny and hugged it.
Daphne Sheldrick made it clear when she told me she admired researchers
like Joyce Poole and Cynthia Moss who had the courage to draw attention
to the emotional lives of animals even at the cost of being labeled by their
scientific brethren as bunny huggers. Peter Beard made it clear where he
stood when he told me there were only a few who had it figured out, and
named Alistair Graham, Richard Bell, and Ian Parker, the early proponents
of culling.

It was Ian Parker, however, who I felt had the final word when, with an
amused twinkle in his eye, he said to me, "I find conservationists a much
more intriguing topic to study than conservation."

Chui, bless his heart, has just brought me a beer from the cold box. Joyce
bounces Selengei on her knee. I think back to the juvenile male elephant we
had stopped to watch day before yesterday, and how Iain had lowered his
binoculars and said, "As long as I've seen elephants in the bush, the one
thing that always gets me is the silence around them, the ability of an animal
of that size to be able to walk with such silence."

"Yes, I know what you mean," Joyce had replied. She then lowered her
binoculars and smiled and said, "I never tire of watching elephants."

Had Jonah Western been there in Joyce's place, I am confident I would
have observed on his face the same admiration for that elephant that I saw
on Joyce's. For that matter, I would have seen the same admiration on the
face of Bill Woodley. Or David Sheldrick, or Daphne Sheldrick, or Pete
Jenkins, or Peter Beard, or Iain Douglas-Hamilton, or Ian Parker, or
Stephen Gichangi, or Richard Leakey. I suspect all these people, captivated
as I am by these lands and the great beasts that inhabit them, have more in
common than, through the passion of their convictions, they only grudg-
ingly acknowledge.

19

Hunting changed man's relation to other animals and his view of what is natural. The human notion that it is normal for animals to flee, the whole concept of animals being wild, is the result of man's habit of hunting.

—Washburn and Lancaster,
"The Evolution of Hunting," 1967

It is eleven P.M. and somewhere downriver, not far from camp, I hear a lion roar. No, two lion. It is not a roar, either, but a primordial exhaling bellow from deep in the animal's maw. It is more than just loud. It is a sound that has weight, a sound you know can come only from an animal of immense power.

The two lion continue bellowing, but they seem to be staying in one area; that is, they don't seem to be getting closer. I fall asleep only to wake again as they continue. At four A.M., from somewhere upriver, an elephant trumpets. I fall asleep again and wake at five A.M. The lion are still at it, and now from across the river comes the descending curlew call of the spotted thick-knee. I sit up and turn on my headlamp and complete my journal entry from the previous day.

After we had finished our interview with David Western and we were driving back to camp, Danny directed our vehicle off the road and through the bush to an opening a few yards from the riverbank where we all hopped out to inspect two markers made of old bricks laid on the ground in an

L-shape; here and there on some of the bricks were remnants of whitewash that presumably had covered all the bricks at one time.

"My father discovered these in the 1950s," Danny said, "Then brought me here when he was posted back to Tsavo West. They are the markers of Denys Finch Hatton's landing strip. This was the location of his hunting camp, where he brought his wealthy clients to Tsavo to look for the big tuskers. No one else knows it's here."

I finish my entry and think about the film version of *Out of Africa,* and about Denys Finch Hatton and his "aeroplane," as Karen Blixen spelled the word in her book. I recall that scene where Robert Redford takes Meryl Streep for a ride in the Gypsy Moth and they fly low over a soda lake and cause thousands of flamingos to take wing. They lean their heads out of the cockpit and see the birds flash in scintillating patterns of pink and white against blue and green. In my opinion, this is the place in the film that most closely evokes the poetic language of the book. "To Denys Finch Hatton," Karen wrote, "I owe what was, I think, the greatest, the most transporting pleasure of my life on the farm: I flew with him over Africa. . . . You have tremendous views as you get up above the African highlands, surprising combinations and changes of light and coloring, the rainbow on the green sunlit land, the gigantic upright clouds and big wild black storms, all swing round you in a race and a dance. The lashing hard showers of rain whiten the air askance. The language is short of words for the experiences of flying, and will have to invent new words with time."

I finish the entry in my journal as the sky begins to lighten, and that finally quiets the lions.

❖

The sun rises in a blinking orange ball behind the line of Tana River poplars that grow like a giant hedgerow along the gravel bar behind camp. The morning air is cool, but it is a cool that is like a medicine that only masks instead of cures a pain, because under the cool, just below the surface, you can already feel the heat. Everyone is up and taking their morning coffee, and at six forty-five we bid farewell to Joyce and Selengei, who are returning today to Nairobi. Then we leave.

Today we will walk the distance to our next camp on the more remote north side of the river. I am still wearing my sandals, which allows me the convenience of stepping in the water and crossing without having to remove my shoes like the others do. The swelling in my ankle where the thorn had entered several days ago has now gone down, thanks to an "operation" two nights before to remove it. "Get Mohamed or Lokiyor to take it out," Iain had suggested. "They grew up with thorns in their feet." Lokiyor performed the operation on the dining table under kerosene light with a large sewing needle. He was amazingly gentle, and after enlarging the hole where the thorn had entered, he was able to reach in with the needle, hook the end, and pull it out. It was just under an inch long and quite thick, but unfortunately the tip was gone, probably broken off by repeated flexing of the ankle.

The river is wide and slow and, I hope, shallow enough to allow a bow wake to form off any approaching crocodile. Ahead of me, one of Iain's staff is wearing a T-shirt that has on the back in large black letters INEDIBLE. We reach the far bank, and while the others dry their feet and replace their shoes, I ask them if they heard the lions last night. Everyone, of course, says they did, but no one elaborates beyond that. We begin walking and we go no more than one minute when Iain says, "Look, over there!" and points across the river where we all see one of the lions standing next to the saltbush. We raise our binoculars just as the second lion steps into view. They are both large, lean, and maneless, and their tawny coats catch the low morning light. "When you see a Tsavo lion," Daphne Sheldrick would tell me later, "you see a real lion. It is not going to sit there with its legs in the air waiting to be photographed. It will instead probably want to eat you, because it is a lion that has had to earn its keep."

The two lions are walking in a desultory start and stop and seem tired (from being up all night roaring, I would like to think). In *Portraits in the Wild*, Cynthia Moss says that a lion's roar has the "dual purpose of communicating to both pride members and strangers. A roar seems to take quite a bit of energy—the lion puts its head forward, its sides contract, and it almost looks as if it were trying to vomit."

We watch these two lions as they continue to amble slowly in and out of the saltbush, and they look sinister without manes. No one is certain why male Tsavo lions have no manes, but it may be an adaptation to thick bush where long hair is a liability. One of them disappears into the saltbush, then the other. As we continue to walk, Danny looks back and asks me if I've ever heard of a lion hair ball.

"No."

"Basically, the lion's roar comes from its stomach," he explains, "but when it growls, it makes a 'took, took, took,' through a hair ball that forms in its throat from licking and cleaning itself. When you shoot or spear a lion the animal usually spits up the hair ball, and they are highly valued as good luck charms. The Wakamba wear them on a leather thong tied around the upper arm, and believe they give you the strength of a lion.

One day Elui was at a water hole," he continues "when he was pounced on by a lion. He gave the lion his arm, pulled his knife, and stabbed him in the aorta. The lion collapsed and spit up its hair ball onto Elui, who from then on wore it around his bicep. Later he killed a female lion and so he had that hair ball on his other arm."

Throughout our trek I have heard from Bongo and Danny a number of Elui stories that together form a catalog of wild encounters with dangerous animals. In addition to the lion attack he had a scar where he was horned by a rhino, another from being knocked down by a buffalo, and yet another from being grabbed by a crocodile when he was sitting on the bank of the Galana washing his feet. In that last encounter he managed to kick free but not before suffering considerable damage to his foot. In yet another story Elui had once been walking through tall grass when suddenly a cobra reared and hit him hard on the leg. He decapitated the snake and carried on to a labor camp three miles farther, where he collapsed. They ran for help and were able to return with an injectible antidote that probably saved his life.

I tried to imagine myself in even one of these encounters, such as the lion attack. The lion must have knocked Elui down when it pounced, and to survive such an attack, Elui must have been drawing his knife while he was toppling with the lion on him. Then, even as the lion was mauling his arm, he kept his cool enough to thrust the knife into the lion's neck.

When I returned to Kenya after our trek, I was in Kamboyo with Bongo and Danny when a middle-aged man greeted the brothers. They talked for a few minutes, then Bongo introduced me.

"This is Peter, Elui's son. He is telling us Elui is doing fine."

"You mean Elui's still alive?"

"Very much so. He lives in Mutha, to the north of the park. He spends his days sitting in the shade of a large tree."

"Can we visit him?"

It was the rainy season, and the dirt roads were impassable. Danny and I took his small bush plane, flying past the Galana that was then in full flood and breaking its banks, across the featureless north country to Mutha, a scattering of wattle-and-daub huts between fields fallow in the off-season and now puddled from the last storm. Landing would have been too risky. We circled several huts, and under a very large tree there was an old man sitting alone. He watched as we passed. We circled again, came back once more and waved. Danny wasn't sure whether or not it was Elui, but as we waved again the old man waved back.

◈

By mid-morning it is hot. There is no wind and under my shirt I feel the drops of sweat run down my skin. To the north, the savanna stretches flat and forever, open save for a few dead acacia with bone limbs that contrast with apocalyptic nakedness against the dry blue sky. On the horizon a long line of zebra shimmer through the heat waves rising off the land. We drop to the river and walk a narrow corridor between the bank and the spear-grass sedge at water's edge (I quickly learn to beware of this plant's knife-sharp blades that can leave deep paper cuts in your hands). To our right, over the water, a green-backed heron lifts from one sandbar to the next trying to stay ahead of our column, until finally it circles and returns upriver. A steep bank forces us up and into the saltbush where everyone with weapons raises them to the Number Two Position. Despite the heat I am very alert and so are my companions.

We stop to watch three zebra cautiously approach the river to drink. They sense danger from two directions: from crocodile in the river, and from lion that could be lying in wait in the bush. Each animal drinks, pauses to look up, then drinks again. If it were not so common, the zebra's graphic beauty would, no doubt, be more widely celebrated, but watching these three is a good chance to consider their fairy-book grace. In temperament, however, zebra are said to be anything but ladylike: All attempts to domesticate them have failed before the zebra's tendency to bite hard and not let go.

We leave the thick bush and once again enter the open plain. The breeze begins to fill, and I lift my arms to cool my torso. To our left one hundred yards we a see a group of elephant. "Do you want to get closer to film?" Iain asks, but Danny counters, saying we would have to make a long detour to stay downwind. The night before I had told everyone I was concerned I wasn't getting enough close-ups of animals for the purposes of the video (we are using only two small digital handicams, and the lenses aren't long enough to get the close-up imagery we would have enjoyed with a large camera, which, of course, would have been very difficult to carry). Bongo and Danny had told me not to worry, that on this last day of our walk through Tsavo East we are sure to see more elephant, especially on this north side, where they congregate this time of year.

As we continue upwind the elephants sense us and group together nervously. To our right a herd of Peter's gazelle prances away. In the last forty years this species has been extending its range in Tsavo East. When David Sheldrick first arrived in Tsavo, Peter's gazelle were limited in distribution to the region north of the Galana, but in 1958 he saw the first animals south of the river, and by the early 1970s he saw them in the Voi River area, even farther to the south. This extension of their range coincided with the destruction of the *Commifora* woodlands by the elephant, allowing an increase in open grass pasture which, presumably, is what lured the gazelle into new areas.

We see another group of elephant grazing on the acacia scrub near the saltbush growing above the riverbank. They are close to the game trail we have followed, and we approach cautiously, taking care to stay behind the scrub cover. We pause while Lokiyor bends and scoops a handful of sandy soil that he then drains through his fingers to test the wind. The direction is favorable. The herd is an extended matriarchal group with three adult females, four juveniles, and two infants. We are only 150 feet from them, but in a perfect downwind position, and they continue to browse, unaware of our presence.

We stand motionless, and I admire the great size of the two largest adults. After the trek, I asked Daphne Sheldrick why the elephant in Tsavo were the largest in East Africa, and she said it was because of the quality of their diet. "The bush looks harsh, but in fact, even with the low rainfall, or perhaps because of it, it is very nutritious, full of minerals. Tsavo elephants have the biggest ivory, too. Let me show you." She then went to another room and returned with an old black-and-white photograph. "David was flying the northern sector when he spotted this tusker, turned around, and flew back to Voi to get his camera." The photograph was grainy and slightly out of focus, but it showed a great male elephant rearing its head at the circling aircraft, its enormous tusks sweeping forward like an artist's depiction of a Paleolithic mammoth. "David reckoned it was 180, 190 pounds, each tusk. It was the biggest elephant he had ever seen."

We lower our binoculars and continue around the herd, careful to stay downwind until we have sufficient distance to resume our route along the animal track. Danny was right: This is the largest concentration of elephant so far on our trek. In another hundred yards we see two more feeding in a grove of juvenile doum palms. We pause to watch, and Danny says, "Do you want a closer look?" I nod affirmatively, and he says, "Let's keep it small, just Bongo, Lokiyor, you, and me."

The four of us stalk cautiously bush to bush, following the edge of a hippo trail that has cut a channel into the red earth. We are now less than a hundred feet from the elephant, and they are still unaware of our presence. The palm grove is thick and we lose sight of one, then the other, as they browse. One of them slowly emerges from the grove, the dried doum fronds snapping loudly with each advancing step. He appears to be a juvenile male. I have my camera on Record, and alternate one eye looking through the viewfinder while the other watches the elephant, the better to gauge its distance. It seems very close, perhaps only seventy-five feet away, and every muscle in my body feels alert and ready.

The animal leaves the grove, turns, and walks away toward the open grass and thornbush. Then the second one emerges, even closer. He too is a juvenile male, and suddenly his ears fan out, he lifts his head, extends his trunk, and looks right at us. Rifles go to Number One Position. I fall behind Danny, Bongo, and Lokiyor and we all begin walking backward. The elephant trumpets, takes several steps toward us, paws the ground, and takes another step forward. We retreat with fast but sure steps. The elephant moves forward two more steps, and I feel every fiber of my body preparing to run. It may be a juvenile, but at this close range it is huge. Its head is still held high, and tusks seem to be aimed directly at us. Then it snorts, shakes its head, turns, and runs toward its companion, its skinny tail held high. I let out a breath and continue to follow the animal with my camera.

"He was close," I say.

"Let's see how close," Danny says as he paces off the distance, dipping down and then up to cross a hippo trail that was between us and the elephant. "About fifty feet." I walk over and look at the elephant prints. "I was quite sure he wasn't going through with his charge," Danny says. "He was young and unsure of himself, and elephants are very cautious crossing a ditch such as we have here."

We return to Iain, Mohamed, and Pete, who had stayed back at Danny's request, then continue along the game trail that parallels the river, now one hundred yards to our right and hidden in its channel lined with riverine bush. We travel only a quarter mile when we spot the head of an elephant revealed above the bank of the river. We stop and the elephant disappears and we walk toward it. We only go a few feet when we see the top of its head again rise above the bank and climb quickly up and now she comes straight at us. I sense immediately this one is different than the others. The elephant is two hundred feet away. I fall behind Lokiyor, Mohamed, Danny, and Bongo, and we start retreating fast. The elephant gains speed as it recovers from its ascent up the riverbank. It is making no noise—no trumpeting, no shouting, no crunching of fronds or leaves. It is not in any way hesitating. Its head is down, and with deadly silence it charges in a direct line toward us. I know this is serious, and every fiber in my body is drawn as tight as a bow-string. The elephant is one hundred feet away, ninety feet, eighty feet, and its trajectory is not veering. We run backward as fast as we can without tripping. I'm ready to break into a full run, but there is no way I can outrun this elephant. Seventy feet. It is closing fast, straight at us with an astonishingly silent intent. She'll catch one of us in five seconds, maybe less. Sixty feet. Danny suddenly stops and turns toward the elephant and Mohamed spins and drops to one knee, shoulders his rifle, and in a quick heartbeat there is the loud pop of rifle fire—five rounds, ten rounds, twenty rounds—a firecracker string of sharp explosions—and the elephant just as instantly plows its front legs to a stop, veers, and runs at an angle away from us.

All the shots have been aimed over its head and past its ears. We follow the elephant and now we see others rising up and over the bank: two more adults, six juveniles, three infants. The great matriarch that charged us moves behind the herd and directs the group toward the open north country. Danny motions us with his hand to follow him as we retreat quickly in the opposite direction. Two more animals climb out of the bank and run to join the herd, which is now in a line heading away from us, all animals with trunks raised like periscopes. Danny waves us on and we continue our own retreat, not stopping until it is clear the herd has regrouped and is still heading for open country.

"Had we remained in position we could have had the whole herd come at us," Danny says. "You have to be very, very careful of that."

"They felt trapped between us and the river," Bongo adds. "That's why she charged."

"That transition from a demonstration charge to a full charge," Danny says, "it happens in a split second. That one was serious, hence the shots."

The herd, now several hundred yards away, is still moving north, but has slowed to a fast walk. "It was a shame to have to put up shots," Danny says. He pauses, then adds, "We had a fright, they had a fright, but the elephants are all together and none of them are hurt."

We resume our walk, and if there were any more elephant in the neighborhood they are now gone. I am behind Iain, and he hasn't said a thing. He is stepping with a gait that is more march than walk, and he is looking straight ahead and not to the sides as he normally does when he tries to spot birds or game. I step up and alongside him. "You don't look happy," I say.

"No, I'm very upset by what just happened."

"You don't think we should have fired?"

"That wasn't necessary at all. Now we've traumatized thirty elephants."

He is referring not only to the matriarch's herd, but to the other elephant we had seen earlier who no doubt also heard the shots. Now I am critical of my own actions, thinking that if I hadn't made the request the night before to get closer to the animals to videotape them, we probably would have given this elephant a wider berth and avoided the charge and the gunfire. We keep walking until we stop to rest at an overlook. Iain is standing by himself and I go over and say, "Why don't I get Bongo and Danny over and let's talk this through."

When we are gathered I say, "Iain has some concern that we unnecessarily traumatized those elephants, and I'm having some second thoughts about my own actions."

"These elephants have been to hell and back," Iain says, "and now, after a few years of peace, they've begun to relax. Joyce has told us this, and so has Jonah. Then here we go shooting at them."

"That's a bunch of shite," Bongo replies, using the long "i" to pronounce "shit." "They're as windy now as they've always been."

"You saw that herd yesterday," Danny agrees. "They were off as soon as they sensed we were there, on foot. It's actually good that they stay wary of humans."

Iain doesn't attempt to reply, and I can see the attempt to air our differences has failed. Later I discuss it further with Iain, just the two of us, and he tells me that he thinks Mohamed fired at the elephant only because he was with Danny and Bongo, and had he been with just us he could have turned the elephant with only a loud hand clap or a shout. "I've seen him do it," Iain says. That's what Abakuna did years ago when he was hunting with Bill, and they were charged by that bull. Perhaps, though, Abakuna knew, in that instance, it was only a demonstration charge. When I later told Danny about Iain's opinion, Danny said, "Without any doubt we were faced with a serious charge which would not have been stopped by clapping hands! So don't give me any bullshit that two experienced game wardens made a blunder."

I remember Peter Beard who in very similar circumstances was tusked by that elephant only a week before we started our own trek. So I'm not sure. I don't know enough about the nuances of elephant behavior to judge whether or not the shots were necessary. I do know, however, that the charging matriarch has produced in me a surge of adrenaline that has honed my senses to a razor sharpness that holds its edge through the remaining hours of our day's walk.

20

Throughout universal history, from Sumaria and Acadia, Assyria and the
First Empire of Egypt, up until the present now unraveling, there have always been men, many men, from the most varied social conditions, who
dedicated themselves to hunting out of pleasure, will or affection. Seen
from this point of view, in its authentic perspective, the topic of hunting ex-
pands until it attains enormous proportions. Consequently . . . aware that
it is a more difficult matter than it seems at first, I ask myself, what the
devil kind of occupation is this behavior of hunting?

—José Ortega y Gasset,
Meditations on Hunting, 1943

We walk the north side of the river. The country is open and wide and the
sky, like a great dome, bends to the far horizon. The land rises gently and a
fringe-eared oryx, solitary and stately, gallops before us and stops next to a
tumulus of gathered stones; the grave and the animal are the only objects
against the stark skyline.

"An Orma grave," Bongo says. The oryx watches as we approach, then
turns and runs. The mound of stones is some six feet in height, and Bongo
stoops and picks up a rock at his feet and carefully adds it to the aggregate.
"It's a tradition when you get to a bush grave to add a stone," he says, and
the rest of us follow his example. We have passed several of these graves the

last few days, and they are even more common farther to the north, beyond the park, where they have been investigated by anthropologists and found to be between six hundred and fifteen hundred years old; and other than a cave inscribed with hieroglyphs that Peter Beard once found on the edge of the Yatta Plateau, these graves may be the only physical evidence of man's prehistoric occupation of Tsavo.

We continue and soon flush a flock of helmeted guinea fowl that takes flight in noisy complaint, then lands again and scurries away "looking like fleas," as Danny says. All the accounts of the early explorers and hunters made reference to frequent shooting of guinea fowl, and when I was a young boy we kept a flock of these plump game birds on the small ranch where I spent part of my childhood in the orange groves of California; I remember the occasional sacrificial victim that would be delivered to our dining table with its skin baked crisp and golden.

One of the main differences between our trek and the marches of the early explorers, or even the walks of hunters as recent as Bill Woodley, was that they shot game to supplement whatever food staples they brought. In the case of Bill, when he was hunting with Elui, or with his Waliangulu trackers, they often brought next to nothing, and lived off the land for weeks at a time. Hunting was never allowed within the national parks, of course, but it was permitted in the surrounding game lands until a complete moratorium on all hunting was installed in 1977.

Now as I watch these guinea fowl scurry and disappear, I have a strong urge to shoot one for supper. It has nothing to do with hunger—there has not been a single meal from Kahin's charcoal hearth that was anything less than stellar—but everything to do with an urge to travel light and unfettered, and, even more, to live wild off the land, like the Waliangulu, or (dismissing the pejorative in the phrase) like a wild animal.

All three of the tribes that lived and traveled in Tsavo in the years before it became a park—the Wakamba, the Waliangulu, the Orma—were able to spend weeks and months in the thornbush living only on what they took foraging and hunting. In his account of his march up the Sabaki in 1890, Lugard described how in this region you could encounter Orma on what sounded like the African equivalent of an aboriginal Australian's walkabout. "You suddenly round an angle in the winding game-path," Lugard wrote, ". . . and find yourself face to face with a Galla [Orma], accompanied by only two or three friends, each with a spear seven feet long. You ask whence he comes and whither he goes, and he replies with absolute nonchalance, and as though he had been expecting you all day . . . that he is 'walking' for pleasure. On inquiry you find that this walk probably began a month or two ago, will continue a month or more yet, that he covers from 20 to 30 miles a day, has no object in his walk except the Galla love of roaming, and no wardrobe or belongings of any sort or kind except his seven-foot spear."

That is not to say that these people could roam this land without making mistakes and without paying the consequences. In 1993 Iain was driving a little-used four-wheel track through this country (cut originally by C. G. MacArthur in the years even before Tsavo was gazetted as a national park) when he saw a donkey standing motionless with what looked like people on its back and a body lying next to it. He was then about a mile north of the river, and he stopped his vehicle to discover two children, one about two and the other about three years old, on the donkey's back, their mother leaning against the animal for support, and their father prone on the ground. The father's eyes were open but they were full of flies, and although not technically dead, he was too far gone to save. Iain gave water to the others, then radioed park headquarters. Mohamed, who could speak the Orma language, found out from the mother that the family had been herding their animals in the north country when their water supply dried, and they had no choice but to march south in a life-or-death attempt to reach the Galana River. When Iain and his party encountered them they had succeeded in covering about eighty miles, but to do so the father had given his share of their water to his children and to his wife. Then he had collapsed, unable to continue, and died one mile from his destination. The park rangers arrived and loaded the body and survivors into their vehicle, and Iain continued, arriving in Malindi three hours later where he sat in a reclining chair at a beach resort and stared out at the ocean, very slowly sipping his cold beer, thinking that all he had to do to get another beer was lay down a few metal coins.

Deserts make you aware of water and aware that without water you soon die. This may sound self-evident, but what I mean is that in the desert, and in particular when you are on foot in the desert, you drink water aware of the sustenance you are feeding your body, and you appreciate it. You even venerate it. In a similar way, I have found traveling long distance by ski or by dog team in the Antarctic leaves the same awareness of how food produces calories that allow your body to defend itself against the cold that is never above freezing, cold that is omnipresently trying to turn your warm body of supple muscle into a frozen brick of hard meat. For Iain, the encounter with the Orma family's desperate effort, seven years short of the beginning of the twenty-first century, gave him an awareness of the material

comforts in his own life that for the rest of his life will cause him now and
again to pause and acknowledge a personal thanksgiving.

◈

I realize that it may be Iain's ability to empathize that has also allowed him
to see the issue of our shooting over the head of the elephant from the animal's point of view. He has imagined the ten years and more of hell that the
elephant must have survived during the poaching wars, only to suffer an additional trauma when we shot at her, and he has imagined the memories of
death and horror that the sound of the rifle fire was likely to have evoked in
her elephantine thoughts.

I look at my own reactions to the charge, and realize I am more concerned
about Iain being upset than I am about the elephant. That's not to say I don't
also empathize with the elephant and its trauma, but that by my nature I
tend to avoid conflict with my fellow humans (my wife tells me this is likely
because I come from a broken family). Iain is less hesitant in this regard and
he continues to walk with a marching gait, his eyes straight ahead as though
he were focused only on our goal of reaching the ocean, the sooner the better. On an intellectual level I can certainly share his concern about awakening this elephant's past traumas, but on an emotional level, if I am truly
honest, I realize I am relishing this close encounter with this monumental
animal. It has produced in me a clarity of senses that is more acute than at
any other time on our walk. I am light on my feet. I hear my sandals crunch
the hardpan gravel. I feel the sun on my leathered skin and the slight breeze
through my shirt. I look to the horizon and, in a kind of cinematic overlay,
see the elephant once again charging at us, head lowered with implacable
intent.

*Her legs trot forward massive yet weightless yet setting down with a force
that would break the bones and back and ribs of every great animal that
walks this wild land and she deserves her name, the matriarch. This monumental weight coming straight at us has slowed time so that each second is
not a second but a minute and so in one of these long seconds I consider how
she is different from the other elephant who have charged us, that she has a
different intent. I run backward at an angle so I am behind Danny as he
spins and drops and in the same motion raises his rifle toward his shoulder.
All with this same slowing of time, all within this one or two seconds that
seem to stretch and stretch and stretch . . .*

The elephant dissolves and I walk across the bushland thinking how this exhilaration is not the same as the seconds you feel as your automobile spins and you swerve toward the cliff, and it certainly is not the days and weeks and months of slow, painful decline in a bed. This danger, this possibility of approaching death, is a closing of a distance between two animals, one intent on damaging the other, and it has produced in me an exhilaration that contains neither fear nor regret, and as a consequence it is an exhilaration that feels clear and pure. I can see that Danny and Bongo share this exhilaration, too, as it is on their faces and in their voices.

I think about the video camera. I raised and pointed it at the elephant even as I ran backward, certainly as a filmmaker's rote response to capture the image. Yet there is something more, something underneath. The camera was a connection between the elephant and me, just as Danny's and Bongo's rifles were connections. Now in my imaginings I see myself holding in my hands a rifle instead of the camera, and spinning and dropping to one knee I raise the gun to my shoulder and aim at the elephant and pull the trigger and shoot. Shoot not over its head, but shoot directly at it. Shoot to kill it.

❀

That's not to say I would ever shoot an elephant in anything less than self-defense. Or that I condone in any way the big-game hunters who pay huge fees to step from their Land Rovers and shoot an elephant. It is to say, however, I am beginning to *feel* how it would be possible to kill an animal that at the same time you respect and even venerate.

This apparent irreconcilability between veneration and destruction of wild game is the underpinning of Peter Beard's *The End of the Game.* (It is also, by the way, the reason I have chosen throughout this book to refer with frequency to the wild animals of Africa as "game"; the word is Old English and originally referred to "animals of the chase" even before it took its derivative meaning of sport, amusement, or pastime.) Peter's book is a photographic catalog of wild animal death and destruction. As I mentioned earlier, many of the images are of elephant that died of starvation in Tsavo during the drought of the early 1970s, but many others are images of dead animals that have been shot by big-game hunters either as sport or as efforts to make room on the expansive estates of the landed gentry for cattle and sheep. Mixed with these images are others of living, healthy rhinoceros, giraffe, lion, bongo, elephant, waterbuck, cheetah, gerunuk, buffalo . . . a se-

lection of images that celebrate the wildness of Africa's wild game, and together re-create what today is referred to with nostalgia as Old Africa.

Then there is a full-page portrait of J. A. Hunter. There are others of
Theodore Roosevelt, Denys Finch Hatton, Philip Percival, Ernest Hemingway, Frederick Selous. These are all men who celebrated Africa's wild
game, who argued for its preservation, who mourned its decline, while, at
the same time, hunted it and shot it and each in his own way—directly and
indirectly—contributed to its unsustainable harvest. The only one missing
from the lineup is arguably the most complex of them all, Richard Meinertzhagen.

◈

In his journal, published as *Kenya Diary 1902–1906*, Richard Meinertzhagen
writes that while steaming across the Indian Ocean on his way to Africa the
German captain had a pet monkey "which is the victim of all sorts of practical jokes by the crew. I hold no brief for monkeys, but I strongly resent any
form of cruelty to any animal." Meinertzhagen then lists a series of tortures
the monkey endures, from being burned with cigarette butts to being
forcefed alcohol until he is drunk, then tied to a line and dipped over the
side into the ocean. "I could stand it no longer, and taking my knife, I cut the
line . . . the Germans jabbered with rage, and I told them they were a lot of
cowardly savages."

Meinertzhagen holds a parallel disdain for what in his personal moral
code he considers unjust cruelty to people. During his first few days in the
colony, he protests vehemently against the flogging of a black orderly for in-
subordination. "The culprit was lashed to a triangle, his breeches removed,
and he was then flogged by a hefty Sudanese with a strip of hippopotamus
hide; he was bleeding horribly when it was over and I was nearly sick. . . . I
hated and resented the punishment so furiously that I went off to the orderly room and expressed my thorough disgust."

With surprising foresight Meinertzhagen also is able to predict the consequences of such brutal subjugation of the Africans. When Lord Delamere,
a British aristocrat with vast inherited wealth who was the unofficial
spokesman for Kenya farmers and settlers, tells Meinertzhagen, "I am going
to prove to you all that this is a white man's country," the twenty-four-year-
old subaltern replies, "But it is a black man's country; how are you going to
superimpose the white over the black?" Delamere retorts impatiently, "The
black man will benefit and co-operate." In another conversation with

Charles Eliot, the colony's high commissioner, Meinertzhagen notes that Eliot "intends to confine the natives to reserves and use them as cheap labour on farms. I suggested that the country belonged to Africans and that their interests must prevail over the interests of strangers. He would have none of it; he kept on using the word 'paramount' with reference to the claims of Europeans. I said that some day the African would be educated and armed [and] . . . that would lead to a clash. . . . I am convinced that in the end the Africans will win and that Eliot's policy can lead only to trouble and disappointment." This entry in his journal is dated July 13, 1902.

There are also many journal entries that make clear Meinertzhagen's passion for natural history. On the train ride from Mombasa to Nairobi he notes a half-dozen genera of butterfly, the Latin name for a land snail common in the area, and many of the birds (he was an avid birder, and later in his career wrote *Birds of Arabia*, a landmark contribution to ornithology). Also on the train ride he takes census of all the game animals he sees on the Athi Plain as they approach Nairobi: "760 wildebeeste, 4006 zebra, 845 Coke's haartebeeste, 324 Grant's gazelle . . ." I have an image of Richard Meinertzhagen sitting in his carriage seat, furiously making hatch marks under each animal's name as his dark eyes sweep the highland plains, missing nothing.

This empathy with Africans, this preternatural ability to foresee the consequences of their subjugation, and this passion and love for wild animals and birds is, however, only one half of Richard Meinertzhagen. The other half is the British soldier sent to a Kikuyu settlement to seek justice for the death of a white settler who had been seized, staked to the ground, and forced to endure the entire village urinating into his mouth until he had drowned. Meinertzhagen had his men surround the village in the predawn and at first light, attack. By his orders he and his men then bayoneted to death every single man and woman; there were no survivors. Later Meinertzhagen seeks to teach a similar lesson to a tribe who is raiding supply caravans and murdering policemen. He stages a series of raids on their villages, and after two weeks he tallies his progress: "Our total captures were 782 cattle and 2150 sheep and goats. We killed 796 of the enemy."

In the same way that Meinertzhagen admires Africans and champions their rights on one hand, while he brutally punishes them for what he sees as their moral transgressions on the other, he also advocates (as I mentioned earlier in the book) the establishment of a game reserve and strictly enforced policies to preserve the colony's wild animals, while at the same time he takes every opportunity to shoot anything that walks on four legs (with the exception of elephant). Every turn in his journal describes another suc-

cessful hunting foray: "Today Hemsted and I went down to the junction of
the Tana and Mathyoia and shot some impala and oribi. . . . Today I shot a
leopard. . . . I went to a pool just above the bridge where I had previously
seen hippopotami, and I shot the largest bull of the four. . . . Killed a waterbuck and oribi near camp." All this in the space of ten days while he is otherwise busy overseeing construction of a new bridge.

The list of game animals that Meinertzhagen shot during the four years he
was posted to British East Africa totals 444 animals and includes hippopotamus, lion, giraffe, leopard, hyena, cheetah, rhinoceros, buffalo, and nearly
every type of antelope save only the rare and elusive bongo (although he did
see one of these while walking in the Aberdares, and he would have shot it
had it not bounded away too quickly). And this list pales, at least in terms of
the rate of killing, alongside the approximately 500 game animals that
Theodore Roosevelt and his son Kermit bagged in the ten months they were
on safari in East Africa. Then we must consider the 996 rhinoceros that J. A.
Hunter shot. That is more than twice the estimated 400 black rhinoceros
that are left alive in Kenya today.

Yet Meinertzhagen, Roosevelt, and the rest of them all had this passionate and genuine regard for wildlife and wildlands (Roosevelt of course
played a large role in the expansion of the national park system in the
United States). Each of them too had his own rationalizations for hunting: It
was to provide meat for the porters or the workers, or it was in the name of
science, or in the name of taming and developing the country, or even when
it was just in the name of sport, it was sport based on the hunter's respect for
the animal and his underlying regard for its long-term well-being, at least as
a species if not as an individual; and furthermore, shooting a few individuals, especially the antelope, was of no consequence.

The latter point, I believe, was the most prevalent rationalization: That
each of them saw himself as taking only a small and sustainable portion of
any animal's total population—not unlike the way the Waliangulu had over
the years found a balance in their harvesting of elephant. But taken together
the total number of animals hunted was having an impact, especially when
game was shot to clear land for cattle or human settlement, because then not
only did a species lose individuals from its population, but it also lost habitat, and that was something that could not be recovered.

Rationalizations are just that: blinders that you wear that after a while,
like any pair of glasses, cover your eyes in a comfortable way that allows you
soon to forget they are there. But these are very intelligent men we are talking about. The list includes great soldiers, writers, naturalists, businessmen,

game wardens, even a president. So what is going on? Is there something in
the act of hunting so compelling, so alluring, so basic to who we are as a
species, perhaps, that they couldn't help themselves, even knowing deep
down (as I believe they all did) that their actions were inconsistent with
their otherwise genuine regard for the survival of Africa's game animals? Is
there something in hunting, perhaps, that is connected to that clarity of
senses, that exhilaration I felt after the elephant had charged and we had
fired over her head?

◈

This question is nothing new. The Spanish philosopher Ortega y Gasset
wrote a book on it, *Meditations on Hunting*, concluding that "the grace and
delight of hunting are rooted in this fact: that man, projected by his inevitable progress away from his ancestral proximity to animals, vegetables,
and minerals—in sum, to Nature—takes pleasure in the artificial return to
it, the only occupation that permits something like a vacation from his
human condition." In *Gardeners of Eden*, Alistair Graham, who was part-
ners with Ian Parker in their game-control company, looked specifically at
how hunting relates to conservation in East Africa. He began with his examination of the relation between hunting and the early game laws of England, and how those laws were transposed to British East Africa. He then
examined how this human urge to conserve animals is historically connected to a desire to hunt them, but then spent the rest of the book arguing,
often with great vitriol aimed at the so-called sentimentalists, "that all efforts to save wild nature are linked psychologically to repressed aggression."

I realized that any extended look into this question of why we hunt,
whether philosophical, Freudian, or simply academic, would in all likelihood end with more theoretical conjecture, but after our walk I couldn't
help digging into it a little further. I decided to start with a topic that David
Western mentioned in passing during our interview. It was when he was
telling us that wilderness is not an African concept, that in Africa men and
animals have always shared the land. He explained that his largest challenge
is to teach Africans to value wildlife. "To me, an even greater danger than
the number of people [overpopulation] is the attitude that wildlife is the
enemy," he said, "because then it will disappear, no matter how many or
how few people there are."

Then he made a statement that was intended to support this, and it was
this statement that had me thinking: "*Don't forget that in the Pleistocene pe-*

*riod in North America only a handful of Amerindians knocked off the very
largest mammals."*

This seemed like a good place to start an investigation into our species's
history as hunters. A library search revealed that the "bible" on this subject
was called *Quarternary Extinctions*, and I sat down and read all 892 pages of
it. The book assumed that anyone cracking the cover already knew that at
the end of the last ice age two-thirds of all the large animals in North America, and four-fifths of all the megafauna in Australia, suddenly (at least by pa-
leozoological measures) became extinct. There were also major extinctions
in South America and, to a lesser extent, Europe. The only place it didn't
happen was in Africa. The goal of the book was to examine why these extinctions happened, and the forty-nine contributing authors divided more or
less evenly into two camps: those who believed the extinctions were due to
climatic changes, and those who believed humans were the culprits.

I thought the best article was the last one, "Historic Extinctions: A
Rosetta Stone for Understanding Prehistoric Extinctions," by Jared Diamond. The main reason the preceding forty-eight authors were so divided
on what had caused these extinctions was that the scientific evidence available about Pleistocene-era hunters was so sketchy. Diamond reasoned that
it made sense to look at the causes of historic extinctions to see if those examples might offer insights into what caused prehistoric extinctions. In Diamond's examination there was very little modern evidence of species going
extinct because of climate changes (there just haven't been enough severe
climatic changes in the historic era to cause many extinctions), but there was
a rich history of cases where man had caused extinctions through hunting,
destruction of habitat, and introduction of predators and disease.

The cases that interested me most were the ones where man had hunted
species into extinction. One of the more interesting was the fate of the Moa
birds of New Zealand. Before the Maoris arrived about a thousand years
ago, at least thirteen species of these giant, flightless birds with thick legs
and huge feet filled varying ecological niches on the two islands. All of them,
however, were relatively defenseless against the newly arrived human
predators, who hunted them down and robbed their nests of eggs. By the
time Europeans arrived eight hundred years later, the Moas of New Zealand
existed only in legends (although a few individuals of one of the species may
have survived into the nineteenth century).

Jared Diamond's inquiry found many other examples of human hunters ex-
terminating to the last individual some of the world's more spectacular
species: the Steller's sea cow, the Japanese sea lion, the quagga (a zebra species

of South Africa), the dodo, the passenger pigeon. Most of these species met their fate within a relatively short period after exposure to human beings. The larger question, then, was whether the same thing had happened to the large animals in North America and Australia when our species first arrived there.

Diamond concluded that indeed that is just what happened. The giant marsupials in Australia all disappeared about the same time man arrived. The same thing happened to the megafauna in North America. (There are still some who argue that *Homo sapiens* arrived in the New World earlier than about eleven thousand years ago, but the evidence is all inconclusive.) Perhaps most telling, argued Diamond, is what *didn't* happen, especially in North America, where the fossil record is more complete: The amphibians, the fish, and the reptiles did *not* go extinct. Neither did the insects, except for two species of dung beetle that (just as they do in Africa) required the presence of large mammals to complete their life cycles. If the large mammals had died because of climate change, then you would expect that at least some of these other species would have suffered the same fate.

Does Diamond then have the last word? Not quite. I found one other researcher, Valerius Geist, who thought Diamond's theory could be stood on its head. Geist argued that the Amerindians could not have populated North America until the large mammals, called by paleozoologists the Rancholabrean megafauna, became extinct, because these animals were simply too fierce to allow people to survive alongside them. One in particular, the short-faced bear, was such a ferocious and fearsome predator that, Geist reasoned, Amerindians armed only with spears and *atlatls* (spear throwers) wouldn't have had a chance against it. Only when this bear had died off (from some kind of environmental change) would human beings have been able to migrate southward from Alaska.

At this point I realized Geist's position was based more on conjecture than fact, so I decided the next phase of my research should be some conjecture of my own. I had walked for one month in the close company of lions, elephant, hippo, and buffalo. I had a visceral feel for these animals, and for our species's ability to hunt them. What I needed now was to stand next to some of these Rancholabrean animals to get a feel for them. I was especially keen to take the measure of this short-faced bear.

❖

Today the Rancho La Brea tar pits in Los Angeles are like a Pleistocene theme park, but twelve thousand years ago they were natural tar seepages that sometimes were covered deceptively by water, and this made them dangerous traps for the local animals. The herbivores that lived in the Los Angeles Basin—giant sloths, horses, bison, lamas, mammoths, camels— would come to the pools to drink, and as they stepped into the ponds their legs began to sink inexorably into the underlying tar. Saber-toothed tigers, American lion, or short-faced bear then pounced from the surrounding bush to feed on the trapped animals, and they themselves sometimes became mired in the sticky goo that then, as the years passed, metamorphosed into asphalt.

In 1870 Major Henry Hancock, then the owner of Rancho La Brea, began mining this asphalt that was refined and then shipped to San Francisco to make cobblestone streets. Soon the Chinese immigrants who labored in the pits started to uncover bones, lots of bones, and when they found a skull with two fearsome saber fangs for incisors, Hancock realized they weren't bones from any living animals. Word of these unusual bones spread, and a professor from Massachusetts, visiting the tar pits in 1875, was first to real- ize their scientific potential. By the beginning of World War I, Rancho La Brea was recognized as the preeminent source in the world for late Pleis- tocene fossils, and that is a distinction it still holds today: More than one mil- lion bones have now been recovered from the tar pits, representing more than six hundred species, including fifty-eight different kinds of mammals.

When I visited Rancho La Brea I entered Hancock Park on a sidewalk that bordered an attractive pond that had been created by restoring one of Han- cock's early asphalt pit mines. Pads of tar floated on the pond's surface, and methane gas, bubbling up from natural seepages on the bottom, popped pri- mordially into the air. There was a life-sized fiberglass replica of an imperial mammoth, standing twelve feet high, at the edge of the pond, and in the cen- ter another replica of a mastodon that was trapped in tar. Real-life dragonflies skirted in Jurassic darts over the water. Behind the pond the Mutual Life In- surance building rose fifty-five stories into the smoggy downtown air.

Behind the pond I entered the George Page Museum that houses skele- tal specimens of all major herbivores and carnivores that have been recov- ered from the tar pits. I stood under the imperial mammoth, the largest of the elephant that lived in North America. This specimen was twelve feet high, and when it was alive it weighed about fifteen thousand pounds, mak- ing these mammoths on average thirty percent larger than African elephant. It had what Bill Woodley would have called very big ivory, and I am certain the tusks weighed well over two hundred pounds each. The saber-toothed tiger, smaller than I imagined, appeared to be about the size of a modern-day leopard. The American lion was about thirty to fifty percent bigger than the present-day African lion, but otherwise looked just the same. While a plaque next to its skeleton said it was "probably the most formidable predator of its time," I thought, from what I had read, that this distinction would have belonged to the short-faced bear. When I arrived at the skeleton of the bear and stood next to it, I suspected the judgment about the lion was wrong.

This short-faced bear, at its shoulder, stood a foot higher than a grizzly bear, but what really set it apart was the length of its legs. They were long, very long. This bear was made to run, and run fast. It was a courser; it was the cheetah of bears. Standing there imagining a bear half again as big as a grizzly, that could run like a cheetah, that was a pure carnivore (unlike grizzlies, who are omnivores), was sufficient to convince me that this was the Pleistocene king of the beasts. I have a story that supports this conjecture, too. I was once on a kayaking trip in the Siberian tiger reserve along the eastern seaboard of Russia—the only place in the world where tigers and brown bear coexist—when I met a field researcher, Dale Miquelle, who told a story of once arriving at a site where a tiger had just made a kill of a large deer. Miquelle knew the tiger was very close; he even assumed the cat was watching him as he stooped to examine the deer. Suddenly a huge brown bear (very closely related to the grizzly) busted out of the bush, and Miquelle, screaming and jumping backward, fell down an embankment that, in all likelihood, saved him from a severe mauling. The startled bear ran off, and once Miquelle calmed himself, he examined the tracks around the deer and reconstructed what had happened. The tiger had killed the deer, but then the bear had arrived and stolen the kill from the tiger. This was the first time that a scientist had ever established the order of dominance between big cats and big bears.

On my way out the museum I stopped in the bookstore, and my eye went to a magazine that gave me pause. I picked it up and stared at the cover. It was a confirmation of something I had begun to realize as I walked through the museum and had in my imagination tried to flesh out the fossils. The magazine was the quarterly publication of the Los Angeles Museum of Natural History, the organization that oversees the Rancho La Brea tar pits, and on the cover was a painting they had commissioned that was titled *Los Angeles Basin 20,000 Years Ago*. What made me stand there and stare was that it looked just like Africa.

As I drove out of the museum parking lot and into the L.A. traffic, I saw the horses that looked very much like zebra. There were long-legged llamas that looked very much like gerenuk antelope. There were mammoths that looked like elephants, lions that were lions, camels that were camels. Then suddenly there was a honking horn and the bison that looked very much like a wildebeest turned into a late-model Suburban piloted by a typically irate L.A. driver, and I realized I needed to snap out of my reverie. But I had seen it: The Los Angeles Basin, most of the Western United States, even the little valley of Ojai where I now live, were once another Africa.

I was out of my reverie, but I still considered the question I had come to the tar pits to answer. Could we as a species, armed with spears and spear throwers, have survived living alongside these Pleistocene animals?

After walking across Africa in the close company of similar, if somewhat smaller, animals, I had the sense that we could. Even though we made our walk with semiautomatic weapons and a Rigby .416 elephant rifle, I had learned, by the time we had finished, enough about the Waliangulu and the Wakamba, armed with their bows and arrows, to appreciate how effectively they lived in the close company of Africa's wild animals. The early Amerindians could have done the same with the animals I had examined at the George Page Museum, even the short-faced bear. But could those same Amerindians, having just arrived on these plains that looked so much like the Serengeti does today, have hunted those animals to extinction?

I think they definitely could have. First, spears thrown by spear throwers are formidable weapons (*atlatl* is a Nahuatl word, and assisted by spear throwers, Aztecs could hurl spears with such force they could pierce Spanish armor). Today there is a group of *atlatl* aficionados based in the United States, and the current record by their members for a spear launched by an *atlatl* is nearly 850 feet. Second, the Amerindians would not have hunted the predators, only the herbivores. Then, too, remember that those herbivores would have evolved with none of the protective instincts against man that the large African herbivores enjoyed, and therefore would have been easy prey. Jared Diamond had a story that illustrated this point. In New Guinea the largest indigenous mammal is the tree kangaroo, and it is highly coveted by local hunters. It is also uncommon, nocturnal, and elusive, and in his many years in New Guinea working as an ornithologist, Diamond had never seen one in the wild. Then he had an opportunity to make a trip by helicopter to the Gauttier Mountains, a range in New Guinea so remote and steep-sided that it was unoccupied by any humans. There the tree kangaroo was common, it was diurnal, and it allowed him to approach within ten meters.

An acquaintance told me a similar story about a journey he made in the early 1070s to a remote pocket of western Tibet, to climb a glacial peak that rose in solitary seclusion out of the desert plateau that was uninhabited in some directions for hundreds of miles. There were no yak herders who lived in this area, and the Chinese had never ventured to this mountain. My friend and his climbing companions traveled in a caravan of four-wheel-drive vehicles, and one day, approaching them in the near distance, they spotted an animal that at first appeared only as a speck. They stopped and watched, through the flawless high-desert air, as the animal continued to trot toward them, never veering in its approach. When it was sufficiently close, they could see it was a fox. It continued to come at them, never changing its pace, until finally it arrived at their vehicles, where it then stopped only a few feet away and stood and looked at them. It continued to stand there, its sharp eyes fixed and unerring, until the Chinese army officer who accompanied the climbers took out his rifle and shot it.

❖

So where is this digression of mine leading? It is to this idea: That possibly we, as a species, whenever we have the opportunity and the capability, hunt to extinction the large animals with whom we share our landscape.

That Meinertzhagen and Roosevelt and Selous and Hunter couldn't help themselves blasting away and killing among them thousands of rhino and hippo and buffalo only positions them in a successive pattern of predation by *Homo sapiens* that has been going on for thirty thousand years and more. But what about traditional hunting and gathering peoples who seem to live in balance with the animals they hunt? There are many examples of cultures who have self-imposed mechanisms that limit their members from taking game (or fish) in numbers beyond what their environment can naturally sustain. When those same cultures, however, are disrupted, or when man is in contact with game animals when there are no cultural restraints, as was likely to have been the case when the Amerindians first arrived in North America, the Aborigines in Australia, the Maoris in New Zealand, and as was definitely the case when the big-game hunters arrived in Africa, it seems that man will then hunt those game animals until they are extinguished from the face of the Earth.

Once in the high Arctic (on that trip with Doug Peacock when he was armed against polar bear with only his spear) we were camped with an Inuit hunter on Somerset Island, a remote place inhabited only by a few of this hunter's relatives. One day the Inuit went out with his shotgun and bagged two eider geese. The geese were out of season because they were raising their fledglings. We confronted the Inuit with this fact, but he said he didn't care, they were his geese. We remained polite (no small feat for Peacock, under such circumstances), and we then asked the Inuit hypothetically if he would still shoot those same geese if they were the only flock left in all the Arctic. "Sure," he said. "They would still be my geese."

"Remember, the African's word for wildlife is *nyama*," Peter Beard had told me. "And *nyama* means 'meat.'"

21

On the face of a cliff deep in the Libyan Desert stands an ancient rock en-
graving depicting a duel between a long-legged elephant and a man, in
which the elephant seems to be winning, for it is holding a small
man . . . high off the ground in the curl of his trunk.

—*Carleton S. Coon,*
The Hunting Peoples, *1971*

The river flows in a horseshoe around a low bluff, and at the apex, marked by a solitary tree, we stop to rest. To the west we can see the river, wide and slow, coming from the direction of the Yatta Plateau, which seems a long ways away; to the east the Galana continues into flat thornbush broken only by an occasional archipelago of distant hills and, closer, the singular cone-shape of Sala Hill marking the boundary of Tsavo East National Park.

"This place is called Jirma Koito," Danny says. "Which means 'Place of Female Circumcision.' Young Orma girls eleven to fourteen come here and there is a big ceremony. No men are allowed. This is also a burial site, and there is one grave near here of an important Orma chief who died in the 1950s. So this place has special significance. On a clear day you can even see Kilimanjaro. If I had my wish, I would like to be buried here. Right now, we're thinking of where to bury our parents, and there's some discussion that it should be here, under this tree. We would place a big rock on their ashes, and engrave their names and dates."

Both Danny and Bongo are confident their father would be pleased to have his ashes rest at this place. Koito had special significance for Bill. It was here that he was camped with Elui when the Wakamba hunter first revealed the secret of the Waliangulu. Sitting on this same bluff Bill had seen the clouds of vultures that marked the carcasses of the poached elephants, and it was here he first began to realize the extent of the challenge he was soon to face.

That was in the fall of 1948. It was seven months later that Tsavo was divided into two parks; David Sheldrick was sent down to be the first warden of the eastern sector, and Bill Woodley was promoted to assistant warden under Sheldrick. Shortly after this Bill took David on a tour of the new park, telling him about the Waliangulu bow hunters and the extent of their poaching.

Like most people in National Parks, David knew nothing about the Waliangulu. Very little had been written about them. The first description of any length came from Charles New, an energetic missionary who, in 1871, organized an expedition to the greater Kilimanjaro region and described the Waliangulu as living in country that was "prairies of high course grass and rushes, far-stretching patches of sometimes dry, but usually flooded sand flats, and considerable portions of unhealthy miasmic mangrove swamps. It is not an inviting piece of country, though, no doubt, stocked as it is with wild beasts, it suits its possessors [who] live entirely by the chase, and are as wild and dexterous a set of nimrods as ever twanged a bow."

There were occasional references in the journals of subsequent explorers, and the early big-game hunters such as Percival and Hunter were aware that the Waliangulu could successfully bring down an elephant with a long bow and poisoned arrows, but they didn't realize the extent of their poaching. C. G. MacArthur, the game warden in the area during the 1930s, had arrested and prosecuted many Wakamba and some Waliangulu bow hunters, but he had been circumspect in passing on his knowledge to the young Woodley.

So David Sheldrick didn't necessarily disbelieve his junior warden, but he wanted to see for himself. The two made a trip to the lower Galana, near the park boundary, and there Sheldrick saw the evidence firsthand: Dozens of elephant carcasses, some of which were still fresh and attracting vultures. He was shocked, and he dispatched a report to headquarters in Nairobi informing his superiors that he estimated the bow hunters in and around Tsavo were killing somewhere around six hundred elephant a year.

But now what? How could he and Bill and a handful of rangers go about trying to capture these poachers? Like any detective work, they realized the first step was to gather information. They turned to Elui, and to a few other Wakamba poachers whom they had captured in the interim, for a beginner's ethnography of these elusive people.

They learned that most of the Waliangulu bow hunters lived in an area to the east of the park, a short day's walk from the boundary. There was another group a little to the north, and a third to the south. Together there were about a thousand of them, of whom about two hundred were active hunters. The most evident distinction between the familiar Wakambas and these lesser-known Waliangulu was the types of bows they used. The Wakambas had short bows about four feet long, but the Waliangulu bows were as long as six feet.

Bill had earlier obtained one of these longbows from a Wakamba informant, and, with several of the local people watching, he had confidently nocked an arrow and then tried to draw the bowstring. To his chagrin he couldn't pull it back more than a few inches. In later years Ian Parker researched the comparative history of these bows and learned that their double-convex curve was the same shape as bows depicted in Neolithic cave paintings in the Sahara and in Spain. Most astonishingly, the Waliangulu longbows had a measured draw weight between 120 and 170 pounds, making them perhaps the most powerful self-bows known, even more powerful than the famed armor-piercing longbows of medieval England. To draw the bow it was first lifted over the head, then as it was lowered the bowstring was drawn in the same motion. Perhaps the most graphic illustration of the Zen-like focus required to do this is the fact that occasionally a man would die while drawing his bow because his heart would rupture.

More deadly than the bow's strength was the power of the poison that was smeared on the arrow's hilt, just behind the head. Both the Wakamba and the Waliangulu used this poison derived from one of several species of *Acokanthera,* a small tree that grows in eastern and southern Africa and contains a variety of extremely potent toxins called cardiac glycosides that are used in medicine as heart stimulants, but in even small doses cause heart failure. Indeed, only two one-thousandths of a gram of the particular strain of *Aconkanthera* used by the Waliangulu is enough to kill a man, and a typical Waliangulu arrow carried enough poison to kill a twelve-thousand-pound elephant seventy times over.

David and Bill learned that this poison was obtained from the Giriama, a coastal people whose territory extended inland up the Sabaki to where these Waliangulu allegedly lived. The Giriama were also makers of palm wine, and it seemed that much of the money the Waliangulu made selling ivory to Giriama middlemen (who then sold it to the Indian and Arab ivory merchants in the coastal towns of Mombasa and Malindi) was used to buy more poison and more palm wine.

From their Wakamba informants, David and Bill learned the Waliangulu had one habit that both men realized was a potential Achilles' heel. Using a series of hatch marks, each hunter autographed his arrows with an individual signature. This was done because even though the arrows were tipped with poison so lethal an elephant would drop dead often within two hundred yards of being shot, arrows sometimes lodged in a victim's intestines where the poison's distribution was blocked by the compacted fecal browse, and it would take hours or even days before the elephant died. But when it did, and someone found it, the rightful owner could be traced by the signature on the arrow. David and Bill were able to obtain a few arrows retrieved from dead elephant, and also from a few Waliangulu hideouts they had discovered where hunters had cached their arrows. With Elui and the other Wakamba informants translating, they began at least to collect names of the more active Waliangulu hunters: Barissa Dara, Boru Debassa, Abakuna Gumundi. They also began to establish a hierarchy of who by reputation were the best hunters. At the top of this list was an individual whose hunting prowess was referred to almost reverentially, even by the Wakamba: Galo-Galo Kafonde.

❖

What they needed now was somehow to capture one of these top hunters. Their break came when David discovered along the Galana River a Waliangulu hideout with signs it had been very recently occupied. He and his rangers staked it out and succeeded in capturing one of the bigger-name hunters. He was about forty years old, and his name was Badiva Kuvicha. David was surprised when this Waliangulu led him to the tusks he had hidden, and then to the carcass of the elephant he had most recently shot. The hunter had a kind of endearing naïveté. He was affable, polite, and answered any question he was asked with apparent straightforward honesty. "How many elephant have you killed all together? Fifty?"

"Oh no," the Waliangulu answered. "More than that. Maybe four hundred."

From the information David and Bill had gathered so far they realized there were at least forty or fifty very good hunters operating in Tsavo East and the adjacent bushlands, and maybe ten of those were regarded as aces. So if this fellow had shot four hundred elephant—and he allegedly was nothing alongside this near-mythical Galo-Galo Kafonde—then the total number of animals being poached out of the greater Tsavo ecosystem was enormous. Before David and Bill could construct a strategy to deal with the problem, however, Bill was called to his mandatory six-month national service, and when the Mau-Mau rebellion broke out a few months later, in 1952, his tour was extended.

❖

It was a tough period for David Sheldrick. He would have enthusiastically joined Bill in the fight against the Mau-Mau, but the government decided it was more important to keep him in Tsavo. His marriage broke apart, and his wife left with their two children. David was fifteen years older than Bill, but he had enjoyed the junior warden's company, and he needed him now more than ever.

It would be two years, however, before the Mau-Mau were contained and Bill would be able to return to help David in the effort to contain the Waliangulu. During this period, it was probably a good thing that David was by temperament a loner. He had grown up an only child in the Aberdares, where his family owned the baronial Mweiga Estate and built the famous Treetops Lodge. His father was something of a martinet and insisted young David address him as "sir." When David was only four he was at a sawmill on their property when his father told the young boy to go home and tell his mother they were going to be late for supper, knowing the boy had to walk through a forest thick with rhino and buffalo. David did as he was told, and the father, without the boy knowing, followed. When David arrived home, his father caught up and told him he was proud that David had done as he was told, and that he had showed no fear. If his father expressed his paternal pride, he failed to display any direct affection: Two years later, at age six, David was sent to boarding school in England, and he didn't see his parents again until he was seventeen.

After serving in World War II with the King's African Rifles in India and Burma, David returned to Kenya and became a professional hunter, but he didn't enjoy the role of playing local hero for the amusement of wealthy clients. His personality was too reserved, so when he saw a notice for a warden's position in National Parks, he applied.

Now he was the first full warden of Tsavo East, and he resolved that even without Bill he would press his pursuit of the Waliangulu poachers. He decided to change strategy. He abandoned the fixed ranger posts he had established in favor of a mobilized field force of thirty men who were on standby to chase poachers whenever they received information of their whereabouts. Then he decided to take the offensive. From information gathered from informants, Sheldrick knew that most of the Waliangulu poachers lived lower on the Galana in a settlement called Kisiki Cha Mzungu, a half-day's walk downriver from the park boundary. Accompanied by a member of the Game Department, which gave him official sanction to operate outside of the park, David planned a surprise raid on the village. He and his rangers drove as far as they could under cover of darkness, then marched the remaining distance, arriving at first light. They surrounded one hut and inside it found bows and arrows and several elephant tails, so they arrested the owner. They stealthily approached another hut where a solitary man was sitting in front watching the sunrise. If he was surprised when Sheldrick appeared, he didn't show it. He was very lean and well muscled, with short-cropped wiry hair and watchful eyes. Sheldrick asked him his name and he said, "I am Galo-Galo Kafonde." David asked if he could search his hut, and with calm dignity the man said, "You may do so."

Inside there was a longbow and some rhino meat, but no ivory. David had his men search the bush surrounding the hut, and they soon uncovered two large tusks. When David asked him if they were his tusks, Galo-Galo said yes, adding that he had taken them off an elephant he had shot along the Galana, near the Yatta Plateau. He told David his four sons were still there, continuing the hunt. David asked him if he would lead them to the hideout, and Galo-Galo said, "Of course." Leaving part of his force to guard the prisoners they had rounded up in the raid, David set off with Galo-Galo and several rangers to the hideout. They drove as far as they could, then, tying a short length of rope to Galo-Galo's handcuffs, asked the hunter to lead the way. Night fell, and for two hours they threaded through the dark *Commifora* toward the river. Suddenly Galo-Galo lurched forward against the rope. The rangers pulled and then fell backward: Galo-Galo had slipped his hands through the cuffs and was gone. There was no hope chasing him, but David wondered why this Waliangulu had taken them so far from his village before trying to escape. He found the answer the next day when he followed Galo-Galo's tracks to a hideout that had been close to the camp from which Sheldrick had staged the raid, and from there Galo-Galo's tracks continued east, along with two other hunters who Sheldrick realized were probably his sons. As much as he hated losing him, David couldn't help but admire Galo-Galo's shrewd strategy in designing his escape and at the same time warning his sons.

During the next year David was more successful in apprehending poach ers in the area south of the Galana, but Galo-Galo and the other top aces began to operate in the north country, which was much more difficult to patrol. When the causeway across the river above Lugard's Falls was completed, David pushed the road to the northern boundary of the park where he worked to build an outpost from which rangers could organize patrols. Still, it was far too large an area to safeguard with the number of men available to him. But David was a creative strategist. He convinced the East African Wildlife Society, the Game Department, and National Parks to collectively give him the manpower, equipment, and authority he needed to break the back of the native bow hunters once and for all. It was then that Bill Woodley returned from the Mau-Mau insurrection.

During the insurrection Bill had been promoted to captain, commanded his own regiment, and became a counterinsurgent, disguising himself as a Mau-Mau by rubbing stove-black on his face and infiltrating into enemy hide-outs. He was awarded the prestigious Military Cross not for any single action, as is usual, but for general leadership, which is very unusual. He returned to Tsavo with a knowledge of guerrilla warfare that would serve him well in the coming campaign that Sheldrick was designing. He also returned a married man. His new bride was Pete Jenkins's younger sister, Daphne.

They moved into a small house at the park headquarters at Voi. Shortly after that she met David Sheldrick.

"David had a presence," Daphne would tell me when I interviewed her after our walk. "A bit aloof and shy, but he exuded power and confidence, and had an air of authority. He wasn't arrogant—he was very quiet and humble—but he had this strength you could feel."

Daphne also saw that David and Bill got along very well. David was pleased to have Bill back, and together they reviewed the plans David had designed for an organized antipoaching campaign against the Waliangulu bow hunters. David had arranged to have several game wardens join the effort, including the young Ian Parker. Pete Jenkins was transferred from Tsavo West to assist the effort. The rangers, now called the Voi Field Force, were divided into three sections. Ian was put in charge of patrols operating in the coastal area, and also north toward the Tana River. Bill and Pete were in charge of the field force that focused on the area around the Galana River, both within the park and downriver of the boundary. David would oversee logistics, and also public relations, which was essential to get Nairobi to support them with personnel and matériel. The colony's governor, Sir Evelyn Baring, gave the effort his personal endorsement. Special police units in Voi and in Malindi were placed under Sheldrick's direction to track down the ivory middlemen and the coastal Arab and Indian trading syndicates.

The pieces were in place. Sheldrick had everything he needed, and the Anti-Poaching Campaign began.

22

*Not every man [in the tribe] is qualified by temperament, boldness and
skill to hunt big game, and those who do are outstanding individuals, both
for the amount of meat they supply to their fellows, and for the respect that
they receive, if they survive.*

—Carlton S. Coon,
The Hunting Peoples, 1971

A herd of oryx run down the skyline like galloping cavalry, their horns like
lances in erect silhouette against the gathering cumulus. I watch the foraging flight of the little bee-eater as it leaves its perch and sallies out to
hawk its insect prey, returning in a wheeling trajectory to the same branch,
while down by the river comes the parakeet-like chatter of a flock of Namaqua doves.

We have only five kilometers before we reach our camp at Sala Gate, so
we cross the river and walk the road on the south bank arriving eventually
at a crossroads with a large rock cairn in the center supporting a flat stone
that has painted on it the kilometer distances to various points in the park.
In the early years David Sheldrick had experimented with cedar roadsigns
but the elephants had knocked them down, or worse, had the habit of turning them around, to the confusion of the tourists; these stone replacements
have held up admirably in the twenty years since he died.

And so has the road on which we walk, and for that matter, all the roads in Tsavo East. And the main park headquarters in Voi, and the northern park headquarters in Ithumba. And the gatehouses at the entry points and the causeway at Lugard's Falls. Nearly every man-made structure in Tsavo East was built under the supervision of David Sheldrick during his long tenure as park warden from 1949 to 1976, and nearly all of them are still serviceable.

❦

In the early years, while Bill was away fighting the Mau-Mau, David pursued these construction projects between his raids and patrols trying to capture the bow hunters. Once Bill was back, however, the main focus of David's and everyone else's efforts was the Anti-Poaching Campaign. They started in earnest in late 1955 when Sheldrick sent the Voi Field Force on patrols through all areas where poachers were suspected of operating. Their first success came when one of the patrols near Sala Hill picked up a hunter's track that led to a hideout where they apprehended Guyu Debassa, one of the top ten Waliangulu aces. As had happened with other Waliangulu they had captured, Debassa was open and friendly, and answered all their questions as though he had no ability to lie or to deceive. He told them that Galo-Galo Kafonde had been very active in the area, and had recently taken more than twenty elephant. More importantly, he was at that moment resting in his hut at Kisiki Cha Mzungu. Bill and Pete decided it was time to plan another raid on the village, and this time they didn't plan on letting the great hunter get away.

"We drove to Lali Hill," Pete Jenkins told me, "and got there in the afternoon. We had ten rangers with us, and about ten porters because we planned to camp at Kisiki Cha Mzungu."

They also had Guyu Debassa who had agreed to guide them to Galo-Galo's hut. "We were very confident we were going to get Galo-Galo," Pete recalled. "We knew he had just sold his ivory, he had money in his pocket, and we were sure we'd find him lying around boozed up on palm wine."

It was over a twenty-mile hike to Kisiki Cha Mzungu. "It was a good thing we had moonlight," Pete continued. "The wait-a-bit was thick. Then suddenly out of the bush this great rhino came charging right at us, puffing and snorting, and Bill dove one direction while I went another, and the porters scattered, utensils and pots clanking, making a frightful noise. Somehow the rhino missed everybody. It took us an hour to regroup, and we didn't arrive at Kisiki Cha Mzungu until five in the morning.

"With our guide showing us the various little footpaths, some of us crept 'round the back of Galo-Galo's hut while others approached from the front. We burst in, but no one was inside. Somehow Galo-Galo had gotten wind we were creeping up, and he had just managed to sneak off into the bush. We did arrest a few others, and we also took Galo-Galo's wife and his son, Hunter Galo-Galo, in for questioning, but this was done more to put the pressure on Galo-Galo himself."

By then Bill had developed a very effective method of interrogating prisoners. With Daphne's assistance, they kept detailed note cards recording every fact they learned, no matter how trivial or irrelevant it seemed at the time. "During the course of questioning," Daphne wrote in her book *Tsavo Story*, "a poacher might reveal that his colleague had turned back because he had been stung by a scorpion on his toe while trailing an elephant. Finally, when the companion was brought to book, he was flabbergasted by only one question, 'How's your toe? Have you recovered from the scorpion bite?' Invariably the poacher would be so dumbfounded that he assumed if this small incident in his life was known, what was the use of beating around the bush . . . and more often than not, he proceeded to pour out a string of confessions."

"The next raid on Kisiki Cha Mzungu," Pete recalled, "was from the south. We drove in a Land Rover as far as we could go, then walked the rest of the way in the early morning hours. At dawn we swept the village one end to the other. We captured twelve poachers that day, but once again Galo-Galo gave us the slip."

With each raid it took several days to interrogate the additional round of prisoners. Daphne continued to catalog the information that was then used to illicit more confessions. The effort was achieving its goal. Hundreds of poachers were arrested and prosecuted, including nearly all of the so-called top ten Waliangulu aces. The magistrate would fly down from Nairobi to try the prisoners. Most of the sentences were between twelve and eighteen months. When the Waliangulu were released, Bill and David did their best to get them jobs as rangers or gun bearers for the hunting outfitters, so they wouldn't return to poaching.

"Bill and David were a formidable combination," Ian Parker said. "David cold and austere, Bill warm and open, but they operated with a strong mutual respect, and together they were perhaps the greatest partnership in the history of colonial African conservation."

◈

Formidable perhaps, but there was one man from their "most wanted list" who continued to elude them. Bill and Pete staged two more raids on Kisiki Cha Mzungu. Each time they approached as stealthily as possible. Each time they had at least ten additional rangers help them sweep the village hut to hut, covering the back and sides in case anybody tried to escape. And each time the wily Galo-Galo Kafonde escaped.

In one raid they found Galo-Galo's hut empty but with indications the occupant would soon return. With his rangers, Bill hid behind a bush and waited. His patience paid off. Galo-Galo came into view, walking toward his hut. But then the hunter stopped and studied his dog standing in front of his hut. The animal was looking toward the bush where Bill was hiding. Bill held his breath, Galo-Galo studied the animal, then suddenly turned and ran.

It was as though Galo-Galo possessed the stalking instincts of a lion and the stealth of a leopard. Bill and Pete began to despair whether they would ever catch him. They were now going out on patrols that lasted as long as six weeks, and it was creating a strain on Bill's marriage. "He never talked about it," Pete said. "But I was aware they were beginning to drift apart. Then there was this relationship between Daphne and David that actually started during the antipoaching operation."

◈

After our trek, when I sat down and talked to Daphne and later to Pete, they were both discreet about how the affair started, Daphne saying only that she had married very young. "Bill and I never had a huge row, but rather we grew apart. Bill was fantastic for me between the ages of fifteen and twenty-five, and David was fantastic between twenty-five and forty-two," she said. Here she paused and looked out over the bushland beyond her house where I was interviewing her. She had to swallow and clear her throat, but then she straightened, smiled, and looked at me but past me, as though she were gazing at something more distant. "I have been very lucky," she said. "I have had two wonderful men in my life."

As I came to know Bill vicariously through his two sons, and then through his friends and his former wife, the picture formed of a man who listened carefully, who sought to see the other's side in any issue, and who, above all, enjoyed people and respected and honored his friendships. He must have already owned those attributes as a young man during this difficult period in his life, for how else to explain that he and David remained steadfast friends, or that once Bill had remarried, he chose to spend his honeymoon with David and Daphne, who themselves had recently married? And that he kept these attributes into older age, for how else to explain that twenty years later at a dinner party at the Woodley household someone said something disparaging about Daphne, and Bill, a man who rarely lost his temper, flushed and said, "No one is *ever* allowed to speak badly of Daphne in this house. No one."

I can also imagine that the inevitable tensions that existed during this time no doubt fueled the wild bacchanals that happened when Bill and Pete came in from their one- to two-month stints in the bush chasing poachers. They would grab David and repair to the nearby Voi Hotel, the principal lodge for tourists visiting Tsavo East. "The parties would go on for several days," Pete said. "Maybe an hour or two of sleep, then back to it. The manager would give us the keys and leave us to the bar. One night we were making a lot of noise and he complained about us disturbing the other guests, so we had to lock him in the cold room. On another occasion he was standing in the lounge reading the paper and David made a very long shot with a dart and got him perfectly in the backside. We had a carpenter who worked full time repairing furniture and other damage, so the place was always kept in good condition.

"One day after Bill and I had been on safari for about six weeks," Pete said, "we were sitting in the hotel having a boozer when a messenger arrived with a telegram that he gave to David. It was from the police down on the coast, and it said, 'Please arrange to pick up Galo-Galo Kafonde at the Malindi Police Station.' Bill said it must be a hoax, and David agreed, saying 'Forget it, let's have another drink.' Then we thought about it some more, and David said that maybe Bill and I should go down to Malindi and see what's going on. It was about five in the evening, and we'd had quite a lot to drink, but we set off and it was after midnight when we arrived. In the morning we went to the police station and they told us this old guy from the bush had just showed up and turned himself in. We found him sitting in a cell, a very dignified old man. He looked at us and said, 'I am Galo-Galo Kafonde. What do you want with me?' "

Bill and Pete then drove the great hunter back to Voi where Bill spent several days interrogating him. It appeared that Galo-Galo had turned himself in because he had simply grown tired of being chased. David asked him why years before, when he had arrested him, Galo-Galo had slipped his handcuffs and escaped, and the old man replied that he felt it was okay to escape because David had failed to ask him *not* to escape.

Galo-Galo was never arrested and never prosecuted. He stayed at Voi for two months, without supervision, and even accompanied Bill and Pete on one of their operations. They eventually released him, and he walked back to Kisiki Cha Mzungu.

◈

He crosses the dried mud pan of the Kanderi Swamp, then picks up the Voi River lugga, and walks toward the morning sun. In the season of the long rains the grass is good in this area, and the elephant leave the river and come here to browse; it takes extra effort to find them as they scatter wide, but what is the use now of thinking of elephant? He feels naked without his bow and arrows, walking with his hands empty, walking as only half a man.

He remembers when he was a boy and he made his first arrows. Not his play arrows, but his first serious arrows. There were three, and they were handsome and well constructed, with flights of feathers taken from the wings of the vulture and four in number, as was the Wata way. He took his arrows and his bow, and he left the village by himself. On his first day he saw in the bush the striped back of the lesser kudu, and as his father had taught him, he moved downwind and then up, slowly, like a leopard, until he was close; he drew his longbow, and the arrow loosed and the antelope fell. The second arrow found its mark on a great female giraffe, and she too fell, and he knew she would offer meat for the entire village for many days. With the third arrow he now decided he would take ivory, and he chose a boro, a male elephant with good tusks and he stalked close as his father had taught him and he had no fear though he knew if he made a mistake he would die.

He made no mistake and he returned to the village with his tusks and with the elephant's tail tied to his arm; the men in the village spoke between themselves and as he was yet a boy they built a small frame and covered it with his elephant's ears and they shaved his head and he sat in the shelter while they rubbed the fat from the elephant on his head and thus he became a man. The words reached his ears that the men in the village said that never before in anyone's memory and never in any stories passed down had a boy proved himself with three great animals taken with his first three arrows, and that the boy was marked to be a great hunter, marked to be perhaps the greatest hunter of all.

He always preferred to hunt by himself, though that was not the custom. He would get within ten paces of the elephant before he loosed his arrow, and once a great male elephant turned on him and charged and he crawled under a fallen tree and as the elephant in its pain and rage smashed the limbs he jumped one way and then the other with the elephant over him, and as the great feet came down and the trunk swung crashing through the branches looking for him he saw the opening between the giant's rear legs and he jumped as the leg came down where he had been half a heartbeat before, and he escaped.

But all that is now story. He walks along the dry streambed lined with the tall river trees and remembers when the mzungus first began to chase them they thought it was a game, and they shifted hunting to the north country, then south again, and it was easy to avoid the patrols, and they thought nothing of it. But the mzungus returned and came to the village with their rifles and arrested them and sent them to jail and his brother had died there from a mzungu disease and, as was the custom, he had taken his brother's sons into his house and they joined his own sons.

And what will these sons do if they cannot hunt? He has taught them well. Young Hunter, named after the great mzungu who called himself J. A. Hunter, what will he do? What will become of them, the Wata, the people? The Elephant People?

PART THREE

Sabaki

23

Theirs had been a life of risk gladly taken—of so few wants, leisurely and communal, intellectual in ways that are simultaneously practical and aesthetic. And most pertinent to our time, it was a life founded on the integrity of solitude and human sparseness in which men do not become a disease on their environment.

—*The great hunter Philip Percivel on the Waliangulu,*
as quoted by Peter Beard in The End of the Game, 1963

We camp between a grove of doums and a lone Tana River poplar, and that night a gathering of hippo on a mid-river sandbar keeps me awake with its nasal grunting and ha-ha-ha chortling that sounds like a group of fat old-boys telling jokes. One of them waddles up the bank and walks through the middle of camp, and a ranger yells at the brute, and its requires no translation to understand what he says.

In the morning, at first light, we eat our breakfast, then leave to walk the half mile between camp and the Sala gatehouse where the ranger on duty, dressed in crisp green fatigues and polished black boots, snaps a salute and opens the iron gate with the metal profile of a rhinoceros welded in the middle. We thank him; then in two columns we march out of Tsavo East National Park and down a road that is as straight as a surveyor's sight line. From the top of one rise we see the road extending through the bushland up the

next rise, down again, up again, in a compass course that is cross-grain to
these hills that are like small ripples on an otherwise flat plain. There is,
however, in the far distance one promontory that looks like the prowhead of
a whale, and over the next days it will very slowly advance on our horizon
and be the benchmark against which we measure our march.

"Aren't there any hippo trails down by the river?" Iain asks in a voice that
everyone hears.

Bongo and Danny don't respond.

"Are we going to walk along the river at all today?" he asks again.

Bongo half turns his head and says, "Negative."

"It had been my understanding when we planned this walk we would follow the river as much as possible."

"The bush is too thick down there. I've walked it."

Iain looks at me and says sotto voce, "I've had about all of this military
nonsense I can take."

We have only four or five days before we reach the coast, and I am hope-
ful this tension felt most tautly between Iain and Bongo doesn't erupt into
open argument before we finish. I have no way of knowing whether or not
there are hippo trails next to the river, and neither does Iain, but we should
have discussed the issue as a group and made a decision as a group.

Even with this undercurrent of discord, and even with the fact we are, at
the moment, following a road—and in this respect removed from the feeling
I had in Tsavo of at least approximating what it would have been like to be
with Thomson or Lugard through these same regions one hundred years
ago—I still feel good. I am enjoying the physical act of spending each day
walking across East Africa.

Another distinction between our trek and those turn-of-the-century safaris
is that they had native porters and we, other than Chui and Bernard, who
help Pete and me with our camera gear, do not. In one way this is unfortunate, because on many of my previous expeditions—especially the mountain climbs in remote ranges—the opportunity to spend days and weeks
(and sometimes months) in the company of local porters during the trek to
base camp has always been an enlivening part of an adventure.

Porters are usually animal herders or farmers who take work in their off-
seasons carrying loads for expeditions, but on one occasion I had the chance
to hire porters who were true hunters and gatherers. With a few climbing

friends we were on our way to scale a mysterious tusk of granite that rose out of an uninhabited fastness near the border between Venezuela and Brazil eighty miles beyond the last Yanomami villages; and those were villages that had been surveyed by anthropologists only in the previous decade. As we continued upriver, we stopped in our dugouts at the last and most remote village to see if we could hire one more person to help us porter our gear to the base of the spire. The villagers gathered around us. The men wore only a single fold of red cloth around their loins, and they each carried either a machete or a bow and arrows. We had with us one Yanomami from downriver who had worked as an informant for an anthropologist, and therefore could speak Spanish; through him we asked the chief if there was anyone we could hire. We explained that once the river we were traveling became too narrow to navigate, we would leave the boats and walk through the jungle; in all, we would be gone about one month. The chief pointed to a young man standing next to us, holding his bow and arrows and nothing else, and said he would go with us.

"Fine," I answered. "Tell him we will wait while he gets his things."

"He has his things," the chief said. "He is ready."

The only peoples in Africa today who might approach the Yanomami's ability to live off of and travel through their landscape with such unfettered ease and skill would be some of the pygmy groups in the Congo, and remnant groups of Bushmen in the Kalahari.

In his book *Ivory Crisis*, Ian Parker says the Waliangulu share many physical features with the Bushmen. From the photographs in his book it appears to me the Waliangulu have a variety of physical shapes, which probably reflect miscegenation with other tribes, notably the Giriama and Orma, but many others of them do look astonishingly like Bushman, with their round, nut-shaped heads, low nose bridges, and chins that take the same curve as their cheeks. They also seem to share the same cheerful temperament and unpretentious honesty that is renowned among Bushmen. (It is interesting to note that two remnants of Khosian-speaking peoples—the famed click-tongued languages of the Bushmen—exist in Tanzania and suggest that prehistorically these peoples ranged not only across southern Africa, but north as well, perhaps as far as the Blue Nile.)

Like the Bushmen, the Waliangulu (at least in the old days) also knew how to walk. In his book *The Elephant People*, Denis Holman told the story of how Sheldrick, on the day he had his first antipoaching success with the capture of Badiva Kuvicha, also caught an eight-year-old boy who had accompanied his elders on their hunt, and was just learning to shoot with an undersize bow and arrows. Sheldrick took him back to park headquarters and gave him a smart uniform to wear, and light chores to perform around the compound. He received a small wage, and he was allowed to accompany the rangers on patrol. Sheldrick hoped in that way to prevent the boy from becoming an elephant hunter, and thereby to save him from the fate he knew the boy's elders must eventually suffer. The boy was a hard worker, but he was also homesick. One day while accompanying the rangers on patrol the boy disappeared, and it was learned later that by himself he crossed the entire breadth of Tsavo East, following the game trails used by hippo and buffalo and lion, fording the river with its population of often very large crocodile, back to his village of Kisiki Cha Mzungu, a distance of eighty miles.

I wonder today if any of the eight-year-old Waliangulu boys from Kisiki Cha Mzungu could repeat this journey. For that matter, I wonder if any of them even remember the days when an eighty-mile walk across bushland full of wild animals was commonplace. Do any of these boys still learn to shoot a bow and arrow? It is of course very improbable that any of them, boys or elders, still shoot even an occasional elephant, but it is possible they still use bows to shoot game for the pot (even though this too can result in a jail sentence). As Danny said during the planning stages of our trek, these are all questions that, until we walk through the area where the Waliangulu live, or at least used to live, no one can answer.

❖

As I learned more about the Anti-Poaching Campaign of 1955 to 1957 that was so successfully organized by David Sheldrick and implemented by Bill Woodley, I realized that the Waliangulu were not poachers, at least not with the pejorative baggage that the word "poacher" carries when separating bad guys from good guys. The Waliangulu were poachers only as defined by the game laws. And those laws were similar (if not the same) as the laws that had disenfranchised native hunters in Britain when first introduced after the Norman conquest. (I chose to refer to them as poachers earlier in the book, however, because the word "poacher" defined their relationship both to the colonial administration and to the African government that followed.)

It became clear to me as well that Bill Woodley knew the Waliangulu were victims of changing times; he used that argument before the magistrate to plead for light sentences for the bow hunters once they had been arrested. He and the others in the campaign subdued the bow hunters because they believed that was the only way to save the elephant. But I began to wonder to what extent he and the others involved, such as Pete Jenkins and Ian Parker, realized that while they were, at least in the prevailing view of the time, assisting the survival of the most emblematic species of Africa's megafauna, they were at the same time condemning to death one of the most inviolate of Africa's native hunting cultures.

When our trek was over, I asked Ian Parker this question, and he said that indeed it had caused them anguish, although perhaps more after they had done it than while they were doing it.

"Even though we all were born and raised in Africa," he told me, "we were all incredibly ignorant of Africans and African culture. It's the way we were brought up. All of us—Bill, David, Pete, myself—were from settler families, from British who came here and founded a system based on the assumption that Africans knew nothing, that they had somehow been benighted while the outside world had progressed around them.

"But this assumption was fallacious. Archaeological and historical evidence has proved that before the European explorations, the interior of Africa down to the edges of the Kalahari had continuous contact with the Indian Ocean coast, and through this with Eastern Arabian and Indian cultures, at least as far back as the time of Roman and Greek traders. How could we have been so ignorant of this? While it is perhaps unfair and even inaccurate to single out an individual as responsible, there was a single character who does illustrate what happened, and that character is David Livingstone. He was not an admirable man. Although he came to Africa as a doctor and a missionary, his interest was fame. He converted one person to Christianity the entire time he was here, and he practiced remarkably little medicine. He wanted to be known as an explorer, and he rigorously suppressed any information that suggested other outsiders had beat him into the interior. When he arrived on the Zambezi, for example, he bumped into an Arab trader who guided him all the way to the Atlantic coast, and this Arab couldn't have done that if he hadn't already made the trip before. Livingstone even encountered two wealthy Portuguese farmers who were exploring the interior of Africa just for the hell of it. There was an Austrian resident in the upper Zambezi who invited Livingstone to join him, but Livingstone refused.

"So Livingstone created this concept of the Dark Continent. In this he was supported strongly by the missionaries who wanted to promote the concept of a continent that needed to be saved from its own ignorance. So we, the children of that same British generation, were brought up with this same attitude, an attitude we carried into our campaign against the Waliangulu, or the Wata, as they call themselves." (Ian prefers to use the name Wata because Waliangulu, meaning "eaters of tortoise," is somewhat pejorative. I chose to keep Waliangulu because it is the name that has common currency, and the Waliangulu themselves don't seem to mind: They say they like eating tortoises, and if other people don't like them, that's too bad.)

"But I'll tell you, the four of us began to realize, as we got further into the Anti-Poaching Campaign, that the Wata had one hell of a show on the road. With what they had available, I don't think today you could possibly come up with a more efficient way to hunt elephant. The more I learned about them in the years that followed, the more impressed I was. It is a very peculiar thing for a hunting-and-gathering tribe to concentrate on one species like the Wata did on elephant. It's understandable if there is only one species—if all you have to hunt is seals—but that wasn't the case. So why only elephant? And why were there no other elephant-hunting cultures on the entire continent? Even when ivory has been valued by all other peoples the world over? Then look at their bows. They were as powerful as medieval longbows, which were developed to penetrate armor, just as the Wata bows were designed to penetrate elephant. Yet for both purposes, you have to have metal arrowheads. The Wata were also known as Wasaini—the Smiths. If you go into a Giriama village today, and ask them where they learned iron-making, they will say, 'From the hunters.' Hunters normally adopt these technologies, they don't develop them. So where did the Wata get metal? They got it by trading ivory.

"Now let's take a moment to look at ivory itself. The demand for ivory occurred in all Mediterranean cultures, the whole bloody lot wanted it. Where did they get it? There was some ivory that came out of North Africa. But where in that area do you get elephant herds of any size to support a vigorous trade? Herds that are within reach of a maritime people who didn't have the resources to penetrate deep into the continent? Where, on the borders of Africa, are the first big elephant populations? Southern Somalia and coastal Kenya, that's where.

"So go read *The Periplus of the Erythrean Sea.*" (When I returned home, I did read it. *Periplus* is Greek for "Sailing Directions," and the Erythrean Sea was the ancient Greek name for the Red Sea and the West Indian Ocean. This captivating book is the sailing directions for Mediterranean sailors trading down the African coast and across to Arabia, and it was written in the first century A.D.) "The *Periplus* makes reference to a trade of iron ingots for ivory along the East African coast, and it mentions a tribe who hunted with bows that required two people to pull them." (If you're not trained to draw a long-bow, you can't just pull it, as Bill Woodley once found out.)

"So my hypothesis is that the Wata were not some group of primitive hunter and gatherers. They were an elephant-hunting culture geared to providing ivory to the outside world, and when we came along they had already been doing it for two thousand years or more.

"But to return to your question about how we felt about them then, when we were all still very young. It was this: The Wata were hunters. They were masters of the bush. They were living off the land, and they were fitting in naturally. So, you see, to be honest, they were living the lives that we ourselves would have liked to live."

◈

Ian told me this in the living room of a friend's house on the outskirts of Nairobi, across from the national park. We were both enjoying an afternoon Tusker, the preferred beer of Kenya, and I suggested a break so I could take a photograph of him in the garden. Ian was a lean man, seventy-one years old, with a sharp nose and narrow chin. He looked fit, energetic, and easily amused, as people are who have an innate curiosity. He is an active writer, and he was just finishing a series of profiles on five African game wardens (two of whom were Bill Woodley and David Sheldrick). His light blue eyes were quick and articulate, and they looked mischievous.

In fact, Ian is well known in African conservation circles as a gadfly, although he sees himself as a realist. "Before examining the trees, I want to see the woods. I see so many people frigging about with the trees." His most contentious position has been his views on culling. He believes culling is appropriate in some circumstances, and he founded the company Wildlife Services Ltd. (chartered with one thousand pounds that Ian received from selling tusks from the biggest elephant he had ever shot) that, among other functions, contracted with Uganda to cull elephants in Murchison Falls National Park. Wildlife Services also was the company selected by Dick Laws to carry out the culling in Tsavo before the park trustees and David Sheldrick stopped the plan. "The media has tried to place me in the camp of pro-culling," he said, "but that's like saying I favor screwdrivers instead of spanners. Culling is a tool appropriate to some tasks."

Such views place Ian firmly in the camp of the scientists, with the "bunny huggers" on the other side; but as is often the case with simplified black-and-white reductions, this one misses the gray tones in between. In this

case, it's that Ian's position on culling has its roots in his early days working
to contain the Waliangulu poachers. Eventually, as he came to understand
that they had been taking elephant for a very long time, he also realized they
were as natural a part of the ecosystem in greater Tsavo as any other predator. The Waliangulu had been hunting elephant for so long that both predator and prey had achieved an equilibrium. When this balance was upset,
there were reverberations that have sounded continuously for forty years:
the increase in the elephant population in Tsavo in the 1960s, the great die-
off in the drought of the early 1970s, the scavenging of the deadfall ivory
that opened the door to the poaching in the 1980s, and now, at the close of
the 1990s, an elephant population that, while appearing to be at a sustainable level, is nevertheless increasing at a rate of about five percent a year, a
little more than what Kenya's human increase was when it had the highest
rate of population growth in the world. As David Western said, the story
isn't over yet.

In addition to realizing the Waliangulu provided this balance to the elephant
population, Ian Parker also realized that without the ability to hunt elephant,
the Waliangulu would wither. He understood they were different from the
Wakambas, for whom hunting was a supplement to herding goats and growing crops. The Waliangulu were pure hunters. Their entire culture revolved
around the return they gained from elephant ivory and elephant meat, and
they had nothing else to turn to. Realizing this was why Bill Woodley at-
tempted, after the Waliangulu had served their sentences, to find them jobs
as rangers or gun bearers. (You can imagine what must have gone through the
mind of a Waliangulu who had spent his life hunting elephant, then spent
eighteen months in prison for hunting elephant, only to be released and paid
a small wage to assist some overweight American in safari clothes with a big
rifle and enough money to buy a license to hunt elephant.)

In general the attempts to convert the Waliangulu to wage earners failed.
There were a few exceptions—the most notable being the great bow-hunting
ace Abakuna Gumundi, who went on to become perhaps the most successful
native big-game tracker of his time—but for most of the others, there either
weren't enough of these jobs to go around; or when there were, many of them
proved, with their weakness for palm wine, to be less than dependable.

Following the completion of the Anti-Poaching Campaign, in 1958, Ian
Parker had been appointed game ranger of the Kilifi District, an area that

included the three-thousand-square-mile region downriver of the Tsavo Dust park boundary known as the Kilifi Game Range. This area also encompassed Kisiki Cha Mzungu and the other Waliangulu villages to the north. Like Sheldrick and Woodley, Ian was aware that something needed to be done to rescue the Waliangulu. The three of them were wrestling with this problem when they learned from a mutual friend how the Canadian government had solved a similar problem with native Inuit hunters in the high Arctic by creating a system that allowed them to continue to hunt and trap in traditional ways that were consistent with wildlife conservation. The government issued quotas on how many animals could be taken, and controlled the sale of the fur that resulted from the hunts. Why couldn't such a system be set up to allow the Waliangulu to continue to hunt on the Kilifi Game Range where there were still abundant herds of elephant?

Ian Parker drafted a proposal outlining a similar plan for the Waliangulu, and it won government approval. It was officially titled the Galana River Game Management Scheme, but became known, more conveniently, as the Waliangulu Scheme. Ian was charged with administering it, and as he outlined it in its original form, the only people who would be allowed to hunt were residents within the region who had depended on hunting for their livelihood. A quota of three hundred elephant a year would be established and apportioned to each of the five villages in the area. It would be up to the hunters to take the elephant as they saw fit, and it would be up to Ian to enforce the quota, and to transfer the ivory to the Treasury Department, which would sell it and remit the money back to the scheme, where it was to be used to support the project and to assist the Waliangulu.

"The first setback came when the government decided that the Wata had to use firearms to take the elephants," Ian said. "They thought bows and poisoned arrows were too cruel. But then the police had a problem with a large bunch of Waliangulu having rifles, and they insisted it be limited to only a select group of individuals who could be trained and monitored. But the most difficult issue was the ivory itself because by definition the ivory would belong to the government, even if the Wata, by theory, were supposed to see money from it." Here David Sheldrick was the most perceptive. "If the ivory isn't theirs," he said, "this thing won't work. Ivory is the linchpin of their culture."

The other problem was that from the beginning the Game Department said the scheme must not only pay for itself, but return a profit to the government. In the first year's accounting, the Game Department refused to include money that international organizations had contributed to the scheme. To increase revenue, Ian suggested that white hunters be allowed in the area to take elephant on license. After the powerful floods of 1961 and 1962 scoured the *Commifora* woodland and allowed fertile grasses to thrive, Ian further suggested that cattle ranching be introduced as an additional revenue source.

"I just wish I knew then what I do now," Ian told me. "I would have listened more to the Wata, to hear what they wanted, and to let them do it. But as the scheme evolved, they became mere employees of the government, and employment was the last thing they needed. They were free spirits who couldn't live under controls and rules. The scheme was as alien to them as if we had asked them to work in a car factory, and even though I couldn't see it then, it was doomed to fail, just as they were doomed to wither away."

From the top of a crest the road stretches in a straight line east. The river is two or three kilometers to our left, and over the tops of the intervening *luggas*, we can see a group of trees—a green oasis in this expanse of dun bush that Danny says is the headquarters of the Kulalu Ranch. We leave the road and cut overland, through the bush, heading for the distant trees.

We weave through the *Commifora* and wait-a-bit, scaring up a white-bellied bustard, then a black-bellied bustard, and later a courser, all birds that look like waterfowl that have adapted to life in dry bush. I pick up a perfectly round mud golf ball that is light and hollow, and Danny says it is the dung beetle ball and explains how the dung beetle lays its eggs and then rolls them in mud to form the ball, which will hatch when the rains return. "They are usually buried," he says, which explains why we haven't seen more of them. I put the ball in my camera bag, intending to take it home for my young son who loves to dig for bugs in the yard; I have no doubt he will be excited to add a dung beetle ball to his collection.

In the bottom of the *luggas* we pass the spear-ended stalks of *Sansevieria*, an agave-looking plant that Danny warns contains poison in its needle tips that is very toxic. We are now on the Kulalu Ranch property, which, in the years since Ian Parker administered the Waliangulu Scheme (and first suggested the introduction of cattle), has evolved into a government-owned corporation, and still operates as a cattle ranch, although big-game hunting for elephant or otherwise has not been allowed since hunting of any sort was banned in Kenya in 1977. Not that the ban would have made any difference, as there are very few animals anyway. We have seen one bat-eared fox, and now we flush a small group of fringe-eared oryx. This is, of course, in great contrast to the companies of ungulates, the herds of elephant, the gatherings of hippo, and the magnificent pair of lion that we saw all within a day's walk inside the boundary of Tsavo East. (And it also appears to be evidence, at least for the greater Tsavo, that counters David Western's claim that seventy percent of Kenya's wild animals live outside the national parks.)

We descend another *lugga* and into a grove of overhead acacia that have dropped small leaves that create an autumn-yellow carpet on the sandy floor of the seasonal streambed. We find a trail that leads to the ranch headquarters, a scattering of perhaps two dozen buildings, including a schoolhouse and a general store, all built of concrete block walls and corrugated metal roofs. A desultory collection of men dressed in thrift-store shirts and pants idle in the shade, as they seem to do in all such settings in the equatorial world. Other than a few young schoolgirls, there are no women (they are probably out working). It is hot, and we are tired. We pause at the store and each drink a syrupy Coca-Cola, which doesn't taste as good as it sounded when someone suggested the idea. The concrete block wall of the store is riddled with pock holes that Danny says are from a shoot-out against Somali *shifta* armed with AK-47s who once tried to raid the ranch. We meet the ranch manager, a tall thin man in his mid-thirties with a patchy goatee and sharp, intelligent eyes. He knows Danny from the days of fighting the Somalis, and he gives us a cordial welcome.

After a rest we leave the headquarters, angling toward the river, which is now a kilometer away, and soon we pick up a hiking path. It is welcome relief from the dirt road we followed in the morning. We pass several kids returning from school, a young man walking his beat and bent bicycle, and now a few women, all freighting baskets on their heads. The trail climbs a short hill and on top we pass a small hut with a frame of woven reed covered haphazardly with thatch. Next to the door is a piece of discarded corrugated metal sheeting. Nearby a middle-aged woman in a stained lavender and green *kanga* wrap is restringing a bed frame with plaited cord. Bongo says, "Jambo!" but the woman is shy and uncomfortable, and doesn't respond. There is a five-year-old boy with a distended belly beside her, and he too keeps his distance. Toward the river we can see a few more huts. Some are thatched beehives and others more rectangular wattle and daub structures, and there are several people milling and lounging under a shade tree. Then a man in his early twenties approaches and we exchange greetings.

"Ask him the name of this place," I say to Bongo. When the young man replies, I don't need a translator to understand.

"Kisiki Cha Mzungu."

24

> *Hunters and gatherers work less than we do; and, rather than a continuous travail, the food quest is intermittent, leisure abundant, and there is a greater amount of sleep in the daytime per capita per year than in any other condition of society.*
>
> —*Marshall Sahlins,*
> Stone Age Economics, 1972

A small crowd has gathered around us. They are a mix of mostly young women and children, although one middle-aged man has joined the company. All are dressed ragamuffin in discarded Western clothes, and one young man has a torn and holed shirt that says Columbia University. (Clothing donated to organizations such as the Salvation Army is often sold to middlemen at rates as low as thirteen cents a pound, who truss it into five-hundred-pound bales that are shipped to Third World countries, where, in remote villages such as this, a shirt may be resold for as much as five dollars.)

Bongo turns to the young man whom we first spoke to and asks if anyone here remembers the old elephant hunters who came from this place.

"Yes," he says, pointing to the ruins of an abandoned hut about thirty feet behind us. "This was the *muji* of Galo-Galo Kafonde."

Bongo and Danny exchange glances.

"Are any of the old people still around?"

"Yes. This woman here," he says, pointing to an old woman who is standing in the crowd next to the boy we saw when we first arrived, "she is Galo-Galo's senior wife."

The old woman has short-cropped, wiry hair that is black and gray, and her skin looks thin over her small-boned body. She has a *kanga* wrap around her waist that is faded indigo. She avoids our eyes, but I sense she knows we are talking about her, and, perhaps because she is nervous, she puts her hand on the young boy's head and pats it.

"And this man here. He is Hunter Galo-Galo." We are introduced to the middle-aged man who has joined the crowd. He is about five foot three, has short, receding hair and a flat nose, and looks to be in his forties (although he must be at least fifty because he was a juvenile when Bill first captured him in this very place, in either 1956 or 1957). Under his eyes is a line of ceremonial beaded scars that extend on each side of his face in a droop from the bridge of his nose, under his eyes and up again, then in another droop that ends at his temples. He has small holes that pierce his lower earlobes and eyes with the red vein lines of someone who drinks. He seems shy.

Bongo nods to Hunter, then to the old woman, and says, "We have come to find you people, and to say hello on behalf of someone who has since died, someone who knew Galo-Galo well. He was someone who did the same work that we now do. He was a game warden."

"Oh, you mean Bwana Bilu," Hunter says.

Bongo smiles and nods. "Yes, Bwana Bilu." Bongo then indicates Danny and says, "We are Bwana Bilu's sons."

There is a murmur in the crowd. Hunter smiles and seems to lose some of his shyness. The other people in the crowd smile too, even the younger ones who never knew Bill Woodley, but who have no doubt heard stories about him. (In his book *The Elephant People,* Holman says that Waliangulu mothers used to scold their children and warn them to be good "or Bwana Bilu will get you.")

"We have also come to pay our respects to any of the old elephant hunters who might still be alive," Bongo says. Hunter tells him there are a couple of old hunters left—Kiribai Balaga and Guyu Mkunzu—but one of them is gone, and the other lives on the north side of the river.

"When did Galo-Galo die?" Danny asks.

"In September of 1989, from being an old man. His grave is there."

"Where?"

"You are almost standing on it."

We turn around and Hunter indicates about three feet behind us a small flat headstone only six inches high, and two small sticks in the ground that mark the foot of the grave. It's covered with a stubble of dry reedy grass. We gather around it, and we are not sure what to say. Then Danny breaks the silence.

"You shoot fifteen hundred elephant with a bow and arrow," he says. "You become the best at it in the world. And it doesn't come to much, does it."

⟐

Hunter invites us to the shade tree about one hundred feet away, which appears to be the village center. It is also the village bar, at least for the moment, because a Giriama wine seller has arrived on his bicycle, which is leaned against the tree's trunk, to peddle his wares. Tied to a rack over the bicycle's back wheel is a five-gallon plastic jug full of wine, and with a siphon hose the wine peddler fills a green soda bottle, and then uses this to fill a small yellow gourd, about the size of an aperitif glass, with the cloudy white liquid. He inserts a reed straw with a filter on the end made from a weave of narrow-bladed grass, and offers it to Danny who then invites Mohamed to take the first drink. Mohamed doesn't hesitate, and empties the shot gourd in three loud, sucking pulls. The wine seller refills the gourd, and in this fashion we all partake. The wine has the sour-mash taste of village-brewed hooches I know from other places: the cactus pulque of Mexico, the potato chicha of Peru, the rice chang of Nepal.

We invite Hunter to join us for another round, on our tab, of course. The Giriama, who is dressed in a safari shirt and pants that are of a significantly higher quality than the rags the Waliangulu wear, seems very pleased with this unanticipated business. We have been in this place fifteen minutes, and already it is easy not to like this wine seller. In his book, Holman called them drug dealers, and I wonder why it is that the most pure of the world's original cultures, the true hunters—and I think of the Plains Indians of North America, the Dayaks of central Borneo, the old Inuit of the Arctic— are also the most fragile, the ones with the least resistance to the demon alcohol.

This palm wine packs a wallop. We have two more rounds and we are all giddy-headed. We agree we'll have one more before hitting the trail. The wine seller refills the gourd. Bongo is last. He inserts the reed straw, lifts the gourd and looks at it, his eyes large behind his substantial glasses, and says, "For old times' sake, to Dad's memory, and to commiserate with a tribe that is dying, if not dead."

He takes a long pull and then adds, "In other words, to Old Africa." He finishes the wine, hands the gourd back to the wine seller, and we leave.

⟐

When I returned to Kenya six months later, Iain, Bongo, Danny, and I came back to Kisiki Cha Mzungu and spent two days with the villagers. It was the rainy season, and everybody was home. Galo-Galo's wife was still alive but complaining of a chest ailment. Hunter was pleased to see us, and then we met the handful of old-timers whom we missed on our first visit: Pununu Barissa, an old man with kind eyes who, after the Anti-Poaching Campaign, had worked for a hunting outfitter as a gun bearer; Kiribai Balaga, with a long, bushy mustache, who had also been a gun bearer; Guyu Mkunzu, with a large scar on his shoulder, who figures in both Holman's and Ian Parker's books.

When Bill first captured Guyu Mkunzu, the Waliangulu had told Bill he had shot hundreds of elephants, but Bill was surprised since he had never heard about him from any of the other hunters. When Bill asked around the others laughed and said Guyu was the village storyteller, and he extended his talent to claims about himself. He enjoyed telling strangers, for example, that his nasty scar was the result of being impaled by a charging rhino, but it was really a machete wound administered by a cuckolded husband. "Normally in the village piss-ups, everyone appreciated a good story," Ian Parker told me. "But you couldn't bullshit, you had to stick to the truth. Guyu, however, broke all the rules so outrageously, and with such style, that everyone would go quiet when he started talking, knowing the true story behind the story he would tell, and they would die laughing."

Guyu was a cordial host. Along with Hunter and the other elders, they took us on a tour of the village, although it was less a village than a collection of huts sprinkled miscellaneously up and down both banks of the river. The interiors of the huts were all Spartan: an earthen floor, a wood-frame bed, five feet by three, strung with a crosswork of plaited pandani, a mill stone, a fire hearth, and a metal chest to hold valuables and heirlooms, although I had the sense these were scarce (in the old days the chests safeguarded such things as leopard skins, rhino horns, and money gained from selling ivory).

We walked through their small subsistence plots along the river. They grew mostly maize, and in 1983 they planted a grove of coconut palms, so they could make their own wine (this was the most inland grove of coconut along the Sabaki). They told us they catch a few fish, but added that food is usually scarce, and things are not getting better. "We used to be able to feed elephant fat to our children," one of the elders told us. "The children grew strong. But now they are thin and they become sick."

Bongo asked if they continued to hunt elephant after the Anti-Poaching Campaign had put most of them in jail, and they said that they did, on infrequent occasions, until the Somalis raided in 1979. "They came and robbed us," the elder said. "They had rifles and we had only bows and arrows. They stole our goats, and the things we kept in our chests. Then they killed Abakuna, and we knew we were finished."

Abakuna had been the most successful of all the Waliangulu who, after the Anti-Poaching Campaign, had gone to work as trackers for the big-game hunters. Bill was first to employ him during that difficult period when, in the interim between his departure from Tsavo East and transfer to Mountain Parks, he had gone on the five-month safari looking for big ivory. (Abakuna was also the one who had once taken the biggest *usho* in the living memory of the tribe, the giant whose tusks had weighed at least 180 pounds.) After the safari with Bill, Abakuna found employment with other famed big-game hunting guides such as Tony Archer. "Abakuna was a very unusual man," Ian Parker told me. "He was an intellectual, and a very good medicine man, an herbalist and a bone setter that doctors here in Nairobi said could do as good a job as they could. He had great aplomb. Once he got to ride in a helicopter, and when he stepped out the other Waliangulu circled him excitedly and said, 'What was it like?' and he said, 'What was what like?' "

In his job as a tracker Abakuna met the rich and famous, and he traveled the world. He was invited by his wealthy patrons to join them on a tiger hunt in India, and they put the former bow hunter up in a grand suite in the most luxurious hotel in Delhi with "a bloody great four-poster and Indian servants in turbans waiting on him," Ian said. "Abakuna saw the irony and humor in it, and couldn't wait to get home to the village to tell the boys."

It all ended in 1979. Abakuna was at home in his village when the bandits arrived. For the Somalis, elephant poaching was by then turning into a very lucrative business, and they didn't want any competition, not even from a few natives using bows and poisoned arrows. They cornered Abakuna, and at gunpoint forced the old bow hunter to swallow his own poison. He died after five minutes of writhing agony.

❖

We walked back to Guyu Mkunzu's hut, and he brought out a longbow, strung it, nocked the arrow, and drew the bowstring. His shoulder might have been deformed from his wound, he might have been old, and he might have been the village jokester, but he pulled the powerful bow with a straight back and legs that were well braced.

"Do you do any hunting with your bow now?" Danny asked.

"If I did, do you think I would tell you?" he said, then smiled and laughed.

"If you are, I'll probably find out."

"If I am, you'll have to catch me."

Danny and Guyu both laughed, and I could see Danny delighted in this conversation, knowing this was the same mischievous cat-and-mouse repartee his father had played with these people forty years before.

Back at the village center, we told the elders we wanted to host a party for all the Waliangulu living in the area. We bought a fat-tailed sheep, an animal described in the Old Testament that looks more goat than sheep, and is named for its fleshy, paddle-shaped tail that functions as a reservoir to store fat. The former owner butchered the animal and quartered it, hanging the pieces in a low acacia next to the village common. Several wood stools were brought out and arranged around a metal-topped table, and the Giriama wine seller showed up and this time we told him we would buy his entire five-gallon inventory.

The sheep was put on to roast and the wine gourd was filled and refilled. The women produced two empty plastic jugs, turned them upside down, and began to sing while they beat out a percussive melody. Guyu Mkunzu and Hunter Galo-Galo stood side by side and, each holding the other's hand while they both extended their free arms, began stomping their feet and issuing a glottal "uuhhggaa, uuhhggaa"; two other women stood and danced opposite them. There was something familiar in the way the men held their arms out like the wings of a gull, and then I recalled a black-and-white photograph in Ian Parker's book. It was taken in 1957 during the Anti-Poaching Campaign when the rangers discovered an elephant dead in the bush and had five Waliangulu prisoners butcher it. The photograph showed the carcass of the elephant and four of the prisoners, all smiling, hacking out the ivory, while the fourth danced round them, his arms held out in the same gull-like way that Guyu and Hunter now held theirs.

The sun set below a sickle moon, lightning in the western sky illuminated a towering nimbo-cumulus, and above the cloud the Hale-Bopp comet was outward bound toward its millennial destiny. The dancers invited us to join, and one at a time we stood holding hands with the elder men while the women danced opposite. Danny told me that his father would sometimes dance this way, and until now he had never realized where it came from. The comet sank into the horizon, the Southern Cross circled above it, and below the village the starlight silvered the waters of the Sabaki.

We continued taking turns dancing with the elders. We had finished a good part of the palm wine, and we had eaten a good portion of the sheep. One old man sitting with us, with gray Brillo hair and cataract eyes, chewed on a piece of meat and looked at the tree where one of the sheep's quarters still hung, and said, "I was once on a hunt with Galo-Galo Kafonde, and we were chased by Bwana Bilu, but we escaped. We shot an elephant and brought the meat back, and we hung it in a tree, just like that sheep."

He paused meditatively, and sat the bone down on his plate. His chin whiskers had grown to a stubble, and his dirty *kikoi* was rolled up so that it exposed his knobby knees. He looked again at the meat in the tree, then picked up the bone and chewed slowly. "In the old days," he said, "we did important things." He paused and looked out toward the river, then back to us, and said, "Now, we only farm."

25

We need another and a wiser and perhaps a more mystical concept of animals. . . . For the animal shall not be measured by man. . . . They are not brethren, they are not underlings; they are other nations, caught with ourselves in the net of life and time, fellow prisoners of the splendor and travail of the earth.

—Henry Beston,
The Outermost House, 1928

We have hired one of the elders named Karissa Marubaya to guide us from Kisiki Cha Mzungu to the next main village, which we expect to gain by mid-day; from there we will retain another local to show us through the myriad of footpaths that parallel the Sabaki. We are surprised to learn that Karissa is Giriama. Similar to many of the Waliangulu, he has skin that looks as though it has been burnished, exposing beneath a black patina a bronze underlayer. He also has the double-loop cicatrix under each eye that he shares with all older Waliangulu men (we asked him why none of the young men had these tribal marks, and he told us it was because the boys would be ridiculed in school). It is probably more accurate to say that it is not he who looks like the Waliangulu, but rather the other way around, because it has been observed that the Waliangulu have an uncanny ability to merge and meld into the other tribes that they not only adjoin, but actually live among.

Karissa points out a wide swath of siafu ants that are on the march across the trail, and cautions us to step over them. Pete, the cameraman, pulls up the rear, and when he gets to the ants he asks the rest of us to stop and says he wants to get a ground-level shot of us stepping over the column. "These things don't bite, do they?" he asks Danny, who shakes his head and says, "No worry." I am debating whether or not to intercede when Pete gets down on his knees and positions the camera on the ground next to the ants. As he looks through the viewfinder I see the entire column shift trajectory and head for him in attack mode. In less than five seconds Pete is on his feet swatting and slapping his legs, thighs, arms, and torso, and cursing Danny, Bongo, and the rest of us, who are having a good laugh at his expense. Then he has to retrieve the camera, which is now black with these very aggressive, stinging ants, and it takes two or three minutes to clean them off.

"In the rainy season the siafu swarm," Bongo says, "and they can take over a house. Back when we lived in Mweiga [headquarters of the old Mountain Parks], and Danny was a baby, my parents were in the lounge when suddenly they saw the curtains next to Danny's crib alive with siafu. Danny was pretty much covered. They were in his eyes and ears and down into his throat. Roughly two more minutes, and he would have been a goner. I was seven years old, and it made quite an impression."

Old Karissa now tells us that it had been foretold by Bwana Bilu that someday he would send his sons walking down the river, just as he himself had done in the old days, and Karissa said it was a good thing he and Danny were now doing it. Bongo asked where the nickname Bwana Bilu had come from, and the old Giriama said "bilu" means "knife," and Bill was named after the knife he always carried. Bongo then tells us he thinks his father received this nickname because it was also a pun on "Bill," and thus a double entendre. (Africans love riddles and puns, and they also love nicknames, especially ones that are revealing. Ian Parker told me that David Sheldrick's nickname was Saa Nane meaning "two o'clock," because David would start the men working at six in the morning, knock off at two, and then start again at six, and, unlike Bill, he was a real stickler for keeping schedules.)

An ancient Waliangulu woman, with an eight-foot log balanced on her head, approaches us and stops when we meet. Her rickety legs are bowed as though they were steam-formed around a barrel. She wears a tattered saffron and burgundy wrap, and her cropped hair is pure gray. Danny and then Bongo shake her hand and ask her what family she is from, and then they explain they are Bwana Bilu's sons, and she says she remembers Bwana Bilu very well. She turns and continues, and we watch her walk slowly down the trail, her impossibly frail legs supporting the long firewood log, and Danny says, "Bloody hell, can't you just imagine her going down the trail, instead of that log a seventy or eighty pounder balanced on her head."

I take a photograph of her as she continues, seeing in my mind the image in black and white, and the log on her head as a great ivory tusk, as Danny has just imagined. I turn and continue, and reload my camera as I walk. In the small compartment of the shoulder bag that holds my camera gear, I feel around for a canister of film and instead I find the round mud ball of the dung beetle that I picked up the day before. I am surprised it hasn't broken, and as I finger it I wonder, with concern, if once at home it will hatch and loose dozens of tiny dung beetles into the fields of Southern California. Later it would occur to me that even if that were to happen, there is not enough dung from wild large mammals in Southern California to nurture baby dung beetles.

After our journey the dung beetle ball sat on my desk, and, while it never hatched, it did become for me, as I continued my research and my thinking into hunting, a kind of talisman of our species's relationships with the other large mammals with which we share our habitats. The connection was the reminder that during the mass extinction of mammals in the late Pleistocene, none of the insects in my own habitat of Southern California went extinct *except* the dung beetle. None of the reptiles went extinct, either. Nor did any of the amphibians. The only birds that succumbed were several species of vultures. If all the insects survived—except the dung beetle that depended on the dung of mammals—and all the birds—except the scavengers that depended on the carrion of mammals—then it would seem to me that most of the large mammals did not go extinct from a climate change. (Especially if you consider that today, as the planet is gradually warming, and the ozone hole growing, the animals that seem most sensitive to these changes are amphibians, especially frogs.) The most likely explanation, supported by the timing of our appearance with their disappearance, is that we hunted them down.

The round mud ball of the dung beetle was my connection to our past, and it was positioned on the windowsill above my desk as I recalled that image of the old Waliangulu woman carrying the log—and I remembered how Danny's suggestion had allowed my own mind to visualize an eighty-pound tusk on her head; as I considered Ian Parker's conclusions that the Waliangulu had been hunting elephant for over two thousand years; as I tried to reconstruct Bill Woodley's life and understand the half of him that was a hunter—an elephant hunter—against the other half that was a conservationist—a lifelong warden or assistant warden of national parks.

It was that last question that was the conundrum. The question presented an apparently conflicting duality (not only in Bill, but in many of his predecessors and his contemporaries) that was like a great mask of Janus that hung above all my considerations of our species's relationships to wild animals. I tried to find what others had written on this subject of man's simultaneous desire to hunt animals and to conserve them. I read *Gardeners of Eden*, but to me the book seemed like so much psychobabble. I listened to Ortega y Gasset meditate on hunting, but that was (I'll just say it) too philosophical. All this was either too academic or too abstract. I needed something I could hold and feel, like I could hold and feel that dung beetle mud ball.

As I continued to research Bill Woodley's life, I contacted everybody I could find who I thought might have insights about him, and those inquiries led to Jay Mellon, who I was told knew Bill quite well. Since Jay was part of the prominent Mellon family, I wasn't sure I could get through to him, but I rang the number I was given and he picked up the phone. "Bill Woodley! Greatest guy that ever walked on two legs."

"That's what everybody says," I replied.

Jay then told me he had written a book on big-game hunting, and that Bill had contributed one of the chapters. "You want to see it?"

It arrived next day by express courier, and Bill's article was titled "The Elephant Country: Pointers on Elephant Hunting in the Voi-Tana River Region of Southeastern Kenya, by Major F. W. Woodley, M.C., Senior Warden, Kenya National Parks." In the article Bill described some of the techniques he had learned to track elephant, tips he had picked up, I imagined, from Elui, from Abakuna, from other Wakamba and Waliangulu, and from Tiger Marriott:

"Look for a track that is worn smooth. The feet of young elephant retain a roughness that shows up in their tracks when they walk on firm sand, powdered dust, or in the ash of a burn."

"Always examine droppings. Remember that an old bull cannot digest his food as well as a youngster and that his droppings are therefore likely to be less cohesive and composed of large, semidigested particles."

"If the tracks lead to a spot where the elephant has rubbed its tusks on a tree, look to see how far down the rubbing marks extend. Very long tusks will often leave marks only a foot or two from the ground."

"Where the tracks show that the elephant has stopped and stood, be sure to notice whether he has rested his tusks on the ground. Occasionally, an elephant will carry long enough ivory to be able to do this."

"The outer edges of his tusks are often the widest part of an elephant, and that if he repeatedly avoids passing through narrow spots, such as between trees or boulders, it may be because his ivory is exceptionally large."

What most captured my interest, however, was a description of the five-month hunt on foot for a big tusker that had started in the Lorian Swamp and ended three hundred miles to the south.

"Some years ago," Bill wrote in his article, "the national parks gave me a long leave between changes of post and I spent all five months of it looking for big ivory. My tracker was Abakuna Gumundi, the famous Waliangulu poacher, whose poisoned arrows had turned so much of the elephant country into a bone yard. During our anti-poaching campaign, I had spent months beating the bush for Abakuna—racking my wits to catch him, while he racked his to stay ahead of me. Yet neither of us lost his sense of humor about the other, and, when finally we met, it was like old friends who have been playing chess through the mail. Our friendship survived Abakuna's going to jail, and when he got out, warden and poacher went elephant hunting together.

"Starting in the Lorian Swamp, I hunted southward right down to Makinnon Road, about 300 miles away. It was no champagne safari, that hunt! There were times when my men and I lived on boiled water lilies and lungfish scooped from mudholes. In the driest areas, we chewed water out of cacti or extracted it from roots and tubers. Our provisions were limited to bare essentials. For the rest, we lived off the land, chopping honey out of trees and shooting game where we could. Most of the time we were short of everything except enthusiasm."

Now I began to understand. The hunt was so much more than the act of pulling the trigger. That was still the climatic moment, but it was only a fraction of the total. The rest of it was what all the old-timers I talked to referred to wistfully as life in the bush, and now, with our walk from Kili to the sea behind me, I too had a sense of that life. Like the dung beetle mud ball, it was something I could feel: the razor edge your senses take when you pass close to a buffalo or hippo, the scintillating blue flash of the gray-headed kingfisher as it takes flight over the river water, the slow-motion gait of the giraffe loping away from your approach, the woodnote call of the tropical boubou in the morning and the plaintiff plea of the spotted thick-knee in the evening, the guttural roar of the lion across the still of the night.

And the charge of a twelve-thousand-pound elephant who means to do you harm.

Our walk gave me a window through which I could imagine with all my senses what it was like for Bill when he was on foot safari with Abakuna and the other Waliangulu, walking for five months across uninhabited bush, from the Lorian Swamp to the Makinnon Road; I could imagine, too, what it was like at the end of those five months when the project condensed to the final five minutes of the stalk, and then the final five seconds as the trigger was squeezed. I had caught a taste of that during the elephant charge: It was only a scent, but like the aroma of a new food, you have an idea what it's like even if you don't eat it.

The two faces of Janus were beginning to turn inward and meld into one. There was still one piece missing to understand fully this attraction to the hunt, and it was to be found in that comment Ian Parker made after I had asked him what he, Bill, and the others really thought of the Waliangulu. "They were hunters," he had answered. "They were masters of the bush. They were living off the land, and they were fitting in naturally. So, you see, to be honest, they were living the lives we ourselves would have liked to live."

Living off the land, fitting in naturally. Of course. That was what you did when you hunted: You lived off the land and you were part of it. You crossed from the passive to the active; you were no longer an observer. Sometimes you were a gatherer collecting honey, sometimes a hunter taking game. But in both roles, you were doing what you were designed to do, and *that* was the ineffable attraction.

❖

If that was the attraction to hunt, what was the compulsion to conserve? Going back to the case of Bill, there was no doubt he was dedicated to the ethic of conservation at an early age. Bongo told me that two days after his father arrived in Tsavo in 1948, he and the warden (the pharmacist from Nairobi) were driving along the Mtito Andei River when they spotted a band of hunting dogs, and the warden ordered the nineteen-year-old junior assistant warden to shoot the entire pack. These were not domesticated animals gone feral, but rather a native species of dog that, like hyena, hunted in packs and often ran down their prey, converging on the first to fall behind and then disemboweling the victim while it was still alive. These were not habits that endeared hunting dogs to people. The hunting dog, like the wolf in North America, was eradicated by the colonialists with such a ferocious disdain that today it is extinct in some areas and uncommon in most.

"Father couldn't understand this," Bongo told me. "He said to the warden, 'I thought in a national park everything was allowed to survive because everything has its role.' The warden ignored him, and father was forced to shoot the hunting dogs, but it was something he remembered for the rest of his life."

"As a hunter," Bongo continued, "Dad early realized that a national park was a place fully protected, where nothing was hunted, where everything lived in a natural state without interference."

Bill was not like the warden who had grown up in a city and had no idea that hunting dogs were as natural a thread in that ecological weave as any other animal in Tsavo. Bill had grown up on the Athi Plains when they were still wild, and from the time he was a small boy he had watched the warp and weft of predator and prey that to the uninitiate seems discordantly violent, but to him was an interweave that created a natural and harmonious fabric.

I am suspecting it was that love for the harmony in nature—a love for a wildness that in its natural state of equilibrium mixes violence with grace—that drew Bill in equal measures to hunting and to conservation. When he was hunting for five months after big ivory, he felt part of that equilibrium, and at the same time he dedicated his life to safeguarding it in the parklands his society had set aside for its preservation.

"As a hunter," Bongo said, "Dad had spent enough time in the bush, even as a young man, to see that without the change in policy [introduced by the creation of the national parks], there would be no wildlife left on the continent."

"He could see the whole picture," Peter Beard had told me. "He had a holistic vision." If Bill had this ability to see things in overview, then I suspect he also came to realize, later in his life, that the Waliangulu were as much a part of the equilibrium as any other predator in the ecosystem. At the time he was arresting them as poachers, he no doubt assumed they were taking elephant at an unsustainable yield: If you imagine yourself as a nineteen-year-old walking along the Galana River and finding carcass after carcass of elephant shot by the bowmen, you can understand reaching that conclusion. But in the 1960s, as the elephant population grew, and later during the great die-off in the 1970s and subsequent poaching in the 1980s, I am reasonably certain Bill came to realize he had played a hand in transforming a condition of natural harmony between animals, including man, into a disharmony that today is still readjusting. (I say this, too, recognizing that in any state of natural "harmony" there are always cycles of change and adjustment—what ecologists call discordant harmony—that in the case of the Tsavo megafauna included factors such as drought and the waxing and waning of tsetse fly phases. My point is that these natural adjustments did not include such unnatural impacts as the Anti-Poaching Campaign and the Somali *shifta* invasion.)

I also wonder if Bill ever thought about the origins of that harmony the Waliangulu enjoyed with the elephant they hunted. Why, for example, didn't the Waliangulu shoot more elephant? Why didn't they hunt them to extinction if, as I speculated earlier, man has a tendency to do that whenever he has the capability or the opportunity? Especially when you take into account that the Waliangulu were not even normal hunter and gatherers, but were, instead, commercial hunters who, while taking a good part of the elephant for food, were principally taking its ivory for money. If present-day fishermen can't stop themselves overharvesting bluefin tuna in the Pacific and lobster in the Atlantic, how then did the Waliangulu resist shooting every elephant in Tsavo?

Part of the answer lies, I believe, in the words "capability" and "opportunity." The Waliangulu may not have had the capability to take more elephant because there were never more than a few hundred of their tribe who were active hunters. It took extensive experience and training to learn how to stalk and shoot an elephant with a poisoned arrow, and to be truly expert—to be an ace—required catlike reflexes that only a select few would have been born with. Further, the Waliangulu may not have had the opportunity to take more elephant because the elephant themselves had developed skills to elude the hunters. Elephant had already been established in Africa for about seven million years when our hominoid ancestors walked across that ash-turned-to-rock on the Laetoli Plain, and as our species evolved, so did the elephant's abilities to survive in our presence. (Extending this idea to North America, it's interesting to speculate that had man evolved on that continent instead of in Africa, Kansas may very well have looked like the Serengeti Plain when Lewis and Clarke crossed the American Midwest, because the giant ground sloths, camels, horses, llamas, mammoths, and mastodons all would have developed capabilities to defend themselves against man the predator.)

Is it fair, therefore, to suspect that if the Waliangulu had had the capability, or the opportunity, to take more elephant, they would have? That if somehow they would have had available semiautomatic weapons, like the Somali *shifta*, they would have decimated the elephant?

If somehow, a Giriama trader *had* sold the Waliangulu a cache of semi-automatic weapons instead of a stash of *Acokanthora* poison, the Waliangulu culture would most likely have started to lose its millennial-old equilibrium. *Shifta*-style assault rifles would have wreaked havoc on the natural balance that had evolved between the elephant's rate of reproduction and the tribe's limited ability, with only longbows and poisoned arrows, to hunt them. Automatic weapons would also arguably have introduced strain and dissension between those who believed they were a threat to traditional ways against those who saw them as a tool to gain wealth. The tribe then probably would have lost some of its taboos that had served to maintain this equilibrium between hunter and prey: One of the elders in Kisiki Cha Mzungu, for example, told us that in the old days they had a rule that forbade young hunters from taking old elephants.

So back to the question: With the opportunity and the capability, would the Waliangulu have decimated the elephant? I think back to the first Amerindians in North America, the first Aborigines in Australia, the first Maoris in New Zealand. I think of the sailors clubbing the dodos on Mauritius, the passenger pigeons, the quaggas, the great auks, the Steller's sea cows, the California grizzlies. I think today of the bluefin tuna and the Atlantic salmon. The American bison and the Siberian tiger. The black rhinoceros, the white rhinoceros, the African elephant. I think of the Somali *shifta* and what might have happened to the elephant in Kenya without the combination of an ivory ban and Richard Leakey's assault troops backed by helicopter gunships. Then once more I think of the question of what the Waliangulu might have done if their traditional equilibrium had been disrupted with modern weapons, and I realize that if history is the only laboratory we have to test such questions, then it seems that the answer is a very probable yes: They too would have decimated the largest mammal with which they shared their landscape.

We reach a crossroads with trails going off toward each of the four corners, and our guide tells us this is the border of the Kulalu Ranch. Kisiki Cha Mzungu and its attendant scattering of huts have a kind of grandfather position within the ranch, which otherwise is open bushland, but from here until we reach the coast we will be walking through villages and farm plots.

As though to welcome us to this next and final section of our trek, a wine seller approaches on his bicycle, dismounts, and smiles at us as we walk by. His large plastic jug is full, his siphon hose ready. The air is still relatively cool, but beads of sweat decorate his ebony face and sparkle in the morning sun as he watches us through goofy red eyes. It is a safe guess that this merchant pockets very little of the gain from his trade, and further, that his life will be a continuous but short stupor.

The river has bent away in a looping oxbow, and we walk through saltbush and vines so thick they connect overhead and form a tunnel. Mixed in is a new acacia with lemon-yellow flowers and budding leaves that seems to have detected the coming rains earlier than its upriver cousins. The saltbush opens onto a grove of bananas framed by lines of coconut palms whose trunks are hatch-marked with steps that allow the wine makers to tap the heart-juice at the palm's crown. There is a background drone of cicadas, and a foreground mourn of doves, a descending "coooo-cooo-coo-coo-co" that evokes a wistful melancholy; it is believed by the locals that with this call the dove is saying, "My daddy died, my mommy died, I am sad, sad, sad."

We notice a group of eight people sitting off the trail under the shade of a spreading fig tree. As we walk by they fail to greet us, and given the open hospitality that everyone has showed so far, their detachment seems strange.

"Shall we visit them?" Bongo suggests.

We turn around and walk back to the tree but none of them gets up as we approach, and none of them offers to shake hands. Most of them are old, but two are middle-aged. They sit languidly, and, except for one who is very slowly plaiting strips of palm frond into a mat, they do nothing. Five of them have elephantiasis, and their legs and ankles are swollen grotesquely. Another's skin is scaling, and I notice he has part of one foot missing. Then I see others are missing fingers and toes.

"They are lepers," Iain says quietly.

Awkward in the silence that follows, we bid them good day, and leave. We walk quietly. Later we would learn that one of the old lepers was named Bajila Barissa, and that in his day he had been a great elephant hunter, and that he died a few months after we saw him under the fig tree. Now my mind wanders in an apparent disconnection to the realization that we are no longer keeping an eye out for hippo and Cape buffalo. There are no more lions roaring at night. Since we left the national park we haven't seen a single dangerous animal. (In fact, we've only seen the one fox and the one small herd of oryx.) Mohamed and Lokiyor keep their rifles in a relaxed Number Three Position throughout the day. It is now possible to walk somnambulantly, allowing your mind to drift. I recall only a few days before in Tsavo East when we flushed a herd of impala, and how in the crosslight over their thin, rich fur you could see their muscles shimmering tautly as they loped into the bush. I think back to the two lions at dawn walking the river's bank, and how their roaring had kept me on edge through the night, awake and alert.

Then back to the lepers under the tree, waiting to die, and the thought that, as a species compared to other species, we are certainly an ignoble lot.

26

Then what is the answer?—Not to be deluded by dreams . . .

To know . . . that however ugly the parts appear the whole
    remains beautiful. A severed hand
Is an ugly thing, and man dissevered from the earth and
    stars and his
    history . . . for contemplations or in fact . . .
Often appears atrociously ugly. Integrity is wholeness, the
    greatest beauty is
Organic wholeness, the wholeness of life and things, the
    divine beauty of
    the universe. Love that, not man
Apart from that . . .

—Robinson Jeffers,
from "The Answer," 1937

Morning air rustles the fronds of the coconut palms, making that nostalgic background noise you hear in the coastal tropics everywhere on Earth. The word "coco" is nearly as universal as the tree, and while the origin is probably from the Portuguese for "seed," or "kernel," a more pleasing story is that "coco" is slang for "clown," and early European sailors to Africa gave it its name after the three dots on the end of the nut that do suggest a clown's face.

The sky is patched with blue-gray cumulus, and overhead I track the see-saw flight of a hornbill. We are gathered at the junction of a trail that leaves the vehicle track we had followed the previous night. Yesterday was our longest day yet—forty-five kilometers— and it was dark by the time we reached camp. Most of the distance we hiked alongside *shambas* and through Giriama villages where the women no longer wrapped their *kangas* only around their waists, but tied them higher on their chests in order to cover their breasts.

This trail that we now consider heads east—the direction we want to go—but we are reluctant to commit to it until we have more information. A small crowd gathers and we ask if anyone would be willing to show us the way from here to the beach, which we estimate is about thirty kilometers away. No one says anything, except one young man who is standing in the back, brushing his teeth. "I will take you," he says, and we negotiate a suitable fee.

Our guide continues to brush his teeth as we walk, and Bongo says, "That will be this chap's name: 'Toothbrush.' " Already a pleasant breeze promises a good day for walking. The trail follows a barbed-wire fence with papaya on one side and coconut on the other, and we all expect, as we near the coast, we will continue to follow such pathways between cultivated plots. We're surprised, then, when Toothbrush takes us into a forest of trees some thirty feet high. This is *Acacia nilotica,* Egyptian thorn, known for its hard, termite-resistant wood that is used for making farm implements. The tree's bark is dark and deeply crevassed, and the branches, decorated with small canary-yellow blossoms, form a canopy that shades the trail.

The forest ends in an open field, covered with wild grass and scrub bush, that shows no sign of cultivation. Again we are surprised the place is as wild as it is, and Bongo says it is probably a seasonal floodplain that has therefore resisted occupation. Seeing this little bit of wild country in this otherwise domesticated region makes me squint my eyes and imagine on one end a herd of elephant browsing on the foliage, and on the other a scattering of tick birds rising in the air and settling down again on the saurian-skinned backs of rhinoceros.

"It gives you an indication what this place could have been with Dad's idea to extend the park all the way to the ocean," Danny says.

Bill Woodley had a vision in the beginning days of Tsavo of somehow extending the park boundaries to encompass the lands on both the north and south sides of the Sabaki as far as the ocean. Even in 1948, this would have been a daunting prospect that would have required the translocation of the Waliangulu, Giriama, and Orma peoples living in this region. Had Bill's vision ever come to pass (which assumes a way could have been found to incorporate at least some of these natives peoples, in an equitable manner, into the plans and functions of such a reserve), Tsavo today would be one of the few parks on Earth to enclose all the lands and migration corridors necessary to preserve what ecologists call a complete ecosystem.

This idea of complete ecosystems has been the subject of intensive debate the last twenty or so years. The basic theory, developed by scientists in the 1960s studying islands, is that the bigger a habitat, the larger the number and diversity of species it can support; a complete ecosystem therefore is one that is big enough to support, over a long term, all the flora and fauna in a geographic region. While the idea was developed through studies that focused on islands, it gained profound importance in the 1970s when ecologists began to realize that as the world was being cultivated by farmers, fenced by ranchers, paved by developers and clear-cut by loggers, the remaining parcels of wildlands were, in effect, islands, and the same rule applied on-shore as it did off-shore: The smaller the island, the fewer the species.

The real arguments came when the theory was applied to the real-world considerations of how big a park or a reserve needs to be to maintain viable populations of all the flora and fauna in a region. Our acquaintance Jared Diamond was also at the center of this debate. In 1975 he proposed that if you have limited resources for reserves (which describes every country in the world), it is better to have one big one than, say, five small ones. Others argued a larger number of smaller reserves is better because you would have a larger variety of habitats. That set off a firestorm of controversy among ecologists that burned hot for over ten years (it was called the "SLOSS Debate" for "Single Large or Several Small," an acronym that falls well short of the poetic flare of the "Pleistocene Overkill Debate"). Tom Lovejoy, an ecologist working with the World Wildlife Fund, had the idea to settle the debate by staging an ecological experiment in the Amazon. He arranged with the Brazilian government to preserve, in an area of rain forest slated to be slashed and burned for a huge cattle operation, plots of original primary forest. Each plot would be a different size, and each would be isolated by the surrounding clear-cut. In 1979 Lovejoy and his colleagues began studying these "islands" to see what happened, over the long term, to the plants and animals that were marooned. The scientists are still there, and so far the results have been mixed. If you are considering small species, such as frogs, a small reserve with good habitat is much better than a large one with poor habitat. But when you are talking about big mammals, like jaguar, the results are what your common sense would suggest: Big animals need big habitats.

In the case of Tsavo, then, the real consideration trying to judge whether or not it is a complete ecosystem is to ask whether or not it is big enough for elephant. Since there have been no definitive studies on the migration patterns of Tsavo's elephant (beyond Dick Laws's initial surveys in the 1960s that were never completed because of the debate over culling, and Iain Douglas-Hamilton's aerial surveys in the 1980s), the opinions of the experts vary in detail but not in overview.

"I think there's enough space," Joyce said. "Tsavo is incredibly lucky that way—twenty-two-thousand square kilometers, one of the biggest parks in the world—and it doesn't have the pressure from people on all sides like so many places do."

"Tsavo is by far the most self-contained park," David Western said, "but it still lacks the variety of habitats it needs to be complete. For that reason I would be very loathe ever to see Tsavo fenced because some of the big movements that still occur between the park and the outside would be limited, and as a result you would ultimately have fewer numbers of animals."

Even if they disagreed on the details, Joyce and David did agree, as did Daphne Sheldrick, that fifty years from now Tsavo is likely still to be the stronghold of wildlife it is today. "Tsavo knows how to take care of itself," Daphne said. "It's difficult country, it's not very accommodating, and it doesn't suffer fools."

❖

I believe there is another reason to be optimistic. On my way home from our trek the aircraft's in-flight video included a segment on Joyce Poole's work in Amboseli with African elephant. During the program I noticed that at least half of my fellow passengers were watching attentively. The plane was full, and I assumed the same pattern was occurring in the other sections of the plane. It was a major airline, so I also assumed that around the world, all day long, probably for the entire month, there were many thousands of passengers listening to Joyce describe the similarities of the emotional lives of elephant to our own. I knew, too, that National Geographic Television had aired a half hour program on Joyce. It also played in Europe. Her book was doing well. Her mentor, Cynthia Moss, had written a popular book on her experiences with elephant, and Cynthia's mentor, Iain Douglas-Hamilton, had written two books on his, and they had both been well received and widely read.

These three field researchers were informing hundreds of thousands of people around the world that elephant lead lives that are similar, in many striking ways, to their own. Most of these same people, in a parallel way, had developed a kindred regard for whales. Many of them were feeling, even if they couldn't articulate specifically or scientifically the reasons, that their own fates, as well as the fates of their families, their friends, and their societies, were tied to the fates of these animals, just as Chief Seattle had prophesied over a hundred years before. Equally important, and best exemplified in the case of whales, popular opinion was beginning to influence political policy; in the case of elephant, the fact that more and more people wanted to go to Africa to see those elephant meant a continued flow of tourist dollars, and therefore a continued interest in preserving elephant on the parts of all parties involved.

This change in our attitude toward whales and elephant is, I think, profound. It represents not only a change toward these two species, but a change in our relationship to all the megafauna, and a change as well in our relationship to the rest of the wild world. In the example of East Africa, this change began a short time after the first British settlers arrived about one hundred years ago. At first it was only a stir. Fifty years ago, led by Mervyn Cowie, the stir became a current strong enough to create a system of national parks founded not as *game* reserves but as *wildlife* sanctuaries.

"We humans require an occasional glimpse of a natural scene to keep our sense of balance," Cowie wrote. "We need often to dwell back on the solid earth from which we have sprung, and like animals we should benefit from the pleasures and lessons of a simple life. That, in my view, is the powerful, basic and abundantly justifiable reason, but not by means the only reason, to preserve wildlife and to isolate wild sanctuaries from the onslaught of modern trends."

The taproot of this shift in our relationship to wildlife was the idea that we no longer had to hunt animals to value them. But this raises the question of whether or not Cowie's "occasional glimpse of a natural scene," or even a more extended "dwelling back to the solid earth" is enough to achieve that sense of oneness with the bush that Bill Woodley had on his five-month safari. Can you go into the bush and achieve that sense of being an active part of the warp and weft of the natural fabric without going in as a hunter?

As I thought about this, I realized the answer might be found in a closer look at this shift in our relationship to wildlands and wildlife, to wildness. When Bill was young, it was true that the hunters were the people who best knew the bush. Bill used to tell Danny that only a hunter truly knows and understands an animal. But I'm not sure that is any longer the case. Today, if you combine the knowledge that Daphne Sheldrick, Joyce Poole, and Cynthia Moss have learned about the emotional lives of elephant, I believe you would have an understanding of those animals that matched and even exceeded the body of knowledge that someone had gained from hunting elephant, even from a lifetime of hunting elephant.

After our trek was finished, when I talked to Daphne Sheldrick, I asked her if she thought what she had learned about elephant from her years in the orphanage was perhaps even a deeper knowledge of these animals than what the Waliangulu had understood. "Yes," she said, "because I've raised fourteen elephant, one from the time it was born. I've known them as well as my children. And those other girls, Joyce and Cynthia, they started their studies as laypeople, and they didn't have the mental block common to scientists of thinking and feeling about these animals in a human sense."

I thought back to my own experiences, especially the charge of the big matriarch. From that—from examining my own reactions—I had come to understand better how someone could hunt and kill an elephant. But I had also come to know that matriarch as an individual. From Joyce, I had learned about her social structure, and more important, I had learned about her bonds to her children and to her grandchildren, about her spirit of fun, her joy of reunions with friends and relatives, her loyalty, her sorrows and mournings in times of death, her sense of self.

This knowledge, I think, gave me a sense of oneness with the thornbush savannas that extend vast and timeless under the shadow of Kilimanjaro, and it was a connection similar, I believe, to what Bill Woodley felt when he crossed the same bush country on his long foot safaris. It was the same sense of being part of the land, not apart from it.

❖

We need no longer to eat animals, tan their hides, grind their horns into aphrodisiacs, and carve their trunks into trinkets in order to work to appreciate them. We can work to preserve them whether or not they add positively to our profit-and-loss statement. This shift in our thinking is a change that, when you examine it alongside the relationship we had to wildlife in the preceding ten thousand years, becomes all the more profound. I am sure that scientific thinkers would agree, however, that fifty years, or even one hundred years, in the measure of biogeographic change and shift, is not enough to create a pattern. But I would think it *is* enough to establish the beginning of one.

What about Africans, however? What about rural agriculturists whose lives are every day in conflict with these wild animals? What about the farmer in Rombo whose field is nightly trampled by marauding elephant? The only way that farmer will value those elephant, David Western argues, is if they can bring him economic benefit. Community Based Conservation is working in Zimbabwe, he says, so it can work in Kenya. (Certainly if the predecessor of all African CBC ideas—Ian Parker's Waliangulu Scheme— would have been given a fair trial, it might have provided those people a more equitable future, but I think it's accurate to conclude that the opportunity has passed, and the traditional Waliangulu culture is irreversibly extinct.)

The funds aren't available anyway, Richard Leakey argues, for such CBC schemes. They would be, Western counters, if rural Africans could use wildlife as a resource. If hunting is allowed to return, others reply, it will only open the door to abuse and corruption.

The arguments go on. When you step back, you can see merits to all sides, but you can also see the central hope for Africa's large mammals—as well as mammals large and small worldwide—is to fight fiercely not only to preserve, but even to expand, their wild habitats. You can see this fight is made more difficult, too, by its conflict with our own species's expansion of our habitats. But at the core of it all, we must remind ourselves what Danny told me when we entered the Rhino Free Release Area: "Rhinos are endangered, but people are not. If one of them charges . . . we will not shoot it." There is a lesson in Danny's admonition that, in my opinion, must frame all these arguments, because, at the end of the day, we must remember Chief Seattle's warning: Whatever happens to the beasts, happens to man.

So when you step back and see in overview the arguments that go on between these conservationists, you can also see they are framed within this larger paradigm shift that is taking place worldwide in our species's relationship to the large animals with whom we share this Earth. You can see, too, that this shift is beginning to encompass not only wealthy Westerners, but Africans as well.

"We have to teach our children the real value of our wild animals," Stephen Gichangi told me. "Not just the surface value. Not that an impala is worth twenty dollars because its meat is this much and its hide that much. It goes beyond that, and that's what our people—our children—need to learn."

It seems to me that Stephen Gichangi is a good reason to hold optimism for the fate of Africa's wildlands and wildlife. If the countries that harbor the last great herds of savanna animals on Earth can develop more Gichangis, there's hope. If not, then Peter Beard's "galloping rot" may very well have the day, and those animals may very well disappear.

"To despair of the entire situation is a reasonable alternative," David Quammen wrote in *The Song of the Dodo*. "But the unsatisfactory thing about despair is that besides being fruitless, it's far less exciting than hope."

"I just wish Bill Woodley was still around," Stephen Gichangi said. "So he could see what I've done. So he could see what I'm going to do."

❖

We follow a road lined with tall neem trees and graveled with broken coral, our first direct indication we are approaching the coast. There are occasional houses, and as we proceed the condition of the road improves, as does the quality of the houses, until we pass one that has a Land Rover parked in front. Beyond the houses we catch an occasional glimpse of the river—wide, slow, and reflecting green along its banks—and as a squall off the ocean looses rain that cools the air, we stand for protection under a spreading bougainvillea.

The squall passes, and as we continue a *mzungu* on a moped put-puts by. He looks like one of the many Italians who in recent years have purchased vacation homes, hotels, and restaurants in Malindi, and I am guessing he ignores us either out of pretension or because he is arrived in the country recently enough that everything around him, including us, is equally unusual. We walk loosely down the gravel road, having long since abandoned the single-file configuration we maintained walking through Tsavo. I am behind Bongo and Danny, and both carry their rifles balanced casually on their shoulders. Everyone seems in a good mood. So far today there have been no pointed words between us, and Bongo and Danny seem to be living up to a family trait Bongo described early in the trip when he told me the Woodleys are quick to temper and also fast to forgive; I've noticed Iain seems more relaxed as well, and I am of course pleased and relieved the journey is ending on an amicable note.

As we walk I wonder what the future might hold for Bongo and Danny. It appears they both have the option and ability to climb the organizational ladder in the Kenya Wildlife Service. Bongo, with his keen attention to detail and his extraordinary memory that I am told he has inherited from his father, has the tools and the temperament to be a very successful warden. And Danny, with his love of hunting and of life in the bush, has skills well suited not only for controlling marauding animals, but for the much more dangerous work of controlling armed poachers.

For both of them, their futures in Africa necessarily contain elements of risk and uncertainty. After our trek, I had a chance to discuss this with a close friend of the Woodley family, an American named Lucile Ford. She was an actress when she met Bill some years back while he was visiting the United States, and she took him up on an offer to come out and see Africa. She fell in love with Kenya and made it her home.

"There is always real danger living out here," she told me. "If you are in the bush, it could be from animals or from bandits or poachers. Anywhere it could be mudslides or flash floods to carjackings and armed robbery. If you grow up here, it's almost like a natural part of the landscape. Remember, Bongo's generation of men was brought up on tales of what happened to people who were caught and tortured to death by the Mau-Mau. I was appalled that small children were told, in graphic detail, those real-life horror stories.

"So white Kenya men tend always to be in some joint competition as to who is best prepared for any threat. Danny told me he carries around an imaginary drill sergeant on his shoulder who, when he screws up, yells in his ear. And with Bongo, it's all in the details. To Bongo, people's lives depend on details. When you screw up the details, you sometimes die."

I realized that explained much of this friction Iain and I had with Bongo: For him, no detail was small. Taking two extra hours coming down Kilimanjaro because Iain didn't know about a fork in the trail was, to Bongo, two hours that could have been either conserved or applied elsewhere. Even though two hours would not have made a difference that day, Bongo lived in a world where two hours sometimes is the distance between life and death.

I realized this was true for Danny as well, especially in his work fighting poachers and bandits, and controlling elephant and lion. "Remember that book about hunting that you quoted from?" Lucile said. She referred to Ortega y Gasset's *Meditations on Hunting*. "There was a passage that I think explains how both Bongo and Danny view the world," she continued. " 'Only the hunter, imitating the perpetual alertness of the wild animals, for whom everything is danger, sees everything and sees each thing functioning as fa-cility or difficulty, as risk or protection.' "

Once more I was returned to what Danny had earlier told me was the most valuable thing he had learned from his father: to live and think like a hunter. But by then I had thought much about what Ortega y Gassett had called "this business of hunting," and it was clear to me that the time of the hunter in Africa was passed. And with this I wondered if perhaps Danny saw himself as someone who had been born in the wrong era.

I had an indication of his feelings when all of us were back in Kasiki Cha Mzungu on our return visit, and we had hosted the sheep roast for the vil-lage. We had danced and drank palm wine for several hours after sunset be-fore we finally decided to return to our camp, which was a quarter mile away. We settled our account with the wine peddler, thanked the Walian-gulu, and said our good-byes.

Then, as we left, Bongo turned to me and said, "That's also good-bye to a tribe of hunters who have lived past their time."

Danny was behind, and I don't think he knew I could hear when, mutter-ing to himself through the haze of the palm wine, he said, "Just like me."

Houses now line both sides of the street, and behind a low stone wall of one an old *mzee* working in the garden sees us and calls to his comrade. Unlike the Italian, these two stand and stare as we pass: It is reasonable to suppose they haven't seen any armed *mzungu* officers dressed in khaki and green, on patrol with Africans dressed in camouflage and also well armed, since Kenya gained independence from Britain in 1963. I wave and the two old men wave back. Then Iain stops, points, and says, "There it is." In the distance, perhaps five kilometers away, mottled by the shadows of the trade wind clouds, is the Indian Ocean.

An hour later, and about a kilometer inland from the beach, we reach the coast highway. We walk the shoulder for a few hundred yards until we reach the Sabaki River. Big trucks loaded with freight and belching diesel, mini-vans full of tourists, buses overloaded with men, women, kids, and animals, all slow or stop as the occupants gawk at us. When we arrive at the river we find a Japanese aid project is constructing a substantial new bridge, and after so many days in wild country the din of earth movers and graders and concrete trucks is a shock. We descend to the water's edge and try to push toward the beach, but the bamboolike elephant grass is impenetrable, and

we are justifiably concerned about snakes. Back on the highway we see two
small boys, maybe eight years old, and Bongo says, "Let's ask those *totos* if
they know a path to the beach."

"Better yet," I say, "let's hire them as guides."

I like the looks of these two kids: They have alert eyes and big smiles.
They laugh when we make them an offer, and say, "Follow us!" I can see
what is going through their minds: Wait until we get home and tell everybody about this!

The *totos* know the way. We are soon on a path along the river's edge. It
is now only a half kilometer to the beach. The river widens into a brackish
lagoon, shallow over the white sand and textured with wavelets drawn up by
the trade wind. We near a flock of flamingos that lifts off in a pink cloud as
we approach and settles again a hundred yards ahead. Closer, there is a
mixed congregation of ibis, egrets, and pelicans. There are no signs of
houses or of humans, and the noise of the highway is long disappeared. I am
surprised and delighted how wild it feels. Bongo stops and points out the
prints of a hippo that crosses our path, then disappears into the delta lagoon,
and I rejoice that here, where the waters of Kilimanjaro meet the Indian
Ocean—within a few miles of the tourist hotels that line the beaches at Malindi—the bovine grunt of the hippo sounds above the muted background
rumble of surf on the outer reef.

We cross a wet flat that edges the lagoon. I feel the warm water over my
toes, and I recall the lines of Thoreau: "Think of your life in nature—daily to
be shown matter, to come in contact with it, rocks, trees, wind in our
cheeks!" I feel the sea breeze and smell the salt air. "Contact!" The flamingos once more lift off in a slow soft cloud of pink and white. "Contact!"

"Contact!" That is what I was looking for on this walk. That is what I came
to one of the few remaining sections of wild Africa to experience. To see it,
to smell it, to taste it, to feel it. To be part of it, not apart from it.

◈

The two *totos* keep looking back to make sure we are coming. I don't want
to rush these last few hundred yards. We hike up sand dunes, leaving footprints in the parallel corrugations engraved by the trade winds. With our
guns and our weathered skin it is easy to imagine we are a Bedouin patrol
with Lawrence crossing Arabia. The boom of the surf grows louder. We
climb the shifting sand of the final dune, the salt wind hits our faces, and
then there it is, the ocean: turquoise beyond the outer sandbars, but tinged

red where the river joins the sea, tinged Tsavo red. We strip, leaving our clothes in piles on the hot sand, and hooting and shouting, run and dive in. Even the rangers follow.

I hit the water and taste the salt in my mouth and come up and dive in again and come up and think, This is the hardest I've ever worked in my life for a swim in the ocean.

I grab Iain and give him a bear hug and drop him in the surf, thinking that someday on some future adventure we will be bivouacked on a high, cold ledge, and we will remember this day, and recall the warm water of the Indian Ocean. I shake Danny's hand and give him a hug too, and splash Mohamed as he sits in the shallows, wearing only his underwear, slapping the water childlike as it ebbs and flows around him.

We continue to dive in the waves and splash, and I turn to look for Bongo. He is back where we left our clothes, against the sand dune. He is sitting alone, and for some reason his solitude allows me to imagine him as a little boy in the Aberdares driving on patrol with his father, just the two of them in the front seat and the .416 propped between. I see him now, fully clothed, sitting on the dune in the equatorial sun, owning his father's dedication and his father's honesty and commitment. But where is his father's sense of play and joy? He's a good man, Bongo, and I wish for a moment he would loosen up and strip and dive in the water and laugh and yell. But he reaches in his pack and takes out his GPS and turns it on and waits for it to gain a fix on the satellites out there somewhere in their geosynchronous orbits, and when he has them locked on, he punches the appropriate buttons and waits to get the fix on our final position.

Glossary of East African and Swahili Words

ayah   A housekeeper, or woman who cares for young children

bandas   Huts or cabins

boma   A wall constructed of thornbush branches built to keep dangerous animals out of a village or a camp

Commifora   A genus of deciduous trees indigenous to East Africa, five to ten meters high, with gray peeling bark and long spiky thorns. These trees are so common in Tsavo that much of the habitat is referred to botanically as "*Commifora* thornbush."

kanga   A piece of cloth of various colors and patterns generally worn by women from chest to knees

kikoi   A swatch of cotton batik printed in bright colors and worn as a wrap by men from waist to ankles

KWS   An acronym for the Kenya Wildlife Service, the agency that administers Kenya's national park system

lugga   A seasonal creek bottom, wash, or drainage that is usually a sandy area free of vegetation

manazi   The local palm wine made either from the heart juice of the doum or coconut palm

mellifera   A shrubby member of the indigenous *Acacia* genus, up to eight meters high, with sharp, hooked thorns. It is common in Tsavo and other lowland bush regions of East Africa.

miraa   An evergreen shrub, known also in Arabia as *qat* and in Somalia as *khat* or *kat,* whose short stalks provide a mild stimulant when chewed

morani   A Masai warrior; the plural is *Il-Moran*

mzee   A senior or elderly man

mzungu   A Caucasian or European

nyika   The bushland wilderness that extends in a belt across East Africa between the coastal zone and the interior highlands

shamba   A farm plot and house

shifta   The Somali bandits who originate both from Somalia and, more commonly, from the northeastern portion of Kenya

shuka   The long colorful toga worn traditionally by Masai men

toto   A young kid

Wakamba   Also known commonly as Kamba, these people are the fourth largest tribe in Kenya and inhabit the extensive bush country north and west of Tsavo East National Park. Traditionally making their living hunting and trapping, today they have converted more or less successfully to farming and animal herding.

Waliangulu   A small tribe of former hunting people who live in a zone between the east border of Tsavo East National Park and the coast. While today they are minimal subsistence farmers who also keep a few goats and sheep, historically they were famed elephant hunters, masters of the long-bow and poisoned arrow.

Wata   The name the Waliangulu give themselves, meaning "The People"

Selected Reading

In addition to information gathered from interviews, my descriptions of the history and natural history of the greater Tsavo were supported by several books that assisted my own effort. I have listed the more important ones, and also added annotations describing further how I used a particular work.

Adams, Jonathan and Thomas McShane. *The Myth of Wild Africa*. Berkeley. University of California Press, 1996. While this book is biased in favor of Community Based Conservation programs—dismissing as "myth" the idea that there ever was an African wilderness, and as misanthropic the concept of national parks—it is stimulating and provocative.

Beard, Peter. *The End of the Game*, revised edition. San Francisco: Chronicle Books, 1988. In some ways this is the pictorial equivalent of *Out of Africa*, but with an edge: Peter does a master's job mixing the magic of Old Africa with the realism of this century's destruction of its large mammals.

Dinesen, Isak (Karen Blixen). *Out of Africa*. London: The Bodley Head, 1937. My copy is a handsome hardback reprint, but it is available in paperback, and it is the standard against which all other descriptions of East Africa must be measured.

Graham, A. D. *Gardeners of Eden*. London: George Allen, 1973. This book was very interesting in its views about how British game laws and hunting traditions influenced Kenyan policies and history (for an even more in-depth look at the history of game laws, read *The Poacher and the Squire*, by Charles Chenevix Trench, London: Longmans, Green & Co., 1967). I had trouble, however, with Graham's vindictive tone and his Freudian conclusions about why man hunts and why he conserves animals.

Holman, Dennis. *Massacre of the Elephants*. New York: Holt, Rinehart and Winston, 1967. Published in England as *The Elephant People*, this history of Bill Woodley's efforts against the Waliangulu was drawn from the author's time with Bill, but I found it to be an overly dramatic and unrealistically heroic portrayal of the life of a warden and hunter. It was nevertheless a very useful source of background information on Elui, as well as giving me anecdotes I otherwise would not have had available, such as the story of the young Waliangulu boy captured by Sheldrick who walked eighty miles back home to Kisiki Cha Mzungu.

Meinertzhagen, Colonel R. *Kenya Diary, 1902–1906*. London: Oliver and Boyd, 1957. Iain Allan was generous to give me an extra copy of this fascinating book. The writing is terse and without embellishment; I imagine the author was that way, too.

Miller, Charles. *The Lunatic Express*. New York: Macmillan, 1971. In addition to being *the* history of the construction of the railroad, this is also an excellent summary of the early exploration of East Africa.

Moss, Cynthia. *Portraits in the Wild*. New York: Houghton Mifflin Co., 1975. While this book, because of its date, misses the research completed in the last twenty years, it still offers excellent profiles of the natural histories of most of East Africa's major mammals.

Parker, Ian. *Ivory Crisis*. London: Chatto & Windus, 1983. Ian has a good description of the Waliangulu bow hunters, taken from his years of living in close proximity to them. I used his profile of Galo-Galo Kafonde to construct that imagined description of the hunter's walk home after release from his arrest.

————. *The Tyranny of Freedom*. This is Ian's new book profiling several African park wardens and conservationists, and while I haven't read the complete book (he was finishing it as I was writing this one), he did share his chapters on Bill Woodley and David Sheldrick, and they were very authoritative, offering a good overview history of Tsavo East and Tsavo West National Parks.

Patterson, Lt. Col. J. H. *Man-Eaters of Tsavo*. London, 1907. I have an illustrated reprint (there have been additional reissues), and if you found the story of these man-eating lions interesting, I strongly recommend you read the original: With just a little imagination you can put yourself in Patterson's place, and it's gripping.

Poole, Joyce. *Coming of Age with Elephants.* New York: Hyperion, 1996. I am biased, because I found Joyce to be spirited and enjoyable company on our walk, but I also enjoyed the candor of her memoir, and how it reveals the depth of her knowledge about the emotional lives of elephant.

Quammen, David. *Song of the Dodo.* New York: Simon and Schuster, 1996. While this book, subtitled "Island Biogeography in an Age of Extinctions," does not focus on Africa, it does give an excellent overview of the debate about minimum sizes of nature reserves. It also seeded my thinking about our species's possible predilection to hunt animals to extinction.

Sheldrick, Daphne. *Tsavo Story.* London: Wm. Collins Sons & Co., 1973. Published in the United States with the insipid title *Animal Kingdom,* this is Daphne's story of her life in Tsavo beginning with her marriage to Bill and ending in the early 1970s, just before the poaching wars began. If you enjoy her descriptions of her work with abandoned wildlife, you should also read *The Orphans of Tsavo:* It has remarkable insights into the emotional lives of Tsavo's megafauna.

Thomson, Joseph. *Through Masai Land.* Boston: Houghton Mifflin, 1885; reprinted London: Frank Cass, 1968. Between Susie Caldwell (my assistant) and me, we read several of the early books about the exploration of East Africa, by authors including J. L. Krapf, Frederick Lugard, Charles New, Sir Frederick Jackson, Arthur Neumann, C. W. Hobley, and Sir Charles Eliot. If you want to read only one, I recommend Thomson: He has the verve, and he was there for all the right reasons.

Western, David. *In the Dust of Kilimanjaro.* Washington, D.C.: Island Press, 1997. Jonah's memoir was released after I finished this book (and just in time to include it here); understanding his personal history helps to understand his views on Community Based Conservation.

Zimmerman, Dale, Donald Turner, and David Pearson. *Birds of Kenya.* Princeton, N.J.: Princeton University Press, 1996. If you are an avid birder interested in Africa, most likely you already know about this book. If you are not, this is the bible, but it weighs a lot. If you want a good lightweight guide, take the *Collins Field Guide to the Birds of East Africa,* by John G. Williams and Norman Arlott.

Acknowledgments

Susie Caldwell, who works as my right-hand associate with the other hats I wear, continued, on this project, to reveal the extent of her multiple talents, working on this book as front-line editor and as a sounding board for my ideas. In that latter capacity she has what Hemingway called an essential tool for good writing: "a built-in, shockproof shit-detector."

Without the initial support from John Wilcox of American Adventure Productions, Peter Englehardt of the Outdoor Life Network, Michael Crooke and George Grabner of the Kelty Pack Company, the Kilimanjaro Summit-to-Sea walk would never have happened. I had invaluable encouragement to write the book from my agent Susan Golomb and my friend Ann Clark. David Sobel of Henry Holt committed to our project before we completed the walk: Like me, he thought this would be a story of an adventure walk across East Africa, and what we both ended with was much different than initially anticipated.

Because of the additional themes that I added to this story, it became necessary to condense the descriptions of the trek itself: There were five people who joined us for parts of our walk who I wish to acknowledge for their camaraderie: Michael Crooke, Dan Emmett, Pete Trevor, Clive Ward, and Dave Simpson. Additionally, Pete Trevor was most helpful in planning and route finding, and Dave Simpson, as editor of *Swara*, the publication of the East African Wildlife Society, helped with research and advice. Although he was mentioned briefly in the story, I want to offer additional thanks to Pete Fuszard, who made the video documentation of our trek and who, despite teasing from Iain Allan about riding in a Land Cruiser for a couple of kilometers out of Loitokitok to get a master shot of Kilimanjaro, walked every step of the way with us. Lucile Ford of Nairobi helped me enormously with research, collected archival photographs, facilitated interviews, and, as a close friend of the Woodleys with a warm affection for Bill, helped me to better understand the kind of man he was.

I thank all who gave their time in interviews: Ian Parker, Pete Jenkins, Stephen Gichangi, Joe Kioko, Daphne Sheldrick, David Western, Peter Beard, Bill Stanley, Ted Goss, Jared Diamond, Jay Mellon, Judy Destri, Richard Leakey, Patrick Hamilton, Jon Bowermaster, Joyce Poole, Benjamin Woodley, Brian Heath, Tony Dyer.

Many of the photographs in this book were contributed by Peter Beard and researched by his assistant, Rick Burkoff: They are an eloquent contribution to this book, and I give Peter my heart-felt gratitude. Pete Jenkins, Ian Parker, Mohamed Salim, Daphne Sheldrick, Clive Ward, Bongo, Danny, and Benjamin Woodley also generously allowed me to use images from their collections. Thank you to the Field Museum of Natural History, for the photograph of Col. J. H. Patterson, and to Curt Grosjean of The Darkroom in Northridge, California, for his always excellent work developing, printing, and preparing films.

Thank you to Jon Bowermaster, Joanna Greenfield, Jay Mellon, Ian Parker, and Daphne Sheldrick for permission to quote excerpts from their works. Further permission acknowledgments are due to: Chronicle Books for *The End of the Game*; Random House UK for *Out of Africa*; Peter Riva of International Transactions; Stanford University Press for "The Answer" by Robinson Jeffers; Joan and Arnold Travis for *Man-eaters of Tsavo*; University Press of New England for "The Heaven of Animals" by James Dickey. Robert Barnes of the Ventura County Public Library System located all our research materials despite difficulties created by state budgetary cuts. The team at Adventure Photo and Film's support for and dedication to the agency in my absence was indispensible. The Kelty Pack Company outfitted us superbly with tents, packs, and sleeping bags. Additional gear was generously contributed by La Sportiva boots, Camelbak hydration systems, Patagonia clothing, Leki walking poles, and Chukar Cherries foods and snacks.

Thank you to Clement Kahin, George Njoroge, Joseph Wanaina, Bernard Kyongo, Evans Mutiso, and Kanau Warui from Tropical Ice in Nairobi for their field and camp support during our trek. A special thank-you to my comrades who walked with me every one of the five hundred kilometers from the top of Kilimanjaro to the Indian Ocean: Mohamed Hamisi, David Lokiyor, Galogalo, Danny Woodley, Bongo Woodley, Iain Allan, Pete Fuszard. A final thank-you is reserved for my wife, Jennifer, and our children—Connor, Cameron, and Carissa—for patiently allowing me to pursue my passions.

Index